Tables and Formulas

**The World Book
Desk Reference Set**

Tables and Formulas

Published by

World Book Encyclopedia, Inc.
a Scott Fetzer company

Chicago

Staff

Contents

3   Home Management   66

4 The Home Handyman — **96**

1 Health care and exercise

TABLES AND FORMULAS begins with information on meeting and/or avoiding emergencies, whether the emergency involves drugs, the ingestion of poisons, or naturally occurring events such as fires, tornadoes, or hurricanes. Also included are answers to questions regarding immunization shots and Medicare coverage. You will find an emergency coping chart, a checklist of things to do when you encounter a highway accident, and lists of measures that can be taken to prevent home accidents. Of particular interest to the vacationer is a how-to table on bites and stings. The same reader will want to study the chart on dangerous plants.

Diseases and drugs are given full attention. You will find the necessary actions to take in cases of drug overdosage and learn the names of common diseases. A table listing the uses of common drugs will be of interest to those who require medication or medical aid of any kind.

Are you interested in losing weight and/or working toward better physical fitness? The first section of TABLES AND FORMULAS lists the exercises and sports that give the best results. Another section gives the 1983 weight tables as compiled by life insurance company actuarial records.

The whole is a perfect introduction to what may become one of the best-read books in your library.

Poisons

Chemical poisoning: symptoms and treatment

Poison and sources	Symptoms	Treatment
Benzene, toluene, and xylene		
These substances are present in many commercial solvents and domestic paint removers. Poisoning may occur after ingestion or inhalation.	Burning sensation in the mouth leading to vomiting; chest pains; coughing; and dizziness. In later stages, lack of coordination; confusion; stupor; and coma. Death is usually from respiratory or heart failure.	Remove the victim from the source of poisoning. Carefully remove the victim's clothing if contaminated. Arrange for hospitalization of the victim. If the victim is unconscious, put in the recovery position. If the victim stops breathing, give artificial respiration using the Holger Nielsen method. If the victim's heart stops, apply external cardiac compression.
Carbon monoxide		
The most common source of carbon monoxide is automobile fumes. Poisoning may occur following inhalation.	The victim may be hyperactive. There may also be mild headache; irritability; fatigue; vomiting; confusion; lack of coordination; transient fainting fits with convulsions; and incontinence. Death is usually from respiratory failure.	Remove the victim from the source of poisoning. Arrange for hospitalization of the victim. If the victim is unconscious, put in the recovery position. If the victim stops breathing, give artificial respiration using the Holger Nielsen method

Poison and sources	Symptoms	Treatment

Carbon tetrachloride

Carbon tetrachloride is present in many solvents used for removing grease. Poisoning may occur following inhalation or ingestion.	There may be vomiting; headache; dizziness; confusion; convulsions; difficulty breathing; and coma. Death is usually from respiratory or heart failure.	Remove the victim from the source of poisoning. Carefully remove the victim's clothing if it is contaminated. Arrange for hospitalization of the victim. If the victim is unconscious, put in the recovery position. If the victim stops breathing, give artificial respiration using the Holger Nielsen method. If the victim's heart stops, apply external cardiac compression.

Chlorate compounds

Chlorate compounds occur in some mouthwashes and weedkillers. Poisoning may occur following ingestion.	There may be vomiting; diarrhea; blood in the urine; jaundice; delirium; convulsions; and coma. Death is usually from kidney failure.	Arrange for hospitalization of the victim. If the victim is conscious, give large drinks of water. If the victim is unconscious, put in the recovery position. If the victim stops breathing, give artificial respiration using the Holger Nielsen method.

Corrosives

Strong acids, such as battery acid; strong alkalis, such as caustic soda; strong antiseptics; and tincture of iodine. Poisoning may occur following ingestion.	There may be burns around the lips and mouth; intense pain in the mouth, throat, and stomach; vomiting, sometimes with blood; shock; and difficulty breathing. Death is usually from respiratory failure.	Arrange for hospitalization of the victim. If the corrosive has been spilled on the skin, place the affected area under running water for at least ten minutes and then treat the injury as an ordinary burn. If the victim is conscious, give small drinks of water. If the victim is unconscious, put in the recovery position. If the victim stops breathing, give artificial respiration using the Holger Nielsen method.

Kerosene and petroleum distillates

These substances are present in many domestic cleaning fluids, paint thinners, and polishes. Poisoning may occur following ingestion or inhalation.	Mild poisoning may produce a state similar to drunkenness. Severe poisoning may cause pain in the mouth, throat, and stomach; vomiting; diarrhea; headache; blurred vision; agitation; lack of coordination; delirium; convulsions; and coma. Death is usually from respiratory failure.	Remove the victim from the source of poisoning. Carefully remove all of the victim's contaminated clothing. Arrange for hospitalization of the victim. If the victim is unconscious, put in the recovery position. If the victim stops breathing, give artificial respiration using the Holger Nielsen method.

Metaldehyde

Metaldehyde is present in slug and snail poison. Poisoning may occur following ingestion.	There may be nausea; vomiting; exaggerated reflexes; convulsions; and difficulty breathing. Death is usually from circulatory failure.	Arrange for hospitalization of the victim. If the victim is conscious, induce vomiting. If the victim is unconscious, put in the recovery position. If the victim stops breathing, give artificial respiration using the Holger Nielsen method. If the victim's heart stops, apply external cardiac compression.

Naphthalene

Naphthalene is present in moth balls and air fresheners. Poisoning may occur following ingestion or contact.	There may be abdominal pain; vomiting; diarrhea; difficulty breathing; delirium; convulsions; and coma. Death is usually from liver or kidney failure.	Arrange for hospitalization of the victim. If the victim is conscious, give sodium bicarbonate in water. If the victim is unconscious, put in the recovery position. If the victim stops breathing, give artificial respiration using the Holger Nielsen method.

Organophosphorus compounds

These substances are present in many insecticides. Poisoning may occur following ingestion, inhalation, or absorption through the skin.	There may be increased salivation; vomiting; abdominal pain; diarrhea; pinpoint pupils; difficulty breathing; convulsions; and coma. Death is usually from respiratory failure.	Carefully remove all of the victim's contaminated clothing. Arrange for hospitalization of the victim. If the victim is conscious, induce vomiting. If the victim is unconscious, put in the recovery position. If the victim stops breathing, give artificial respiration using the Holger Nielsen method.

Poison and sources	Symptoms	Treatment

Oxalic acid

| Oxalic acid is present in some bleaches and metal cleaners.

Poisoning may occur following ingestion. | There may be pain in the mouth; vomiting; thirst; twitching; convulsions; and coma. Death is usually from heart failure. | Arrange for hospitalization of the victim. If the victim is conscious, give milk of magnesia or ordinary milk to drink. If the victim is unconscious, put in the recovery position. If the victim's heart stops, apply external cardiac compression. |

Phenol and cresol

| These substances are present in many strong antiseptics.

Poisoning may occur following ingestion, inhalation, or absorption through the skin. | If inhaled or absorbed there may be difficulty breathing, and unconsciousness. If ingested there may also be burning of the mouth and throat, and vomiting. Death is usually from respiratory failure. | Remove the victim from the source of poisoning. Carefully remove all of the victim's contaminated clothing. Arrange for hospitalization of the victim. If the victim is unconscious, put in the recovery position. If the victim stops breathing, give artificial respiration using the Holger Nielsen method. |

Phosphorus

| Phosphorus is present in some rat poisons.

Poisoning may occur following ingestion. | There may be burning of the mouth; a smell of garlic on the breath; vomiting; diarrhea; delirium; and coma. | Arrange for hospitalization of the victim. If the victim is unconscious, put in the recovery position. If the victim stops breathing, give artificial respiration using the Holger Nielsen method. |

Sodium hypochlorite

| Sodium hypochlorite is present in domestic bleach.

Poisoning may occur following ingestion. | There may be vomiting; pain and inflammation of the mouth and throat; difficulty breathing; delirium; and coma. | Arrange for hospitalization of the victim. If the victim is unconscious, put in the recovery position. If the victim stops breathing, give artificial respiration using the Holger Nielsen method. |

Poisonous plants and symptoms

Name	Poisonous parts	Symptoms of poisoning
Aconite	Roots; leaves; seeds.	Nausea; vomiting; slow pulse; burning sensation in the mouth, throat, and skin; collapse.
Baneberry	Roots; sap; berries.	Vomiting; rapid pulse; diarrhea.
Bittersweet	Leaves; berries.	Burning sensation in the mouth; dizziness; weakness; convulsions.
Blood root	Stem; roots.	Burning sensation in the mouth and stomach; nausea; vomiting; slow heart rate; coma.
Castor bean	Beans; seeds.	Diarrhea; vomiting; abdominal cramp; convulsions; collapse.
Daphne	Bark; leaves; berries.	Burning sensation in the mouth and stomach; severe cramp.
Deadly nightshade (belladonna)	Roots; leaves; seeds.	Dry mouth; dilation of the pupils; irregular hearbeat; nausea; vomiting; coma.
Death cup	All parts.	Abdominal pain; nausea; vomiting; excessive thirst; jaundice; convulsions.
Foxglove	Leaves; seeds.	Dizziness; nausea; vomiting; slow pulse.
Fly agaric	All parts.	Diarrhea; vomiting; delirium; convulsions.
Hellebore	Roots; leaves; seeds.	Salivation; abdominal pain; clammy skin; coma.
Jack-o'-lantern fungus	All parts.	Nausea; vomiting; diarrhea.
Jequirity bean	Seeds.	Vomiting; diarrhea; chills; convulsions; heart failure.

Name	Poisonous parts	Symptoms of poisoning
Jimson weed	Roots; seeds; leaves.	Pupil dilation; dry mouth; irregular heartbeat; vomiting; coma.
Larkspur	Leaves; seeds.	Tingling sensation in the mouth; agitation; severe depression.
Lily of the valley	Roots; leaves; fruit.	Irregular pulse; nausea; vomiting; dizziness.
Manchineel	Fruit; sap.	Sap causes burning of the skin; bleeding of the eyes. Fruit causes vomiting; diarrhea; burning sensation in the mouth and throat.
Mountain laurel	All parts.	Salivation; tingling sensation in the skin; vomiting; convulsions; paralysis; coma.
Panther mushroom	All parts.	Abdominal pain; nausea; vomiting; diarrhea.
Poison hemlock	Leaves; fruit.	Burning sensation in the mouth; slow pulse; paralysis; coma.
Poison ivy, oak, and sumac	All parts; leaves irritate the skin.	Redness and blistering of skin; burning sensation; severe itching.
Pokeweed	All parts.	Vomiting; drowsiness; impaired vision; coma.
Water hemlock	All parts.	Stomach cramp; vomiting; excitation; irregular breathing; frothing; convulsions.
Yew	Roots.	Abdominal pain; nausea; vomiting; diarrhea; difficulty in breathing.

Plant poisoning: do's and don't's

If the victim has been in contact with an irritant plant, ensure that your hands are protected before removing the victim's contaminated clothing.

Do not touch other parts of the victim's body, especially the eyes.

Wash the affected area several times with soap and water and apply calamine lotion.

If the victim has eaten a poisonous plant or mushroom, summon emergency medical aid.

If the victim is conscious:

Ask which plant was eaten.

Induce vomiting by making the victim drink a glass of salt water, or mustard and water, or give syrup of ipecac. Tickling the throat will also cause vomiting. Save any specimen of vomit for medical analysis. Do not induce vomiting if the victim is convulsing.

Give milk or water to drink, to dilute the substance.

If the victim is unconscious:

Place the victim in the recovery position. *Do not* leave the victim alone. *Do not* give any food or drink. *Do not* induce vomiting.

If the victim stops breathing, give artificial resuscitation.

If the victim's heart stops, get a trained person to apply external cardiac compression.

Insect and animal bites and stings: symptoms and treatment

Name	Toxic substance	Symptoms	Treatment
Ant Genus: *Pogonomyrmex; Solenopsis.*	enzyme; formic acid; vasodilator	Sharp stinging pain; whiteness at point of bite; itching; in severe cases, fever and ulceration; multiple bites may cause death.	1. Identify insect. 2. If reaction is severe, take victim to a hospital. 3. Apply antihistamine cream or cold compress.
Bee For example: honeybee; bumblebee. Genus: *Apis; Bombus; Xylocopa.*	acidic venom; enzymes; hemolytic agents; neurotoxin; vasodilator	Local pain; burning sensation; whiteness at site of sting; swelling and redness; multiple stings may cause generalized swelling, respiratory distress, and shock; rarely, death.	1. Identify insect. 2. Remove stinger. 3. Apply antihistamine cream. 4. Sodium bicarbonate neutralizes poison. 5. Multiple stings require immediate hospitalization.
Hornet or **wasp** Genus: *Polistes; Seliphron; Vespa; Vespula.*	alkaline venom; enzymes; hemolytic agents; neurotoxin; vasodilator	Similar to the signs and symptoms of a bee sting.	1, 2, 3, and 5. Treat as a bee sting. 4. Vinegar or lemon neutralizes poison.
Mosquito Genus: *Aedes; Anopheles; Culex.*	anticoagulant in saliva; disease-causing organisms in saliva	Slight local pain; swelling; itching. Organisms in mosquito bite may cause a variety of diseases, including malaria and yellow fever.	1. Antihistamine cream relieves irritation. 2. Do not scratch. 3. Antimalaria drugs, and insect repellents, if in malarial region.
Scorpion Genus: *Centruroides; Tityus; Leiurus.*	cardiotoxin; enzymes; hemolytic agents; neurotoxin	Acute burning sensation at site of sting; swelling; restlessness; confusion; chest and abdominal pain; respiratory distress; in some cases, convulsions and death.	1. Identify scorpion. 2. Take victim to a hospital or poison-control center for treatment with antivenin. 3. Apply cold compress or ammonia dressing.
Tick Genus: *Dermacentor; Ixodes; Ornithodoros.*	not known	Itching; local skin irritation. Poisonous species cause pain; redness; swelling; muscle cramps. Some species carry typhus and Rocky Mountain spotted fever.	1. Apply petroleum jelly, alcohol, or gasoline to tick, to loosen its jaws. 2. Use tweezers to remove tick. Do not leave jaws embedded. 3. Wash carefully.
Jellyfish For example: Portuguese man-of-war. Genus: *Physalia.* Other species have less serious effect.	sea anemone toxin; vasoconstrictor	Acute stinging or burning sensation; rash; blistering; shock; rarely causes death, unless from drowning as a result of shock.	1. Remove all tentacles. 2. Wash area with seawater, then with alcohol or ammonia. 3. Take victim to a hospital.
Black widow spider Genus: *Latrodectus.*	neurotoxin	Swelling around bite; cramplike pain in chest, abdomen and legs; muscle rigidity; nausea; fever; bite is sometimes fatal.	1. Identify spider. 2. Take victim to a hospital. 3. Lay the victim down; let bitten arm or leg hang down.
Brown spider Genus: *Loxosceles.*	cytotoxin; enzyme; hemolytic agent	Sharp burning sensation; whiteness at bite, surrounded by red swelling; blistering; bleeding into tissues; vomiting; fever; rarely, heart failure, and death.	1. Identify spider. 2. Take victim to a hospital. 3. Lay the victim down. 4. Let a bitten arm or leg hang down.
Tarantula spider Genus: *Aphonopelma; Eurypelma.*	variable, depending on species and location	Slight pain like a pinprick; poison is usually mild and may be harmless.	1. Identify spider. 2. Wash bite with warm salted water.
Gila monster Genus: *Heloderma.*	neurotoxin (heloderma venom)	Local pain; swelling; nausea; respiratory distress; heart failure; in some cases, death.	Treat as snakebite.

Name	Toxic substance	Symptoms	Treatment
Copperhead Genus: *Agkistrodon*.	enzymes	Shock; local pain; swelling; vomiting; blood in stools; may be fatal.	General treatment is the same for any snakebite. 1. Lay the victim down. 2. Calm and reassure the victim.
Coral Snake Genus: *Micrurus*; *Micruroides*.	enzymes	Shock; numbness; headache; vomiting; swollen face; sore throat; rapid heartbeat; may be fatal.	3. Keep the bitten part still. 4. If the bitten part is an arm or leg, let it hang down.
Fer-de-lance Genus: *Bothrops*.	enzymes	Shock; local pain; bleeding from bite; blood does not clot; bleeding into tissues; respiratory distress; may be fatal.	5. Take victim to a hospital or poison-control center for treatment with the specific antivenin. 6. If the victim cannot be moved, summon medical help at once.
Rattlesnake Genus: *Crotalus*.	enzymes	Shock; local pain; swelling; bleeding into tissues; vomiting; dry mouth; problems with speech and vision; may be fatal.	7. Clean the bite, but do not apply a tourniquet, and do not cut or suck the bite. 8. If victim is unconscious, place in recovery position.
Water moccasin Genus: *Agkistrodon*.	enzymes	Shock; local pain; vomiting; blood in stools; tiny bleeding spots on skin; may be fatal.	

Emergencies

What to do in a medical emergency

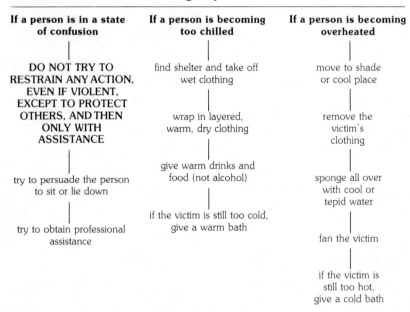

If a person is in a state of confusion	If a person is becoming too chilled	If a person is becoming overheated
DO NOT TRY TO RESTRAIN ANY ACTION, EVEN IF VIOLENT, EXCEPT TO PROTECT OTHERS, AND THEN ONLY WITH ASSISTANCE	find shelter and take off wet clothing	move to shade or cool place
try to persuade the person to sit or lie down	wrap in layered, warm, dry clothing	remove the victim's clothing
try to obtain professional assistance	give warm drinks and food (not alcohol)	sponge all over with cool or tepid water
	if the victim is still too cold, give a warm bath	fan the victim
		if the victim is still too hot, give a cold bath

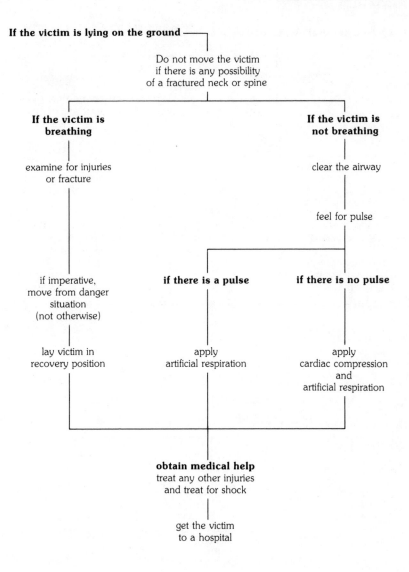

If the victim is lying on the ground

Do not move the victim
if there is any possibility
of a fractured neck or spine

**If the victim is
breathing**

examine for injuries
or fracture

**If the victim is
not breathing**

clear the airway

feel for pulse

if imperative,
move from danger
situation
(not otherwise)

if there is a pulse

if there is no pulse

lay victim in
recovery position

apply
artificial respiration

apply
cardiac compression
and
artificial respiration

obtain medical help
treat any other injuries
and treat for shock

get the victim
to a hospital

If a person has swallowed a poison or a chemical

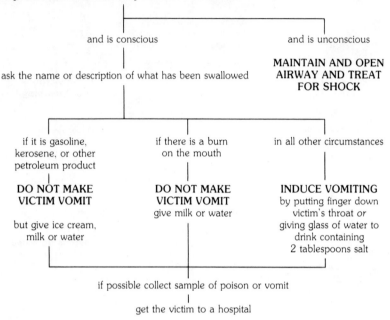

and is conscious

and is unconscious

ask the name or description of what has been swallowed

MAINTAIN AND OPEN AIRWAY AND TREAT FOR SHOCK

if it is gasoline, kerosene, or other petroleum product

if there is a burn on the mouth

in all other circumstances

DO NOT MAKE VICTIM VOMIT

but give ice cream, milk or water

DO NOT MAKE VICTIM VOMIT

give milk or water

INDUCE VOMITING

by putting finger down victim's throat *or* giving glass of water to drink containing 2 tablespoons salt

if possible collect sample of poison or vomit

get the victim to a hospital

If a person has a head injury

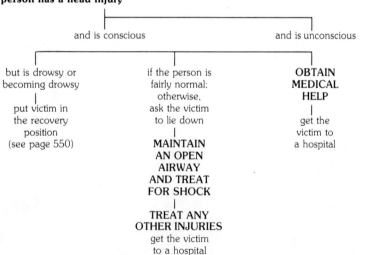

and is conscious

and is unconscious

but is drowsy or becoming drowsy

put victim in the recovery position (see page 550)

if the person is fairly normal; otherwise, ask the victim to lie down

MAINTAIN AN OPEN AIRWAY AND TREAT FOR SHOCK

TREAT ANY OTHER INJURIES

get the victim to a hospital

OBTAIN MEDICAL HELP

get the victim to a hospital

If a person is drowning

in a lake, in the sea, etc.

having fallen through ice

where there is a rope or life buoy

throw it to the victim

haul the victim to safety

where there is no rope or life buoy

observe position of victim carefully

in case the victim sinks, swim to the victim and give artificial respiration; tow the victim to safety

DO NOT GO ONTO THE ICE UNLESS SECURELY ATTACHED AND THERE IS NO ALTERNATIVE

throw a rope *or* push a ladder *or* form a human chain to reach victim and pull to safety

If a person is lying inert in a gas-filled room

DO NOT ENTER THE ROOM

see that professional assistance is called

obtain a rope and, if possible, breathing apparatus

tie the rope around your waist, leaving the other end in the hands of assistants

enter the room (with breathing apparatus, if possible)

open the doors and windows

remove the victim

(If you yourself are overcome by the gas, the rope will enable you to be hauled out immediately.)

If a person is wedged tight

DO NOT TRY TO MOVE THE VICTIM

shout for assistance

protect victim from any possible further injury as much as possible

If a person is stuck at a dangerous height

reassure the victim by talking slowly and calmly

DO NOT ATTEMPT A RESCUE ON YOUR OWN

if you are alone, explain to the victim that you must go and get help

If a person is in contact with an electric current

DO NOT TOUCH THE VICTIM

turn off the electric current *or* remove the fuse *or* if the victim is blocking the means of turning off the current, push the victim away, using a **wooden** chair or **dry** stick, and standing on a dry surface

If a person is lying inert surrounded by fire

wet a cloth

if the heat is too much, cover your nose and mouth with the cloth and crawl along the floor to the victim; pull the victim to safety

17

Home accident prevention checklist

Falls

☑ Provide adequate lighting for all areas of the house.

☐ Install handrails on stairways and in the bathroom.

☐ Secure firmly all loose carpets and rugs.

☐ Do not leave toys or other small objects lying around on the floor.

☐ If there are children in the house, install safety bars at the top of stairways.

☐ Do not allow young children to remain alone near open windows.

Fires and burns

☐ Place sparkscreens around all open fires.

☐ Check regularly that all electrical appliances, sockets, plugs, and leads are in good repair.

☐ Switch off all electrical appliances when they are not being used.

☐ Keep all flammable liquids out of the reach of children.

☐ Do not hang clothes or towels over cookers or heaters to dry.

☐ Buy children's clothes, especially night clothes, made of flame-resistant fabric.

Poisoning

☐ Keep all medicines and other potentially dangerous substances and liquids in locked cabinets.

☐ Keep all medicines and tablets in their original containers, clearly labeled.

☐ Check the correct dosage for all medicines and tablets before taking them.

☐ Destroy or return to the pharmacy all unused medicines and tablets.

☐ Check regularly that all gas appliances are in good repair and make sure that there is good ventilation when using them.

Suffocation

☐ Keep all plastic bags inaccessible to children.

☐ Check that all blankets in a baby's crib are secure and cannot be pulled over the baby's face. Do not allow a young baby to sleep on a soft pillow.

☐ Watch over a baby when he or she is feeding and take appropriate action in case of choking.

Home fires: emergency action

Type of fire	What to do
Deep-fat fryer	Turn off the heat and cover the fryer with a metal lid if you can approach it. Do not attempt to move the appliance. Do not fight the fire. Evacuate; then call the fire department.
Food in the oven	Close the oven door. Turn off the heat.
Small pan fire on the stove	Cover pan with a lid or plate. Turn off the heat.
Smoke from an electric motor or appliance	Pull the plug or otherwise turn off the electricity. If the appliance is flaming, use water *after* the electricity is off.
Smoke from a television	Keep clear—the picture tube may burst. Call the fire department. Shut off power to the circuit.
Someone else's clothing	Do not let the person run. Get the victim on the ground—grab and push if necessary. Use anything handy to smother the flames—a rug, coat, blanket, drapes, towel, bedspread, or jacket. If outside, use sand, dirt, snow, or anything else handy. Do not wrap the victim's face—only the body. Try to remove the burning clothing, but do not pull it over the victim's head.
Your own clothing	Do not run—it fans the flames. Lie down; roll over and over; remove the clothing if you can do so without pulling it over your head. Act fast.

Highway accident checklist

Prevent further accidents

☑ Turn off your engine and ensure other drivers do the same; ensure that the engine of any vehicle involved in the accident is turned off.

☐ Put out cigarettes.

☐ Place a warning signal (such as a red triangle) at least fifty yards (meters) back down the highway.

☐ Switch on your hazard warning lights.

Highway accident checklist—*continued*

☐ Shine your dimmed headlights either at oncoming traffic or at the accident scene.

☐ Check around the accident scene for any victim who may have been thrown clear of the crash, who may be lying where he or she could be hit by moving traffic.

☐ Remove debris from road.

Carry out first-aid procedures

☐ Quickly check each victim and then tend to the most seriously injured.

☐ Undo all motorcycle crash helmet straps and remove helmet in order to assess injury and to prevent suffocation. Do not do this if neck or back injuries are suspected.

☐ Do not move any victim unless there is serious danger of fire or fumes or of being run over.

☐ Treat victims with appropriate first aid.

Alert the rescue and hospital services

☐ The information they will require includes the exact location; the nature of the accident; the number of victims; the type of injuries sustained; whether there are any victims trapped; whether there are any special hazards, such as fire, acid, gas, etc.

Weather: emergency precautions

General	Inside	Outside
Earthquakes usually strike unexpectedly and leave no time for preparation. If the area has a history of earthquakes, survival may depend on knowing these rules and following them as soon as an earthquake begins. It is essential not to panic. Although the tremors can be frightening, the main danger is from falling debris.	Stay indoors. Doorways are the strongest parts of the interior of any building and are the safest indoor places to shelter. Other safe places are against walls or beneath a table, desk, or bed. Stay away from windows and any other glass. Douse all fires and do not use an open flame, because there may be gas leaks.	Outdoors, move away from buildings and overhead cables. Stay out in the open until the tremors stop. The greatest danger is from falling masonry outside doorways and beneath overhanging roofs and walls. A tidal wave may follow an earthquake in low-lying coastal regions. Anticipate this consequence and move to higher ground, away from the coast. Stay out of the danger zone until authorized to return. There may be a whole series of waves.
Floods are perhaps the most common of all natural disasters. Learn the flood history of the locality and find out the elevation of the surrounding areas. In lower areas, keep on hand sandbags, plywood, and plastic sheeting. Store adequate supplies of drinking water in clean utensils. Even the bathtub can be used as an emergency container.	Do not use gas or electric appliances; water may have seeped into burners and wiring.	Do not enter a flooded area unless it is necessary. Cross a stream that is deeper than knee-level only with utmost caution. Avoid driving on flooded roads. If this is unavoidable, check the depth of the water and the road surface. Be especially cautious at night, when the dangers of floodwater are difficult to see. If the vehicle stalls, abandon it at once and move to higher ground.

General	Inside	Outside
Hurricanes are forecast well in advance, so stay tuned for a hurricane warning. The hurricane may not strike for twenty-four hours, and there should be time to move to a community shelter.	If the home is sturdy and on high ground, remain indoors throughout the storm. Board up or shutter all windows. Stay tuned for bulletins. If the eye of the hurricane passes overhead, there will be a lull lasting for perhaps half an hour. Stay indoors during this lull if possible.	Leave low-lying areas that may be swept by high seas. Abandon mobile homes, campers, and boats, but lash them down securely. Seek refuge in a community shelter. Secure all loose outdoor objects, such as garbage cans, porch furniture, and tools.
Thunder and lightning occur during periods of strong rising air currents. Watch for darkening skies, thunderclouds, lightning, and increasing winds. A person who is struck by lightning receives a severe electric shock and may suffer burns. The person retains no electric current. Burns may require treatment. A person who is knocked unconscious by lightning can often be revived by prompt artificial respiration or, if necessary, with cardiac pulmonary resuscitation.	Stay indoors. Keep away from windows, fireplaces, and all metal objects. Do not use the telephone or any electric appliance. A battery radio should be kept tuned for warnings of tornadoes or flash floods that may develop in stormy conditions.	If in an automobile, stay there. If using machinery, leave it. Do not touch or go near any metal object. If in water, get out. Beach and abandon small boats. Seek shelter in a building, a cave, ditch, or large clump of tall trees. Where there is no shelter, stay below the skyline and keep far away from any isolated tree or other tall feature in the vicinity. If an electric charge is felt, causing the hair to stand on end, drop to the ground at once.
Tornadoes occur seasonally. If the area has a history of tornadoes, it is wise to build a storm cellar near the home. Build it with reinforced concrete and cover the roof with three feet of dirt, sloped for drainage. The door should be heavy and open inward. Add a ventilating shaft. Slope the floor to a drainage outlet or dig a dry well. Keep a flashlight, crowbar, shovel, and pickaxe in the cellar.	Seek shelter immediately after a tornado warning. If the building has neither basement nor storm cellar, take refuge in any small interior room. If there is only one large room, shelter near a sturdy wall. Stay away from windows. Crouch under heavy furniture.	If in a vehicle try to drive away from the tornado at right angles to its path. If you cannot outrun the tornado, park the vehicle and seek shelter. If there is an underpass or a bridge nearby, crouch behind its supports. If caught out in the open with no shelter, lie flat on the ground or in any depression.
Winter storms may cause weeks of isolation, and this must be kept in mind when making preparations. There is plenty of time to stock up with adequate food, fuel, and other supplies.	Stay inside as much as possible during cold weather and storms. Children must be taught that although snow looks inviting it can prove dangerous to play in, because of deep unnoticeable drifts.	Avoid overexertion when working outside in the cold. Wear several layers of loose-fitting warm clothing and outer garments that are both waterproof and windproof. Always cover the head.

Drugs

Drug use: short- and long-term effects

Drug	Medical use	Short-term effects	Long-term effects
Alcohol	Rarely used.	Relaxation; euphoria; drowsiness; lack of coordination; loss of emotional control.	Habituation; liver and brain damage; obesity with excessive use; addiction with prolonged use.
Amphetamines (Benzedrine; Methedrine; Dexedrine)	Relief of depression; reduction of fatigue; occasionally, for treatment of obesity.	Increased alertness; loss of appetite; insomnia; euphoria; large doses can produce hallucinations.	Habituation; irritability; restlessness; weight loss; mental disturbances.

Drug	Medical use	Short-term effects	Long-term effects
Antidepressants (dibenzodiazepines; MAO inhibitors)	Treatment of depression.	Mental stimulation; elevation of mood; occasionally, trembling, insomnia, confusion, and hallucinations. MAO inhibitors may interact adversely with some foods and other drugs.	Dry mouth; blurred vision; fatigue; skin rashes; palpitations; occasionally, jaundice.
Barbiturates (Amytal; Nembutal; Seconal; phenobarbital)	Treatment of insomnia and relief of nervous tension.	Intoxication; relaxation; drowsiness; lack of coordination; loss of emotional control; relief of anxiety; occasionally, euphoria. An overdose or a combination of barbiturates and alcohol can be fatal.	Habituation; irritability; weight loss; addiction. Severe withdrawal symptoms if the drug is suddenly discontinued.
Cocaine	Anesthesia of the eyes, ears, or nose.	Increased alertness; reduction of fatigue; reduction of appetite; insomnia; euphoria. Large doses may cause hallucinations, convulsions, and death.	If sniffed, ulceration of the nose. Other long-term effects similar to those of amphetamines.
Hallucinogens (LSD; psilocybin; STP; DMT; mescaline)	Rarely used.	Hallucinations; lack of coordination; nausea; dilated pupils; irregular breathing; sometimes anxiety.	May precipitate mental disturbance in susceptible individuals. Occasionally, recurrence of original hallucinatory experience without taking further doses of the drug. May also cause chromosome damage.
Marijuana	Rarely used.	Relaxation; euphoria; alteration of time perception; lack of coordination. Large doses may produce hallucinations.	Long-term effects have not been definitely established. Prolonged, heavy use may lead to insomnia and depression on sudden withdrawal.
Narcotics (Opium; heroin; codeine; Demerol; methadone)	Treatment of severe pain.	Sedation; euphoria; relief of pain; lack of coordination; impaired mental functioning.	Constipation; loss of appetite; weight loss; temporary sterility; addiction, producing painful withdrawal symptoms on stopping use of the drug. The use of unsterilized hypodermic needles may cause severe infections.
Nicotine	None.	Mental stimulation; relaxation; relief of tension.	Cancer, particularly of the lungs; heart and blood vessel disease; bronchitis.
Tranquilizers (Librium; phenothiazines)	Treatment of anxiety and other mental disorders.	Relaxation; relief of anxiety; general depression of mental functioning.	Drowsiness; dry mouth; blurred vision; skin rashes; tremors; occasionally, jaundice.
Miscellaneous (Amyl nitrite; antihistamines; toluene and other solvents - "glue sniffing")	None, except for antihistamines for allergies and amyl nitrite for angina.	Euphoria, lack of coordination; impaired mental functioning.	Variable. Some of these substances can cause liver and kidney damage.

Major drugs: medical usage

Drug	Medical usage	Drug	Medical usage
Amphetamines	To treat narcolepsy and depression	**Diuretics**	To treat edema and high blood pressure
Analgesics	To reduce pain		
Anorectics	To reduce appetite	**Hematinics**	To treat anemia
Antacids	To counteract excess stomach acidity	**Insulin**	To treat diabetes
		Muscle relaxants	To relax muscles, especially during surgery
Antibiotics	To treat micro and organismal infections		
		Pediculicides	To destroy lice
Anticoagulants	To treat thrombosis	**Respiratory stimulants**	To treat breathing stoppage
Antidepressants	To treat depression		
Antihistamines	To treat allergies	**Scabicides**	To destroy mites
Antinauseants	To treat nausea	**Sedatives**	To treat anxiety or insomnia
Antipruritics	To relieve itching	**Thyroid preparations**	To treat goiter, hypothyroidism, hyperthyroidism, and thyroiditis
Antipyretics	To reduce fever		
Barbiturates	To treat insomnia	**Tranquilizers**	To treat anxiety and various mental disorders
Bronchial dilators	To treat bronchial asthma		
Chelating agents	To treat poisoning by heavy metals	**Uricosuric agents**	To treat gout
Contraceptives	To prevent conception	**Urinary acidifiers**	To increase the effectiveness of certain drugs and to increase the elimination of drugs by the kidneys
Digitalis	To treat heart failure		

Drug emergencies

The first aid treatment of a drug overdose is the same for all drugs. *Act swiftly.* If time is wasted, more of the drug will be absorbed. Do not leave the victim alone. Ask somebody else to summon emergency medical aid.

If the victim is conscious, ask what happened. Try to keep the victim conscious. If the victim is a child give him or her syrup of ipecac to induce vomiting. Watch that the child does not choke from inhaling the vomit.

If the victim is unconscious, place him or her in the recovery position. If the victim vomits while unconscious, check that the victim's air passage is clear.

Look for evidence to determine whether the victim has taken a drug. An overdose of some drugs may cause convulsions. There may be pills in the victim's mouth or empty pill containers nearby. Drug addicts may have a hypodermic syringe; they may also have needle marks on their skin, usually on the inside of the forearm. Keep pill containers, pills, and specimens of the victim's vomit. These will help in finding out which drug was taken.

Step-by-step emergency action

1. *If the victim is conscious,* induce vomiting by putting your fingers down the victim's throat. Do not give salt water to drink. This may be positively harmful. *Do not attempt to induce vomiting if the victim is unconscious,* nor if the victim has taken a drug overdose by either injection or by inhalation.

2. *Keep a close check on the victim's breathing and pulse at all times.* If the victim stops breathing, give artificial resuscitation.

3. *If the victim's heart stops,* give external cardiac compression. If the victim has also stopped breathing and help is unavailable, you will have to alternate between external cardiac compression and resuscitation.

4. *If the victim's heart and breathing have both stopped* and help is available, one person should kneel at the victim's shoulder and give cardiac compression; another person should kneel at the victim's other side and give mouth-to-mouth resuscitation.

5. *The person giving external cardiac compression should press* the victim's chest at a rate of 15 times in 11 seconds. Only a trained person should use this method. The person giving resuscitation should ventilate twice within 15 seconds.

Drug overdose: examples and symptoms

Generic name	Examples	Signs and symptoms of overdosage
Acetaminophen	Tylenol* Parafon forte*	Nausea; vomiting; pallor; sweating; kidney failure; jaundice; difficulty breathing; delirium; and unconsciousness.
Alcohol	Beers; wines; spirits	Changes of mood; lack of coordination; slurred speech; sweating; rapid pulse; vomiting; drowsiness; and unconsciousness.
Amphetamines	Benzedrine* Dexedrine* Methedrine*	Excitement; dilated pupils; talkativeness; insomnia; tremors; exaggerated reflexes; bad breath; vomiting; diarrhea; fever; irregular, rapid heart rate; hallucinations; delirium; convulsions; and unconsciousness.
Anticoagulants	Dicumarol* Coumadin* Panwarfarin* Danilone* Prothromadin* Dindevan*	Nosebleeds; pallor; bleeding gums; bruising; blood in the urine and feces; shock; and coma.
Antidepressants	1) Tricyclic compounds—Tofranil* Elavil* 2) MAO inhibitors—Nardil*; Parnate*	1) Dry mouth; dilated pupils; vomiting; irregular heart rate; retention of urine; hallucinations; lack of coordination; exaggerated reflexes; agitation; convulsions; unconsciousness; and hypertension. 2) Agitation; hallucinations; exaggerated reflexes; irregular heart rate; sweating; retention of urine; convulsions; and muscular rigidity.
Antihistamines	Tripelennamine diphenhydramine chlorpheniramine promethazine	Excitement or depression; drowsiness; headache; irregular heart rate; nervousness; disorientation; lack of coordination; high fever; hallucinations; fixed, dilated pupils; delirium; convulsions; and coma.
Atropine	Hyoscyamine scopolamine stramamine	Dry mouth; hot, dry skin; flushing; high fever; dilated pupils; irregular heart rate; excitement; confusion; convulsions; delirium; and unconsciousness.
Barbiturates	Amytal* Nembutal* Seconal* phenobarbital	Drowsiness; headache; confusion; lack of coordination; slurred speech; lack of reflexes; slow breathing rate; and coma.
Benzodiazepines	Librium*; Valium* Mogadon*	Drowsiness; dizziness; lack of coordination; and, in rare cases, coma.
Caffeine	Coffee; tea; No-Doz* APC	Restlessness; excitement; frequent urination; rapid pulse; nausea; vomiting; fever; tremors; delirium; convulsions; and coma.

Generic name	Example	Signs and symptoms of overdosage
Cannabis		Overdose usually causes only sleepiness.
Chloral hydrate	Noctec*; Somnos*	An overdose of chloral hydrate produces symptoms similar to a barbiturate overdose, but chloral hydrate may also cause vomiting.
Cocaine		Stimulation followed by depression; nausea; vomiting; anxiety; hallucinations; sweating; difficulty breathing; and convulsions.
Contraceptive pill		Overdose may cause nausea and vomiting. It does not usually require emergency medical aid, but it is advisable to consult a physician.
Digitalis	Lanoxin* Crystodigin* Purodigin*	Vomiting; excessive salivation; diarrhea; drowsiness; confusion; irregular heart rate; delirium; hallucinations; and unconsciousness.
Diuretics	Hygroton*; Lasix* Edecrin*	Massive urine output and irregular heart rate. Rarely there may also be skin rashes and abnormal sensitivity to light.
Glutethimide	Doriden*	Drowsiness; lack of reflexes; pupil dilation; slow breathing rate; and coma.
Hallucinogens	LSD; psilocybin; STP DMT; mescaline	The symptoms of an overdose are not readily distinguishable from the normal effects of these drugs, which vary between individuals. The effects include hallucinations; nausea; and lack of coordination. In some cases, there may be extreme anxiety and delusions.
Ipecacuanha	Ipecac syrup	Nausea; vomiting, sometimes bloodstained; diarrhea; abdominal cramps; irregular heart rate; and cardiac arrest.
Iron		Nausea; vomiting, sometimes bloodstained; abdominal pain; pallor; headache; confusion; convulsions; and unconsciousness.
Meprobamate	Equanil*; Miltown*	Drowsiness; relaxation and muscular weakness; sleep; lack of reflexes; and coma.
Narcotics	Opium; heroin morphine; methadone codeine	Pinpoint pupils; drowsiness; shallow breathing; muscular relaxation; coma; slow pulse and respiratory arrest.
Phenothiazines	Chlorpromazine prochlorperazine trifluoperazine	Sleepiness; dry mouth; lack of coordination; muscular rigidity; tremors; uncontrollable facial grimacing; low body temperature; irregular heart rate; convulsions; and coma.
Quinine	Antimalarial drugs	Vomiting; deafness; blurred vision; dilated pupils; headache; dizziness; rapid breathing; irregular heart rate; and unconsciousness.
Rauwolfia alkaloids	Reserpine	Flushing; dry mouth; abdominal cramps; diarrhea; irregular heart rate; tremors; muscular rigidity; and unconsciousness.
Salicylates	Aspirin and many aspirin-containing painkillers.	Abdominal pain; nausea; vomiting; restlessness; noises in the ears; deafness; deep, rapid breathing; fever; sweating; irritability; confusion; delirium; convulsions; and coma.

*Registered trademark

Medical care

Common communicable diseases

Disease	Symptoms	Incubation period	Period of communicability	Preventive measures
Chicken Pox	Headache, fever, recurrent skin rashes that form crusts.	14 to 21 days.	From day before symptoms appear until 6 days after first rashes form.	None. Attack gives permanent immunity.
Diphtheria	Sore throat, hoarseness, fever.	2 to 5 days.	About 2 to 4 weeks.	Diphtheria toxoid injections, started at 2 months of age. Repeated doses throughout childhood.
German Measles	Headache, enlarged lymph nodes, cough, sore throat, rash.	14 to 21 days, usually 18 days.	From about 7 days before rash appears until about 5 days after.	German measles (rubella) vaccine. Attack usually gives permanent immunity.
Gonorrhea	Irritation of sex organs, with discharge of pus. More noticeable in males than females.	Usually 3 to 4 days, sometimes 9 days or longer.	Months or years.	Avoid sexual contact with infected individuals.
Influenza	Fever, chills, muscular aches and pains.	1 to 3 days.	When symptoms appear until 7 days after.	Influenza vaccine protects for only a few months.
Measles	Fever, body aches, cough, rash, eyes sensitive to light.	10 to 14 days.	From 4 days before rash appears until 5 days after.	Measles vaccines.
Mononucleosis (Glandular Fever)	Sore throat, enlarged lymph glands, fatigue.	4 to 14 days.	Unknown.	None.
Mumps	Chills, headache, fever, swollen glands in neck and throat.	14 to 21 days, usually 18 days.	From 7 days before until 9 days after symptoms, or until swelling disappears.	Mumps vaccine. Gamma globulin protects after exposure.
Poliomyelitis	Fever, sore throat, muscle pain, stiff back, paralysis.	Paralytic, 9 to 13 days. Nonparalytic, 4 to 10 days.	Last part of incubation period and first week of acute illness.	Poliomyelitis vaccines.
Scarlet Fever	Sore throat, rash, high fever, chills.	2 to 5 days.	Beginning of incubation period until 2 or 3 weeks after symptoms appear.	None. Attack usually gives permanent immunity.
Syphilis	Chancre sore, usually on sex organs; followed in 3 to 6 weeks by sores in mouth and a rash.	10 days to 10 weeks, usually 3 weeks.	Variable and indefinite during 2 to 4 years after infection.	Avoid sexual contact with infected individuals.

Immunizations
Traveler's immunization

Immunization	Schedule and protection	Areas recommended for
Cholera	International certificate valid for six months beginning 6 days after one injection.	All Asian countries; Australasia; many African countries.
Gamma globulin (immune serum globulin)	One injection just prior to departure. Gives three to four months' protection, but only partly against infectious hepatitis.	Countries outside northwestern Europe and Australasia where sanitation is of a low standard.
Poliomyelitis	Three doses of oral vaccine at four- to six-week intervals. Valid for five years.	All countries.
Tetanus	Three injections; the second, one month after the first; the third, six months later. Valid for five years, and usually combined with the typhoid immunization.	All countries.
Typhoid	Two injections a couple of weeks apart. Valid between one and three years.	All countries except northwestern Europe.
Typhus	Two injections seven to ten days apart. Valid for one year.	Southeastern Asia; India; Ethiopia.
Yellow fever	International certificate valid for ten years beginning 10 days after one injection.	Some central African countries; some South American countries.

Children's immunization

Age	Vaccine
2 months	Diphtheria, tetanus, and whooping cough*; polio†
4 months	Diphtheria, tetanus, and whooping cough; polio
6 months	Diphtheria, tetanus, and whooping cough
15 months	German measles, measles, mumps**
18 months	Diphtheria, tetanus, and whooping cough booster; polio booster
4–6 years	Diphtheria, tetanus, and whooping cough booster; polio booster
14–16 years	Diphtheria and tetanus booster‡
Every 10 years thereafter	Diphtheria and tetanus booster

*Diphtheria, tetanus, and whooping cough (pertussis) vaccines generally are combined in one dose of DTP vaccine.
†Oral (Sabin) polio virus vaccine.
**German measles, measles, and mumps vaccines may be combined in one dose.
‡Adult-type diphtheria-tetanus vaccine.
Source: United States Public Health Service.

Recommended immunization for children not immunized in infancy

Schedule	Age < 7 years	Age > 7 years
First Visit	DTP, OPV	Td, OPV
Interval after first visit		
1 month	Measles, Mumps, Rubella	Measles, Mumps, Rubella
2 months	DTP, OPV	Td, OPV
4 months	DTP	
8–14 months		Td, OPV
10–16 months or preschool	DTP, OPV	
14–16 years		TD

Medicine cabinet checklist

☑ **Adhesive dressings, assorted**
For various minor injuries such as cuts, bites, stings, and blisters

☐ **Adhesive strip, breathing**
For allowing air to reach minor wounds.

☐ **Adhesive tape, waterproof**
For minor wounds that must be kept dry.

☐ **Bandages, conforming**
These are stretchy cotton bandages useful for bandaging awkward places.

☐ **Bandages, one-inch wide**
For bandaging fingers and toes.

☐ **Bandages, triangular**
For keeping dressings in place and to use as slings.

☐ **Bandages, two-inch wide**
For bandaging hands and feet.

☐ **Cotton**
For cleaning and drying wounds and awkward places such as the ear.

☐ **Cream, antihistamine**
For insect bites and stings.

☐ **Cream, antiseptic**
For applying to small wounds after they have been washed with antiseptic lotion.

☐ **Eyebath**
For bathing or washing the eyes. Rinse the eyebath out to remove any grit before using it.

☐ **Eye pads, sterile**
For placing over the eye underneath a bandage.

☐ **First-aid book**
Note the telephone number of a hospital.

☐ **Flashlight**
Test the batteries and bulb regularly.

☐ **Gauze, absorbent**
For tying over bleeding wounds.

☐ **Gauze, sterile**
For covering more serious wounds until emergency medical help arrives.

☐ **Lotion, antiseptic**
For cleaning wounds prior to bandaging them.

☐ **Lotion, soothing**
A preparation such as calamine lotion to relieve sunburn, rashes, and skin irritations.

☐ **Measuring cup**
A measuring cup should always be used for accurate dilution of lotions and medicines.

☐ **Notepad and pencil**
For noting information that may be useful to a physician, such as pulse rate and rate of breathing.

☐ **Painkillers**
For the relief of minor pains such as headaches. Acetaminophen or aspirin is suitable. Persistent pain needs medical attention.

☐ **Petroleum jelly**
For applying on gauze to prevent sticking.

☐ **Safety pins**
At least six.

☐ **Scissors, blunt-ended**
Blunt-ended for safety.

☐ **Thermometer**

☐ **Throat lozenges**
For sore throats.

☐ **Tissues**
A spare box should be kept in the first-aid box.

☐ **Travel sickness pills**
Try several of the different brands available for choosing the most suitable.

☐ **Tweezers, spade-ended**
For removing splinters.

☐ **Upset stomach preparation**
Any of the various antacids suitable.

Hospitalization

Choosing a hospital for your child

☑ Does the hospital offer pre-admission tours?

☐ Does the hospital send out information booklets about the facilities? Any special booklets for children?

☐ What is the hospital policy about parents staying overnight with children? What are the sleeping arrangements for parents?

☐ Can parents participate in the care of their children? Can they bathe their children? Take their temperatures?

☐ What are the visiting rules?

☐ Does the hospital have a playroom or arrangements for other children when parents come to visit the hospitalized child? If so, what are the hours?

☐ What can the child expect as a routine part of being admitted to the hospital? What kind of tests? Who will conduct the tests?

☐ Does the hospital have medical students, interns, and residents working in it? Who will examine the child?

☐ What kind of room will the child be in? How many other children will be there?

☐ Are there TV's in all of the rooms? Can arrangements be made to rent one?

☐ Are children allowed to wear their own clothes in the hospital?

☐ Are there hospital rules regarding bringing toys or teddy bears?

☐ Does the hospital have special policies about parents being in the recovery room with their children? Policies about parents being with the child while he or she is given anesthesia?

☐ Is there a children's activities department or a play program of any kind?

Medicare coverage

Major services covered when you are a hospital inpatient
1. A semiprivate room (2 to 4 beds in a room)
2. All your meals, including special diets
3. Regular nursing services
4. Costs of special care units, such as an intensive care unit, coronary care unit, etc.
5. Drugs furnished by the hospital during your stay
6. Blood transfusions furnished by the hospital during your stay
7. Lab tests included in your hospital bill
8. X-rays and other radiology services, including radiation therapy, billed by the hospital
9. Medical supplies such as casts, surgical dressings, and splints
10. Use of appliances, such as a wheelchair
11. Operating and recovery room costs, including hospital costs for anesthesia services
12. Rehabilitation services, such as physical therapy, occupational therapy, and speech pathology services

Some services *not* covered when you are a hospital inpatient
1. Personal convenience items that you request such as a television, radio, or telephone in your room
2. Private duty nurses
3. Any extra charges for a private room, unless it is determined to be medically necessary

Major services covered when you are in a skilled nursing facility
1. A semiprivate room (2 to 4 beds in a room)
2. All your meals, including special diets
3. Regular nursing services
4. Rehabilitation services, such as physical, occupational, and speech therapy
5. Drugs furnished by the facility during your stay
6. Blood transfusions furnished to you during your stay

7. Medical supplies such as splints and casts
8. Use of appliances, such as a wheelchair

Some services *not* covered when you are in a skilled nursing facility

1. Personal convenience items you request such as a television, radio, or telephone in your room
2. Private duty nurses
3. Any extra charges for a private room, unless it is determined to be medically necessary

Major doctors' services covered by medical insurance

1. Medical and surgical services, including anesthesia
2. Diagnostic tests and procedures that are part of your treatment
3. Other services which are ordinarily furnished in the doctor's office and included in his or her bill, such as:
   X-rays you receive as part of your treatment
   Services of your doctor's office nurse
   Drugs and biologicals that cannot be self-administered
   Transfusions of blood and blood components
   Medical supplies
   Physical therapy and speech pathology services

Some doctors' services *not* covered by medical insurance

1. Routine physical examinations and tests directly related to such examinations
2. Routine foot care
3. Eye or hearing examinations for prescribing or fitting eyeglasses or hearing aids
4. Immunizations (except pneumococcal vaccinations or immunizations required because of an injury or immediate risk of infection)
5. Cosmetic surgery unless it is needed because of accidental injury or to improve the functioning of a malformed part of the body

Major outpatient hospital services covered by medical insurance

1. Services in an emergency room or outpatient clinic
2. Laboratory tests billed by the hospital
3. X-rays and other radiology services billed by the hospital
4. Medical supplies such as splints and casts
5. Drugs and biologicals which cannot be self-administered
6. Blood transfusions furnished to you as an outpatient

Some outpatient hospital services *not* covered by medical insurance

1. Routine physical examinations and tests directly related to such examinations
2. Eye or ear examinations to prescribe or fit eyeglasses or hearing aids
3. Immunizations (except pneumococcal vaccinations or immunizations required because of an injury or immediate risk of infection)
4. Routine foot care

Home health services covered by Medicare
1. Part-time skilled nursing care
2. Physical therapy
3. Speech therapy
   If you need part-time skilled nursing care, physical therapy, or speech therapy, Medicare can also pay for:
   Occupational therapy
   Part-time services of home health aids
   Medical social services
   Medical supplies and equipment provided by the agency

Home health services *not* covered by Medicare
1. Full-time nursing care at home
2. Drugs and biologicals
3. Meals delivered to your home
4. Homemaker services
5. Blood transfusions

Exercise

Major sports: exercise and conditioning

Sport	Special exercises	Complementary exercises
Archery	grip exercise: squeeze a rubber ball hard in each hand; also: one arm dumbbell rowing; shoulder turns, with bar.	bench press; pushups.
Badminton	wrist exercise: hold a dumbbell rod in each hand, with the forearms horizontal, and rotate the wrists; holding a dumbbell rod like a racket, move as during a game; also: seesaw movement; skipping.	exercise the other arm; chinning; one arm dumbbell rowing.
Baseball	sprinting exercise: run hard for thirty yards (27.4 meters), lie down, do two pushups, sprint thirty yards; also: grip exercise; shoulder turns with bar.	exercise the other arm.
Basketball	squat jumps: squat down with the hands on the floor, then jump up, stretching the arms as high as possible over the head; also: squat; press with dumbbells.	basketball exercises all muscle groups.
Canoeing	situps; shoulder turns with bar; bench press, press with dumbbells; flying exercise; chinning.	leg exercises; skipping; facedown, legs raise.
Cycling	squat; deep kneebends with dumbbells; legs curl; situps; stepups; leg exercises.	chinning; hanging; reverse arch; shoulder turn.
Football	pushing exercises against an immobile object; all advanced exercises; weight training with professional supervision; sprinting exercises.	football exercises all muscle groups.
Golf	knee exercise: stand with feet slightly apart, and turn the hips and knees in one direction, then the other, simulating golfing movements; also: grip exercise.	golf uses most muscle groups to a slight extent; a more vigorous, aerobic exercise is also recommended.
Handball	wrist exercises; leg exercises; seesaw movement.	handball exercises all muscle groups.
Hiking	thigh and hip exercise: while standing, balance a weight, such as a sandbag, on the foot, and lift the leg as high as possible, bending the knee; also: leg exercises; seesaw movement.	hiking exercises all muscle groups.

Sport	Special exercises	Complementary exercises
Horseback riding	thigh grip exercise: squeeze a large medicine ball hard between the knees; also: wide kneebends; squat; leg parting; one arm dumbbell rowing.	abdominal exercises; back and chest exercises.
Rock climbing	grip exercise; bench press; shoulder turns with bar; hanging, reverse arch; situps; chinning; leg side raise; squat; seesaw movement.	rock climbing exercises all muscle groups.
Rowing	squat jumps; chinning; situps; pushups; skipping; running, for stamina.	shoulder raise; facedown, legs raise; leg back raise.
Running (Jogging)	leg exercises; legs raise, on angled board; shoulder turns, with bar; straight arm pullover.	running exercises all muscle groups.
Skating	ankle exercise: stand with feet slightly apart, and rock the ankles from side to side; also: deep kneebends with dumbbells; seesaw movement.	back and chest exercises; press with dumbbells.
Skiing	thigh strength exercise: lean the back flat against a smooth wall, with the feet together, about 2 ft (0.6 meters) away, then bend the legs so that the back slides down as low as possible, and push up again; adapt ankle exercise and knee exercise to the movements of skiing; also: leg exercises; seesaw movement.	skiing exercises all muscle groups.
Soccer	ankle exercise; knee exercise; leg exercises; legs curl; neck exercises; shoulder turns, with bar.	soccer exercises all muscle groups.
Squash and Racquetball	wrist exercises; leg exercises; seesaw movement; skipping; situps.	exercise the other arm.
Swimming	straight arm pullover; shoulder turns, with bar; situps; shoulder raise; alternate legs raise.	chinning.
Tennis	wrist exercises; leg exercises; skipping; straight arm pullover; hanging, reverse arch; seesaw movement.	exercise the other arm.
Volleyball	squat jumps; press with dumbbells; hanging, reverse arch; straight arm pullover.	one arm dumbbell rowing; chinning.
Waterskiing	squat; deep kneebends with dumbbells; one arm dumbbell rowing; chinning.	hanging, reverse arch; shoulder raise.

Height and weight table

Male
Weight at ages 25-59 based on lowest mortality. Weight in pounds according to frame (in indoor clothing weighing 5 lbs., shoes with 1" heels).

Female
Weights and ages 25-59 based on lowest mortality. Weight in pounds according to frame (in indoor clothing weighing 3 lbs., shoes with 1" heels).

Height Feet	Inches	Small Frame	Medium Frame	Large Frame	Height Feet	Inches	Small Frame	Medium Frame	Large Frame
5	2	128-134	131-141	138-150	4	10	102-111	109-121	118-131
5	3	130-136	133-143	140-153	4	11	103-113	111-123	120-134
5	4	132-138	135-145	142-156	5	0	104-115	113-126	122-137
5	5	134-140	137-148	144-160	5	1	106-118	115-129	125-140
5	6	136-142	139-151	146-164	5	2	108-121	118-132	128-143
5	7	138-145	142-154	149-168	5	3	111-124	121-135	131-147
5	8	140-148	145-157	152-172	5	4	114-127	124-138	134-151
5	9	142-151	148-160	155-176	5	5	117-130	127-141	137-155
5	10	144-154	151-163	158-180	5	6	120-133	130-144	140-159
5	11	146-157	154-166	161-184	5	7	123-136	133-147	143-163
6	0	149-160	157-170	164-188	5	8	126-139	136-150	146-167
6	1	152-164	160-174	168-192	5	9	129-142	139-153	149-170
6	2	155-168	164-178	172-197	5	10	132-145	142-156	152-173
6	3	158-172	167-182	176-202	5	11	135-148	145-159	155-176
6	4	162-176	171-187	181-207	6	0	138-151	148-162	158-179

2 Diet and nutrition

The second section of TABLES AND FORMULAS is designed to aid in your campaign for better health. Covering diet and nutrition, Section 2 includes tables of common, and not-so-common, weights and measures. Charts are offered to illustrate how recipes can be adjusted to accommodate more dinner guests than expected, perfect for those emergencies when every guest brings a friend.

There are special tables for the home canner and preserver. A GRAS, "generally regarded as safe," chart lists food additives that can be used with confidence. Two tables give the cholesterol content of many types of foods and the fat content quotients of various dishes you may wish to avoid if on a diet. A calorie and energy-consumption equivalencies chart also serves the reader who is calorie conscious. Included are tables for the reader on a special diet; these offer ingredient exchanges and substitution ideas.

Another special table compares costs between convenience and homemade foods. "Diet and Nutrition" is rounded off with tips for more economical and convenient meal planning. The cook who uses the oven consistently will find the United States Department of Agriculture tables on roasting and broiling times an encyclopedic and indispensable aid to better cooking results.

Weights and measures

Metric conversion table

When you know:	Multiply by:	To find:
Length and distance		
inches (in.)	25.0	millimeters
feet (ft.)	30.0	centimeters
yards (yd.)	0.9	meters
miles (mi.)	1.6	kilometers
millimeters (mm)	0.04	inches
centimeters (cm)	0.4	inches
meters (m)	1.1	yards
kilometers (km)	0.6	miles
Weight and mass		
ounces (oz.)	28.0	grams
pounds (lb.)	0.45	kilograms
short tons	0.9	metric tons
grams (g)	0.035	ounces
kilograms (kg)	2.2	pounds
metric tons (t)	1.1	short tons

When you know:	Multiply by:	To find:
Volume and capacity (liquid)		
fluid ounces (fl. oz)	30.0	milliliters
pints (pt.), U.S.	0.47	liters
pints (pt.), imperial	0.568	liters
quarts (qt.), U.S.	0.95	liters
quarts (qt.), imperial	1.137	liters
gallons (gal.), U.S.	3.8	liters
gallons (gal.), imperial	4.546	liters
milliliters (ml)	0.034	fluid ounces
liters (l)	2.1	pints, U.S.
liters (l)	1.76	pints, imperial
liters (l)	1.06	quarts, U.S.
liters (l)	0.88	quarts, imperial
liters (l)	0.26	gallons, U.S.
liters (l)	0.22	gallons, imperial

Kitchen unit equivalencies

Units	Tea-spoon-fuls	Table-spoon-fuls	Fluid ounces	Cup-fuls	Liquid pints	Liquid quarts	Milli-liters	Liters
1 teaspoonful equals	1	1/3	1/6	*	*	*	11	*
1 tablespoonful equals	3	1	1/2	1/16	1/32	*	15	*
1 fluid ounce equals	6	2	1	1/8	1/16	1/32	30	*
1 cupful equals	48	16	8	1	1/2	1/4	240	0.24
1 liquid pint equals	*	*	16	2	1	1/2	470	0.47
1 liquid quart equals	*	*	32	4	2	1	950	0.95
1 milliliter equals	1/5	*	*	*	*	*	1	1/1000
1 liter equals	*	*	34	4.2	2.1	1.06	1000	1
1 gallon equals	*	*	*	16	8	4	*	3.8

Kitchen conversion table

To convert	multiply	by
ounces to grams	the ounces	28.35
grams to ounces	the grams	0.035
liters to quarts	the liters	1.057
quarts to liters	the quarts	0.95
inches to centimeters	the inches	2.54
centimeters to inches	the centimeters	0.39

Weights per cup

Ingredient by cup	Ounces
Beans (dry)	6½
Butter, margarine, cooking oils	8
Citrus fruit juice (fresh)	8½
Cornflakes	1
Corn meal	5
Eggs (whole)	8½
Flour (wheat, all-purpose sifted)	4
Flour (cake, sifted)	3½
Milk (whole, fluid)	8½
Milk (dry)	4½
Nutmeats (pecan)	4
Oatmeal	3
Pancake mix	5
Prunes (dried)	5½
Raisins (seedless)	5
Rice	7
Shortening (vegetable)	7
Sugar (brown, moist, firmly packed)	7½
Sugar (granulated)	7
Water	8⅓

Can sizes by weight

Industrial term	Net weight
8 oz.	8 oz.
No. 1 or Picnic	10½ to 12 oz.
No. 303	16 to 17 oz.
No. 2	20 oz. (1 lb. 4 oz.)
No. 2½	29 oz. (1 lb. 13 oz.)
No. 3 Special	46 oz. (2 lb. 14 oz.)

Miscellaneous recipe measurements

Units	
a few grains equals	less than 1/8 teaspoon
1 jigger equals	3 tablespoons (1½ fluid ounces)
1 dash equals	6 to 7 drops (less than 1/8 tsp)
8 (dry) quarts equals	1 peck
4 pecks equals	1 bushel
16 (dry) ounces equals	1 pound

Recipe conversion factors

Conversion factors provide keys to adjustment of recipe sizes for feeding larger or smaller groups. Simply multiply the amount of each ingredient by the factor listed in the right-hand column of the table.

Number of servings desired	Factor
15 servings	0.6
20 servings	0.8
30 servings	1.2
35 servings	1.4
40 servings	1.6
50 servings	2.0

Adjusting recipe sizes

15 servings	20 servings	25 servings	30 servings	40 servings	50 servings

Volume measures

15 servings	20 servings	25 servings	30 servings	40 servings	50 servings
Dash	Dash	⅛ teaspoon	⅛ teaspoon	¼ teaspoon	¼ teaspoon
⅛ teaspoon	¼ teaspoon	¼ teaspoon	¼ teaspoon	⅜ teaspoon	½ teaspoon
¼ teaspoon	⅜ teaspoon	½ teaspoon	½ teaspoon	¾ teaspoon	1 teaspoon
½ teaspoon	½ teaspoon	¾ teaspoon	1 teaspoon	1¼ teaspoons	1½ teaspoons
½ teaspoon	¾ teaspoon	1 teaspoon	1¼ teaspoons	1½ teaspoons	2 teaspoons
1¼ teaspoons	1½ teaspoons	2 teaspoons	2½ teaspoons	3¼ teaspoons	4 teaspoons
1¾ teaspoons	2½ teaspoons	1 tablespoon	3½ teaspoons	4¾ teaspoons	2 tablespoons
2½ teaspoons	3¼ teaspoons	4 teaspoons	4¾ teaspoons	6½ teaspoons	8 teaspoons
3½ teaspoons	4¾ teaspoons	2 tablespoons	7¼ teaspoons	3 tablespoons	4 tablespoons
5½ teaspoons	7¼ teaspoons	3 tablespoons	11 teaspoons	5 tablespoons	6 tablespoons
7¼ teaspoons	3 tablespoons	¼ cup	⅓ cup	6 tablespoons	½ cup
3 tablespoons	¼ cup	⅓ cup	6 tablespoons	½ cup	⅔ cup
⅓ cup	6 tablespoons	½ cup	⅔ cup	¾ cup	1 cup
6 tablespoons	½ cup	⅔ cup	¾ cup	1 cup	1⅓ cups
½ cup	⅔ cup	¾ cup	1 cup	1¼ cups	1½ cups
⅔ cup	¾ cup	1 cup	1¼ cups	1⅔ cups	2 cups
1¼ cups	1⅔ cups	2 cups	2½ cups	3¼ cups	1 quart
1¾ cups	2⅓ cups	3 cups	3⅔ cups	4¾ cups	1½ quarts
2⅓ cups	3¼ cups	1 quart	4¾ cups	6½ cups	2 quarts
4¾ cups	6½ cups	2 quarts	9½ cups	3¼ quarts	4 quarts
7¼ cups	9½ cups	3 quarts	14½ cups	4¾ quarts	6 quarts
9½ cups	3¼ quarts	4 quarts	4¾ quarts	6½ quarts	8 quarts
3 quarts	4 quarts	5 quarts	6 quarts	8 quarts	10 quarts
14½ cups	4¾ quarts	6 quarts	7¼ quarts	9½ quarts	12 quarts

Weight measures

15 servings	20 servings	25 servings	30 servings	40 servings	50 servings
½ ounce	¾ ounce	1 ounce	1¼ ounces	1½ ounces	2 ounces
1¼ ounces	1½ ounces	2 ounces	2½ ounces	3¼ ounces	4 ounces
1¾ ounces	2½ ounces	3 ounces	3½ ounces	4¾ ounces	6 ounces
2½ ounces	3¼ ounces	4 ounces	4¾ ounces	6½ ounces	8 ounces
3½ ounces	4¾ ounces	6 ounces	7¼ ounces	9½ ounces	12 ounces
4¾ ounces	6½ ounces	8 ounces	9½ ounces	13 ounces	1 pound or 16 ounces
7¼ ounces	9½ ounces	12 ounces	14½ ounces	19 ounces	1½ pounds or 24 ounces
9½ ounces	13 ounces	1 pound or 16 ounces	19 ounces	25½ ounces	2 pounds or 32 ounces
12 ounces	1 pound or 16 ounces	1¼ pounds or 20 ounces	24 ounces	32 ounces	2½ pounds or 40 ounces
14½ ounces	19 ounces	1½ pounds or 24 ounces	29 ounces	38½ ounces	3 pounds or 48 ounces
17 ounces	22½ ounces	1¾ pounds or 28 ounces	33½ ounces	45 ounces	3½ pounds or 56 ounces
19 ounces	25½ ounces	2 pounds or 32 ounces	38½ ounces	51 ounces	4 pounds or 64 ounces
29 ounces	38½ ounces	3 pounds or 48 ounces	58 ounces	77 ounces	6 pounds or 96 ounces
38½ ounces	51 ounces	4 pounds or 64 ounces	77 ounces	102 ounces	8 pounds or 128 ounces
48 ounces	64 ounces	5 pounds or 80 ounces	96 ounces	128 ounces	10 pounds or 160 ounces
58 ounces	77 ounces	6 pounds or 96 ounces	115 ounces	154 ounces	12 pounds or 192 ounces

Nutrition

Recommended daily allowances of chief food elements

	Age	Weight In lbs.	In kg.	Calories	Protein (gm)	Calcium (mg)	Iron (mg)	Vitamins A (I.U.)	C (mg)	D (I.U.)	Thia-mine (mg)	Ribo-flavin (mg)	Niacin (mg N.E.)
Children	1-3	28	13	1,300	23	800	15	2,000	40	400	0.7	0.8	9
	4-6	44	20	1,800	30	800	10	2,500	40	400	0.9	1.1	12
	7-10	66	30	2,400	36	800	10	3,300	40	400	1.2	1.2	16
Males	11-14	97	44	2,800	44	1,200	18	5,000	45	400	1.4	1.5	18
	15-18	134	61	3,000	54	1,200	18	5,000	45	400	1.5	1.8	20
	19-22	147	67	3,000	54	800	10	5,000	45	400	1.5	1.8	20
	23-50	154	70	2,700	56	800	10	5,000	45		1.4	1.6	18
	51+	154	70	2,400	56	800	10	5,000	45		1.2	1.5	16
Females	11-14	97	44	2,400	44	1,200	18	4,000	45	400	1.2	1.3	16
	15-18	119	54	2,100	48	1,200	18	4,000	45	400	1.1	1.4	14
	19-22	128	58	2,100	46	800	18	4,000	45	400	1.1	1.4	14
	23-50	128	58	2,000	46	800	18	4,000	45		1.0	1.2	13
	51+	128	58	1,800	46	800	10	4,000	45		1.0	1.1	12

Nutritional values of common foods

Food	Portion	Calo-ries	Pro-tein (g)	Cal-cium (mg)	Iron (mg)	Vitamins A (I.U.)	C (mg)	D (I.U.)	Thia-mine (mcg)	Ribo-flavin (mcg)	Nia-cin (mg)
Apple, raw	1 large	117	0.6	12	0.6	180	9	0	80	60	0.4
Banana, raw	1 large	176	2.4	16	1.2	860	20	0	80	100	1.4
Beans, green, cooked	1 cup	27	1.8	45	0.9	830	18	0	90	120	0.6
Beef, round, cooked	1 serving	214	24.7	10	3.1	0	0	0	74	202	5.1
Bread, white, enriched	1 slice	63	2.0	18	0.4	0	0	0	60	40	0.5
Broccoli, cooked	⅔ cup	29	3.3	130	1.3	3,400	74	0	70	150	0.8
Butter	1 tablespoon	100	0.1	33	0.0	460	0	5	tr.	tr.	tr.
Cabbage, cooked	½ cup	20	1.2	39	0.4	75	27	0	40	40	0.3
Carrots, raw	1 cup, shredded	42	1.2	39	0.8	12,000	6	0	60	60	0.5
Cheese, cheddar, American	1 slice	113	7.1	206	0.3	400	0	0	10	120	tr.
Chicken, fried	½ breast	232	26.8	19	1.3	460	0	0	67	101	10.2
Egg, boiled	1 medium	77	6.1	26	1.3	550	0	27	40	130	tr.
Liver, beef, fried	1 slice	86	8.8	4	2.9	18,658	10	19	90	1,283	5.1
Margarine, fortified	1 tablespoon	101	0.1	3	0.0	460	0	0	0	0	0.0
Milk, whole, cow's	1 glass	124	6.4	216	0.2	293	2	4	73	311	0.2
Oatmeal, cooked	1 cup	148	5.4	21	1.7	0	0	0	220	50	0.4
Orange, whole	1 medium	68	1.4	50	0.6	285	74	0	120	45	0.3
Pork, shoulder, roasted	2 slices	320	19.2	9	2.0	0	0	0	592	144	3.2
Tomatoes, raw	1 large	40	2.0	22	1.2	2,200	46	0	120	80	1.0
Potatoes, white, baked	1 medium	98	2.4	13	0.8	20	17	0	110	50	1.4
Rice, white, cooked	1 cup	201	4.2	13	0.5	0	0	0	20	10	0.7
Sugar, white, granulated	1 tablespoon	48	0.0	0	0.0	0	0	0	0	0	0.0

g = grams; mg = milligrams; mcg = micrograms; I.U. = International Units; tr. = trace.

Foods suited and unsuited for diet plans

Foods allowed	Amount	Foods not allowed
Meat and fish group	3-4 oz. twice a day	
Lean roast meat		Pork
Chicken		Bacon
Turkey		Goose
Lean fish		Duck
Shellfish, prepared without fat		Fat fish (tuna and salmon)
Dairy group		
Egg, boiled or poached	1 per day	Whole milk
Milk (skim or buttermilk)	1½ pints daily	Cream
Cottage cheese (dry)	4 oz. daily	Butter
		Oleomargarine
		Cheese (other than cottage)
Vegetable and fruit group	Unlimited	Any not specified in allowed foods.
Asparagus		
Green beans		
Beets		
Broccoli		
Brussels sprouts		
Cabbage		
Celery		
Carrots		
Dandelion greens		
Lettuce		
Mushrooms		
Greens		
Cucumber		
Eggplant		
Endive		
Leeks		
Onions		
Okra		
Radishes		
Sauerkraut		
Sea kale		
Sorrel		
Spinach		
Squash, summer		
Squash, yellow		
Turnips		
Swiss chard		
Tomato		
Watercress		
Fresh fruit	2 servings daily	Sweetened fruit
Citrus fruit	1 serving daily	Dried fruit
Bread and Cereal Group		
Bread (enriched or whole wheat)	1 slice daily	Cakes
		Pastries
Miscellaneous		
Spices and condiments	In moderation	Gravies
Lemon	Unlimited	Sauces
Vinegar	Unlimited	Dressings
Saccharin or Sucaryl	As needed for sweetening, in moderation	Olives
		Pickles
Tea	Unlimited	Nuts and nut butter
Coffee	Unlimited	Carbonated beverages
Clear broth or bouillon	Unlimited	Alcoholic beverages

Cholesterol content of common foods

Food	Amount	Cholesterol (mg)
Milk, skim, fluid or reconstituted dry	1 cup	5
Cottage cheese, uncreamed	½ cup	7
Lard	1 tablespoon	12
Cream, light table	1 fl oz	20
Cottage cheese, creamed	½ cup	24
Cream, half and half	¼ cup	26
Ice cream, regular, approximately 10% fat	½ cup	27
Cheese, cheddar	1 oz	28
Milk, whole	1 cup	34
Butter	1 tablespoon	35
Oysters, salmon	3 oz cooked	40
Clams, halibut, tuna	3 oz cooked	55
Chicken, turkey, light meat	3 oz cooked	67
Beef, pork, lobster, chicken, turkey, dark meat	3 oz cooked	75
Lamb, veal, crab	3 oz cooked	85
Shrimp	3 oz cooked	130
Heart, beef	3 oz cooked	230
Egg	1 yolk or 1 egg	250
Liver, beef, calf, hog, lamb	3 oz cooked	370
Kidney	3 oz cooked	680
Brains	3 oz raw	More than 1700

Calculating protein, carbohydrate, fat content

The common diets in the United States provide 15% of the energy from proteins, 45% from carbohydrates, and 40% from fats. If this were the case for a 6700 kJ diet, then:

Protein provides $6700 \times \dfrac{15}{100}$ kJ/day = 1000 kJ/day and since 1 g protein = 17 kJ of energy then:

1000 kJ of protein = $\dfrac{1000}{17}$ g = 59g/day

Carbohydrate provides $6700 \times \dfrac{45}{100}$ kJ/day = 3000 kJ/day = $\dfrac{3000}{17}$ g/day of carbohydrate = 176 g/day

Fat provides $6700 \times \dfrac{40}{100}$ kJ/day = 2700 kJ/day = $\dfrac{2700}{37}$ g/day of fat = 73 g/day

From Montgomery, Dryer, Conway, and Spector: BIOCHEMISTRY, ed.4, St. Louis, 1983, The C.V. Mosby Co.

Fat content of selected foods

| Food | Fatty acids | | | |
	Total	Saturated	Monoun-saturated	Polyun-saturated
Animal fats				
Chicken	100.0	32.5	45.4	17.6
Lard	100.0	39.6	44.3	11.8
Beef tallow	100.0	48.2	42.3	4.2
Avocado	15.0	2.0	9.0	2.0
Beef products				
T-bone steak (cooked, broiled—56 percent lean, 44 percent fat)	43.2	18.0	21.1	1.6
Chuck, 5th rib (cooked or braised—69 percent lean, 31 percent fat)	36.7	15.3	17.5	1.5
Brisket (cooked, braised, or pot roasted—69 percent lean; 31 percent fat)	34.8	14.6	16.7	1.4
Wedge and round-bone sirloin steak (cooked or broiled—66 percent lean; 34 percent fat)	32.0	13.3	15.6	1.2
Rump (cooked or roasted—75 percent lean; 25 percent fat)	27.3	11.4	13.1	1.2
Round steak (cooked or broiled—82 percent lean; 18 percent fat)	14.9	6.3	6.9	.7
Cereals and grains				
Wheat germ	10.9	1.9	1.6	6.6
Oats (puffed, without added ingredients)	5.5	1.0	1.9	2.2
Oats (puffed, with added nutrients, sugar covered)	3.4	.6	1.2	1.4
Barley (whole grain)	2.8	.5	.3	1.3
Domestic buckwheat (dark flour)	2.5	.5	.8	.9
Cornmeal, white or yellow (whole-ground, unbolted)	3.9	.5	.9	2.0
Shredded wheat breakfast cereal	2.5	.4	.4	1.3
Wheat (whole grain; Hard Red Spring)	2.7	.4	.3	1.3
Wheat flakes breakfast cereal	2.4	.4	.3	1.2
Rye (whole grain)	2.2	.3	.2	1.1
Wheat meal breakfast cereal	1.4	.3	.1	.7
Wheat flour, all purpose	1.4	.2	.1	.6
Rice (cooked brown)	.8	.2	.2	.3
Bulgur from Hard Red Winter wheat	1.5	.2	.2	.7
Oatmeal or rolled oats, cooked	1.0	.2	.4	.4
Rye flour	1.4	.2	.1	.6
Cornstarch	.6	.1	.1	.3
Rice (cooked white)	.2	.1	.1	.1
Farina (enriched, regular, cooked)	.2			.1
Corn grits, cooked	.1			.1
Dairy products				
Nondairy coffee whitener (powder)	35.6	32.6	1.0	
Cream cheese	33.8	21.2	9.4	1.2
Cheddar cheese	32.8	20.2	9.8	.9
Light whipping cream	32.4	20.2	9.6	.9
Muenster cheese	29.8	19.0	8.7	.7
American pasteurized cheese	28.9	18.0	8.5	1.0
Swiss cheese	27.6	17.6	7.7	1.0
Mozzarella cheese	19.4	11.8	5.9	.7
Ricotta cheese (from whole milk)	14.6	9.3	4.1	.4
Vanilla ice cream	12.3	7.7	3.6	.5
Half and half cream	11.7	7.3	3.4	.4
Chocolate chip ice cream	11.0	6.3	2.6	.4
Canned condensed milk (sweetened)	8.7	5.5	2.4	.3
Ice cream sandwich	8.2	4.7	2.6	.5
Cottage cheese (creamed)	4.0	2.6	1.1	.1

Food	Fatty acids			
	Total	Saturated	Monoun-saturated	Polyun-saturated
Yogurt (from whole milk)	3.4	2.2	.9	.1
Cottage cheese (uncreamed)	.4	.2	.1	
Eggs				
Fried in margarine	15.9	4.2	7.2	1.9
Scrambled in margarine	12.6	3.7	5.5	1.4
Fresh or frozen	11.3	3.4	4.5	1.4
Fish				
Eel, American	18.3	4.0	9.0	2.7
Herring, Atlantic	16.4	2.9	9.2	2.4
Mackerel, Atlantic	9.8	2.4	3.6	2.4
Tuna, albacore (canned, light)	6.8	2.3	1.7	1.8
Tuna, albacore (white meat)	8.0	2.1	2.1	3.0
Salmon, sockeye	8.9	1.8	1.5	4.7
Salmon, Atlantic	5.8	1.8	2.7	.5
Carp	6.2	1.3	2.7	1.4
Rainbow trout (United States)	4.5	1.0	1.5	1.4
Striped bass	2.1	.5	.6	.7
Ocean perch	2.5	.4	1.0	.7
Red snapper	1.2	.2	.2	.4
Tuna, skipjack (canned, light)	.8	.2	.2	.2
Halibut, Atlantic	1.1	.2	.2	.4
Fowl				
Chicken (broiler/fryer, cooked or roasted dark meat)	9.7	2.7	3.2	2.4
Turkey (cooked or roasted dark meat)	5.3	1.6	1.4	1.5
Chicken (broiler/fryer, cooked or roasted light meat)	3.5	1.0	.9	.9
Turkey (cooked or roasted light meat)	2.6	.7	.6	.7
Lamb and veal				
Shoulder of lamb (cooked or roasted, 74 percent lean; 26 percent fat)	26.9	12.6	11.0	1.6
Leg of lamb (cooked or roasted, 83 percent lean; 17 percent fat)	21.2	9.6	8.5	1.2
Veal foreshank (cooked or stewed, 86 percent lean; 14 percent fat)	10.4	4.4	4.2	.7
Nuts				
Coconut	35.5	31.2	2.2	.7
Brazil nut	68.2	17.4	22.5	25.4
Peanut butter	52.0	10.0	24.0	15.0
Peanut	49.7	9.4	22.9	15.0
Cashew	45.6	9.2	26.4	7.4
Walnut, English	63.4	6.9	9.9	41.8
Pecan	71.4	6.1	43.1	17.9
Walnut, black	59.6	5.1	10.8	40.8
Almond	53.9	4.3	36.8	10.1
Pork products				
Bacon	49.0	18.1	22.8	5.4
Sausage, cooked	32.5	11.7	15.1	3.9
Deviled ham, canned	32.3	11.3	15.2	3.5
Liverwurst, braunschweiger, liver sausage	32.5	11.0	15.5	4.1
Bologna	27.5	10.6	13.3	2.1
Pork loin (cooked or roasted, 82 percent lean; 18 percent fat)	28.1	9.8	13.1	3.1
Ham (cooked or roasted, 84 percent lean; 16 percent fat)	22.1	7.8	10.4	2.4
Fresh ham (cooked or roasted, 82 percent lean; 18 percent fat)	20.2	7.1	9.5	2.2

Food	Fatty acids			
	Total	Saturated	Monoun-saturated	Polyun-saturated
Canadian bacon (cooked and drained)	17.5	5.9	7.9	1.8
Chopped ham luncheon meat	17.4	5.7	8.3	2.2
Canned ham	11.3	4.0	5.3	1.2
Salad and cooking oils				
Coconut	100.0	86.0	6.0	2.0
Palm	100.0	47.9	38.4	9.3
Cottonseed	100.0	26.1	18.9	50.7
Peanut	100.0	17.0	47.0	31.0
Sesame	100.0	15.2	40.0	40.5
Soybean, hydrogenated	100.0	15.0	23.1	57.6
Olive	100.0	14.2	72.5	9.0
Corn	100.0	12.7	24.7	58.2
Sunflower	100.0	10.2	20.9	63.8
Safflower	100.0	9.4	12.5	73.8
Shellfish				
Eastern oyster	2.1	.5	.2	.6
Pacific oyster	2.3	.5	.4	.9
Ark shell clam	1.5	.4	.3	.3
Blue crab	1.6	.3	.3	.6
Alaska king crab	1.6	.2	.3	.6
Shrimp	1.2	.2	.2	.5
Scallop	.9	.1		.4
Soups				
Cream of mushroom (diluted with equal parts of water)	3.9	1.1	.7	.8
Cream of celery (diluted with equal parts of water)	2.3	.6	.5	1.0
Beef with vegetables (diluted with equal parts of water)	.8	.3	.3	
Chicken noodle (diluted with equal parts of water)	1.0	.3	.4	.2
Minestrone (diluted with equal parts of water)	1.1	.2	.3	.5
Vegetable (diluted with equal parts of water)	.9	.2	.3	.4
Clam chowder, Manhattan style (diluted with equal parts of water)	.9	.2	.2	.5
Table spreads				
Butter	80.1	49.8	23.1	3.0
Margarine (hydrogenated soybean oil, stick)	80.1	14.9	46.5	14.4
Margarine (corn oil, tub)	80.3	14.2	30.4	31.9
Margarine (corn oil, stick)	80.0	14.0	38.7	23.3
Margarine (safflower oil, tub)	81.7	13.4	16.1	48.4
Vegetable fats (household shortening)	100.0	25.0	44.0	26.0

Converting calories into pounds

A simple formula indicates how many calories (kcal) equal one pound of added weight: 3500 kcal = 1 pound.

Applying the formula, if John eats food valued at 3000 kcal per day, and his daily energy need is 2700 kcal/day, he will add a pound as follows:

$$\frac{3500 \text{ kcal}}{300 \text{ kcal/day}} = 11.67 \text{ days}$$

Calorie energy equivalents

Food	kcal	Activity			
		Walking (min)	Riding bicycle (min)	Swimming (min)	Running (min)
Apple, large	101	19	12	9	5
Bacon (2 strips)	96	18	12	9	5
Banana, small	88	17	11	8	4
Beans, green (1 cup	27	5	3	2	1
Beer (1 glass)	114	22	14	10	6
Bread and butter	78	15	10	7	4
Cake (1/12, 2-layer)	356	68	43	32	18
Carbonated beverage (1 glass)	106	20	13	9	5
Carrot, raw	42	8	5	4	2
Cereal, dry (1/2 cup) with milk and sugar	200	38	24	18	10
Cheese, cottage (1 tbsp)	27	5	3	2	1
Cheese, cheddar (1 oz)	111	21	14	10	6
Chicken, fried (1/2 breast)	232	45	28	21	12
Chicken, "TV" dinner	542	104	66	48	28
Cookie, plain (148/lb)	15	3	2	1	1
Cookie, chocolate chip	51	10	6	5	3
Doughnut	151	29	18	13	8
Egg, fried	110	21	13	10	6
Egg, boiled	77	15	9	7	4
French dressing (1 tbsp)	59	11	7	5	3
Halibut steak (1/4 lb)	205	39	25	18	11
Ham (2 slices)	167	32	20	15	9
Ice cream (1/6 qt)	193	37	24	17	10
Ice cream soda	255	49	31	23	13
Ice milk (1/6 qt)	144	28	18	13	7
Gelatin, with cream	117	23	14	10	6
Malted milk shake	502	97	61	45	26
Mayonnaise (1 tbsp)	92	18	11	8	5
Milk (1 glass)	166	32	20	15	9
Milk, skim (1 glass)	81	16	10	7	4
Milk shake	421	81	51	38	22
Orange, medium	68	13	8	6	4
Orange juice (glass)	120	23	15	11	6
Pancake with syrup	124	24	15	11	6
Peach, medium	46	9	6	4	2
Peas, green (1/2 cup)	56	11	7	5	3
Pie, apple (1/6)	377	73	46	34	19
Pie, raisin (1/6)	437	84	53	39	23
Pizza, cheese (1/8)	180	35	22	16	9
Pork chop, loin	314	60	38	28	16
Potato chips (1 serving)	108	21	13	10	6
Sandwiches					
Club	590	113	72	53	30
Hamburger	350	67	43	31	18
Roast beef with gravy	430	83	52	38	22
Tuna fish salad	278	53	34	25	14
Sherbert (1/6)	177	34	22	16	9
Shrimp, french fried	180	35	22	16	9
Spaghetti (1 serving)	396	76	48	35	20
Steak, T-bone	235	45	29	21	12
Strawberry shortcake	400	77	49	36	21

Food marketing

Fruits and vegetables: seasonal availability

Fruits	When available	Vegetables	When available
Bananas	all year	Beans, lima	all year (pole beans, vary locally)
Lemons	all year	Cabbage	all year
Grapefruit	all year, most plentiful January through May	Carrots	all year
Rhubarb	January to June	Celery	all year
Pineapples	March to June, most plentiful April and May	Potatoes	all year
		Sweet potatoes and yams	all year, low May through July
Strawberries	peak May and June		
Cherries	May through August	Mushrooms	all year, low in August
Cantaloupe	May through September	Asparagus	mid-February through June
Limes	all year, peak June and July	Tomatoes	most plentiful early spring (March) to fall
Apricots	June and July	Peas	most plentiful in spring (March onward)
Raspberries and blackberries	June through August		
		Summer squash	most plentiful in spring (March) through fall
Watermelon	peak June through August		
Blueberries	June through September	Spinach	best in early spring (March)
Nectarines	June through September	Lettuce	all year, most plentiful in spring (March onward)
Peaches	June through September		
Plums	June to September	Artichokes	peak April and May
Grapes	July through October	Radishes	most plentiful May through July
Cranshaw melon	July through October		
Honeyball and honeydew melons	all year, best July to October	Cucumber	most plentiful all summer (May onward)
Casaba melon	July to November	Corn	most plentiful early May through mid-September
Persian melon	August and September		
Pears, Bartlett	August through November	Beans, green and wax	May through October, best June and July
Cranberries	September through January	Beets	all year, peak June through August
Apples	all year, peak October through March (look fo best local varieties early summer through early winter)	Onions	all year, peak June through September
		Peppers	most plentiful late summer (July onward)
Pears, other than Bartlett	November through May	Broccoli	all year, peak October to May (least abundant July and August)
Tangerines	peak November through January	Eggplant	most plentiful late summer (July onward)
Avocados	all year, peak December through June	Cauliflower	most plentiful September through January
Oranges	all year (depending on variety), peak December through June	Winter squash	early fall (October) through late winter
Apricots	some imports available December and January	Brussels sprouts	peak October through February
		Spinach	late fall (November onward)

Meat and vegetables: servings per pound

	Servings per pound*		Servings per pound
Meat		**Fresh vegetables**	
Much bone or gristle	1 or 2	Asparagus	3 or 4
Medium amounts of bone	2 or 3	Beans, lima	2
Little or no bone	3 or 4	Beans, snap	5 or 6
		Beets diced	3 or 4
Poultry (ready-to-cook)		Broccoli	3 or 4
Chicken	2 or 3	Brussels sprouts	4 or 5
Turkey	2 or 3	Cabbage:	
Duck and goose	2	Raw, shredded	9 or 10
		Cooked	4 or 5
Fish		Carrots:	
Whole	1 or 2	Raw, diced or shredded	5 or 6
Dressed or pan-dressed	2 or 3	Cooked	4
Portions or steaks	3	Cauliflower	3
Fillets	3 or 4	Celery:	

*Three ounces of cooked lean meat, poultry, or fish per serving.

	Servings per package (9 or 10 oz.)	Celery:	
		Raw, chopped or diced	5 or 6
Frozen vegetables		Cooked	4
Asparagus	2 or 3	Kale	5 or 6
Beans, lima	3 or 4	Okra	4 or 5
Beans, snap	3 or 4	Onions, cooked	3 or 4
Broccoli	3	Parsnips	4
Brussels sprouts	3	Peas	2
Cauliflower	3	Potatoes	4
Corn, whole kernel	3	Spinach	4
Kale	2 or 3	Squash, summer	3 or 4
Peas	3	Squash, winter	2 or 3
Spinach	2 or 3	Sweetpotatoes	3 or 4
		Tomatoes, raw, diced or sliced	4

Comparing meat costs

Find the packages of meat, poultry, and fish that give enough servings for a family meal—or more if you plan to use the meat for additional meals. Compare the costs of various meats for a meal. Example: For a family of four, a 1⅓-pound round steak that costs $3.20 may be compared with half the cost of a 4-pound pork loin roast costing $6.00 ($1.50 per pound) that can be used for two meals

$$\frac{\$6.00}{2} = \$3.00.$$

Compare the costs of a serving from different types and cuts of meat. Using the example above, divide the price per pound by the number of servings a pound will provide.

Round steak at $\dfrac{\$2.40 \text{ per pound}}{3 \text{ servings per pound}}$ = 80 cents per serving.

Pork loin roast at $\dfrac{\$1.50 \text{ per pound}}{2 \text{ servings per pound}}$ = 75 cents per serving.

45

Estimating meat costs: ground beef

To calculate the actual cost of cooked ground beef derived from 70 percent "lean" beef, use the following formula:

You know that 70 percent of every pound is actual meat, giving you .7 pound. You want 100 percent meat in each pound, giving 1.0 pound. So you have the ratio $\dfrac{.7}{1.0}$.

Similarly, you spend $1.30 for each pound of 70 percent ground beef, giving $1.30. You want to find the cost, x, for a pound of 100 percent beef. So you have the ratio $\dfrac{1.3}{x}$.

These two ratios can be set into a new proportion: $\dfrac{.7}{1} = \dfrac{\$1.3}{x}$.

Now solve the proportion: $.7x = \$1.3$; so $x = \$1.86$ for a pound of pure beef.

Costs of 'convenience' vs. home-made foods

Product	Cents per serving			Product	Cents per serving		
	Fresh or home-made	Frozen	Canned		Fresh or home-made	Frozen	Canned
Fruits and berries				**Fish and shellfish**			
Cherries, red sour, pitted–4 oz.	22		22	Crabcakes–3 oz.	60	52	
Coconut–3 oz.	2		3	Crab—deviled–3 oz.	29	40	
Cranberry sauce, strained–2 oz.	7		6	Haddock dinner–12 oz.	56	100	
Cranberry sauce, whole–2 oz.	6		6	Pollock fish sticks–3 oz.	34	22	
Grapefruit sections–3 oz.	12		14	Shrimp, cooked–2 oz.	61	50	50
Lemon juice–1 oz.	8			Shrimp, breaded–3 oz.	40	45	
Orange juice–4 oz.	12	4		Shrimp, newburg–4 oz.	69	113	
Orange drink–4 oz.		3		Shrimp, breaded–7 oz.	38	60	
Peaches–4 oz.	15	27	17	Tuna noodle casserole–8 oz.	26	67	
Pineapple–3 oz.	12		13				
Raspberries–3 oz.	23	34	24				
Strawberries, sweetened, whole–4 oz.	20	22	45				
Strawberries, sweetened, sliced–4 oz.	20	27					

Food preservation

Food storage guide

Food	Refrigerator (at 35–40°F.)	Freezer (at 0° F.)
Fresh meats		
Roasts (beef)	3–5 days	6–12 months
Roasts (pork, veal, and lamb)	3–5 days	4–8 months
Steaks (beef)	3–5 days	6–12 months
Chops (lamb)	3–5 days	6–9 months
Chops (pork)	3–5 days	3–4 months
Ground and stew meats	1–2 days	3–4 months
Variety meats (liver, kidney, etc.)	1–2 days	3–4 months
Sausage (pork)	1–2 days	1–2 months
Processed meats		
Bacon	1 week	1 month
Hot dogs	1 week	2 week
Ham (whole)	1 week	1–2 months
Ham (half)	5 days	1–2 months
Ham (slices)	3 days	1–2 weeks
Luncheon meats	3–5 days	2 week
Sausage (smoked)	1 week	2 weeks
Cooked meats		
Cooked meat and meat dishes	3–4 days	2–3 months
Gravy and meat broth	1–2 days	2–3 months
Fresh poultry		
Chicken and turkey (whole)	1–2 days	12 months
Chicken (pieces)	1–2 days	9 months
Turkey (pieces)	1–2 days	6 months
Duck and goose (whole)	1–2 days	6 months
Giblets	1–2 days	3 months
Cooked poultry		
Pieces (covered with broth)	1–2 days	6 months
Pieces (not covered)	1–2 days	1 month
Cooked poultry dishes	1–2 days	6 months
Fried chicken	1–2 days	4 months

Food	Refrigerator (at 35–40°F.)	Freezer (at 0° F.)
Fresh fish	1–2 days	6–9 months
Commercially frozen fish		
Shrimp and fillets of lean fish	—	3–4 months
Clams (shucked) and cooked fish	—	3 months
Fillets of fatty fish and crab meat	—	2–3 months
Oysters (shucked)	—	1 month
Fruits and vegetables		
Fruits	1 day–2 weeks	8–12 months
Dairy products		
Milk (whole, skim, 2%)	1 week	—
Cream	1 week	—
Ice cream and other frozen desserts	—	1 month
Cottage cheese	1 week	—
Hard cheeses (like cheddar)	1–2 months	6 months
Soft cheeses (like Brie or cream)	2 weeks	1 month
Cheese spreads	1–2 weeks	—
Butter, margarine	2 weeks	2 months
Eggs (in shell)	1 week	—
Prepared foods		
Breads, prebaked and cake batters	5–7 days	2–3 months
Cakes, custard pies	1–2 days	4–9 months
Fruit pies, combination main dishes	3–4 days	3–6 months
Cookies	—	6 months

SOURCE: U.S. Department of Agriculture, taken from THE HOUSEHOLD HANDBOOK, Meadowbrook Press

Fruit and vegetable storage guide

Hold at room temperature until ripe; then refrigerate, uncovered

Apples	Cherries	Peaches
Apricots	Melons, except water-	Pears
Avocados	melons	Plums
Berries	Nectarines	Tomatoes

Store in cool room or refrigerate, uncovered
Grapefruit   Limes
Lemons   Oranges

Store in cool room, away from bright light
Onions, mature   Rutabagas   Sweetpotatoes
Potatoes   Squash, winter

Refrigerate, covered
Asparagus   Cauliflower   Parsnips
Beans, snap or wax   Celery   Peas, shelled
Beets   Corn, husked   Peppers, green
Broccoli   Cucumbers   Radishes
Cabbage   Greens   Squash, summer
Carrots   Onions, green   Turnips

Refrigerate, uncovered
Beans, lima, in pods   Grapes   Pineapples
Corn, in husks   Peas, in pods   Watermelons

Home drying chart

Fruit	Preparation	Treat before drying. Choose one of the following three methods.			Drying times		Test for dryness (Cool before testing)
		Sulfur	Steam blanch	Water blanch	Sun drying	Dehydrator	
Apples	Peel and core, cut into slices or rings about ⅛ thick.	45 minutes	5 minutes, depending on texture	—	3-4 days	6-12 hours	Soft, pliable, no moist area in center when cut
Apricots	Pit and halve for steam blanch or sulfuring. Leave whole for water blanch. Pit and halve after blanch.	2 hours	3-4 minutes	4-5 minutes	2-3 days	24-36* hours	Same as for apples
Figs	In dry, warm, sunny climates, it is preferable to partly dry on the tree. Figs normally drop from the tree when ⅔ dry. In coastal areas, pick fruit when ripe.	No treatment necessary			4-5 days	12-20 hours	Flesh pliable, slightly sticky, but not wet
Grapes: Muscat, Tokay, or any seedless grape	Leave whole. Grapes dry in less time if dipped in lye 10 seconds.* Or blanch ½ to 1 minute.	No treatment necessary			3-5 days	12-20 hours	Raisin-like texture, no moist center

Fruit	Preparation	Treat before drying. Choose one of the following three methods.			Drying times		Test for dryness (Cool before testing)
		Sulfur	Steam blanch	Water blanch	Sun drying	Dehydrator	
Nectarines and peaches	When sulfuring, pit and halve; if desired, remove skins. For steam and water blanching, leave whole, then pit and halve.	2-3 hours	8 minutes	8 minutes	3-5 days	36-48* hours	Same as for apples
Pears	Cut in half and core. Peeling preferred.	5 hours	6 minutes (peeled, will be soft)	—	5 days	24-36* hours	Same as for apples
Persimmons	Use firm fruit when using the long, softer variety, and use riper fruit when using the round, drier variety. Peel and slice with stainless steel knife.		No treatment necessary		5-6 days	18-24 hours	Light to medium brown, tender, but not sticky
Prunes	For sun-drying, dip in boiling lye solution* or blanch in boiling water or steam for 1 to 1½ minutes, to "check" skins. For oven-drying, rinse in hot tapwater. Leave whole. If sulfuring, pit and halve.		No treatment necessary. However, sulfuring for one hour will produce good flavor.		4-5 days (3-4 days when using lye.)	24-36 hours	Leathery; pit should not slip when squeezed if prune not cut.

*Drying times can be shortened by cutting fruit into slices.

GRAS (generally regarded as safe) food additives

Name	Function	Often used in
Acacia (gum arabic)	thickener	chocolate drinks, confections, ice cream, dressings, cheese
Acetate	sequestrant, buffer	general
Acetic acid	acid	flavoring, syrups
calcium diacetate	emulsifier	baked goods
sodium acetate	antioxidant	licorice candy
sodium diacetate	mold inhibitor	baked goods, breads
Acetone peroxide	maturing & bleaching	flour
Adipic acid	buffer neutralizing	confections
Agar-agar	thickener, stabilizer	beverages, baked goods, ice cream

Name	Function	Often used in
Alginic acid & salts ammonium calcium potassium sodium	stabilizers, water retainer	beverages, ice cream, desserts, meat, condiments, dressings
Aluminum compounds ammonium sulfate potassium sulfate sodium sulfate sulfate	acid	milling, baking, cereals, baking powder
Ammonium salts		
bicarbonate	alkali	leavening agent, thin baked goods
carbonate	alkali	leavening agent, thin baked goods
chloride	yeast food, dough conditioner	bread, rolls, buns
hydroxide	alkali	cacao, leavening agent
phosphate, dibasic	buffer	leavening agent, bakery goods
phosphate, monobasic	buffer	leavening agent, bakery goods
sulfate	buffer	leavening agent, bakery goods
Ascorbic acid ascorbyl palmitate calcium ascorbate sodium ascorbate	antioxidant	fruit juices, carbonated beverages, candy, milk products, cured meats, flavorings, beer, canned mushrooms
Beeswax	glaze	candy glaze & polish
Benzoic acid (sodium benzoate)	antimicrobial preservative	baked goods, beverages, icings, candy
Butylated hydroxyanisole (BHA)	antioxidant	beverages, ice cream, candy, dry cereals, dry mixes, gelatins
Butylated hydroxytoluene (BHT)	antioxidant	chewing gum base, potato flakes, dry breakfast cereal
Caffeine	stimulant	beverages
Calcium citrate	firming agent, buffer	jelling ingredient
Calcium salts	firming agent, nutrient	potatoes, canned tomatoes
Caprylic (octanoic) acid	flavoring	beverages, baked goods, candy
Carnauba wax	glaze	candy
Carbonate, calcium	alkali	baking powder, confections
Carboxymethyl-cellulose	stabilizer	beverages, confections, baked goods, chocolate, cheese spreads
Carob bean gum (locust bean)	thickener, stabilizer	chocolate milk, syrups, cheeses, confections, ice cream
Carrageenan	stabilizer, emulsifier	chocolate products, syrups, cheeses, milks, salad dressings
Caseinate, sodium	texturizer	ice cream, sherbets
Cellulose	stabilizer, thickener, emulsifier	non-dairy topping, beverages, baked goods, beer, dietetic products
Chloride, calcium	firming agent, alkali	jelling ingredient, cheeses, confections
Cholic acid desoxycholic acid glycocholic acid ox bile extract taurocholic acid	emulsifier	dried egg whites
Dextrin	stabilizer	beer foam
Diacetyl tartaric acid	emulsifier	bakery products, animal fat
Dilauryl thiodipropionate	antioxidant	general food use
Erythorbate, sodium	color fixative, antioxidant	processed meats, ham, beverages, baked goods
Erythorbic acid	antioxidant	pickling brine, beverages, baked goods
Ethyl formate	yeast & mold inhibitor	raisins, nuts, chewing gum
Ghatti gum	flavoring	butter, butterscotch, fruit

50

Name	Function	Often used in
Gluconate	sequestrant	salad & cooking oil
calcium		
sodium		
Glucono-delta-lactone	acid	leavening agent, jelly
Glutamic acid & salts	flavoring	intensifiers, salt substitutes, meats, spices
monoammonium		
monopotassium		
monosodium		
Glycerin (glycerol)	humectant, solvent, coating	marshmallows, solvents for colorings, flavorings, beverages, confections
Glyceryl triacetate (triacetin)	flavoring	butter, butterscotch, fruit, spice
Guar gum	thickener, stabilizer	frozen fruit, icings, binder for meats, confections, cheeses
Gum gualac	antioxidant	beverages, rendered animal, vegetable fat
Hydrolyzed vegetable protein (HVP)	flavor enhancer	soup, beef stew, gravy
Isopropyl citrate	sequestrant, antioxidant	margarine, salad oil
Karaya gum	flavoring	citrus, spice
Lactic acid	acid, flavoring	brewing, brines, cheeses, breads, butter, lime, chocolate
Lecithin	antioxidant, emulsifier	breakfast cereals, candy, chocolate, breads, margarine
Magnesium salts		
carbonate	alkali, drying agent, color fixative, bleaching, anticaking agent	cacao products, bleaching, neutralizer, salt, flour, cheeses
chloride	color fixative, firming agent	canned peas
hydroxide	drying agent, color fixative	curd formation in cheese
oxide	alkali	neutralizer, dairy products
sulfate	water corrective	brewing industry
Mannitol	dusting, anti-sticking agent, texturizer	chewing gum, candy
Methyl cellulose	thickener, stabilizer	beverages, dietetic products, toppings, beer foam
Mono- and diglycerides	emulsifier, defoaming agent	beverages, lard, toppings, ice cream, margarine, chocolate, bakery products
Nitrous oxide	propellant	dairy & vegetable-fat toppings
Papain	tenderizer	meat
Pectinate, sodium	stabilizer, thickener	cyclamate beverages, syrups, confections, jelly
Phosphate	buffer	prepared mixes, leavening ingredient,
calcium mono-		chocolate products, beverages, confections, baked goods
sodium		
di-calcium		
tri-phosphoric acid	sequestrant acid	animal & vegetable fat, self-rising flour, & prepared mixes
Potassium citrate	buffer	confections, jellies, preserves
Potassium salts		
carbonate	alkali	baking powder, neutralizer, confections
chloride	yeast food	brewing industry, jelly
	salt substitute	dietetic foods
hydroxide	alkali	peeling agent, extraction of color
iodate, iodide	dietary supplement	table salt
phosphate	yeast food	beer, champagne, sparkling wines
sulfate	water corrective	brewing industry
Propanoic acid	flavoring	butter, fruit
Propyl gallate	flavoring	lemon, lime, fruit, spice
	antioxidant	lard, prepared cereal, candy
Propylene glycol	solvent, wetting agent, humectant	confections, chocolate, ice cream, flavor & color solvent

Name	Function	Often used in
Sillicates	anti-caking agent	table salt, vanilla powder, baking powder, dried egg yolk, meat dry-curing
aluminum calcium		
calcium		
magnesium		
silica gel		
sodium alumino		
sodium calcium alumino		
tricalcium		
Sodium citrate	buffer	frozen dairy products, frozen fruit drinks, confections
Sodium salts		
aluminum phosphate	buffer emulsifier	self-rising flour, prepared mixes, cheeses
bicarbonate	alkali	leavening
carbonate	alkali	neutralizer for butter, milk products
hexametaphosphate	emulsifier, sequestrant texturizers	breakfast cereals, angel food cake beverages, cheese, jelly, pudding
phosphate (mono-, di-, tri-)	emulsifier, texturizer, sequestrant	evaporated milk
pyrophosphate	emulsifier, texturizer	cold water puddings, processed cheese
thiosulfate	antioxidant	protect sliced potatoes from browning
Sorbic acid & salts	fungistat	beverages, baked goods, chocolate, syrups, fruit cocktail, cheesecake, cake, jelly
calcium potassium		
sodium		
Sorbitol	sequestrant, bodying agent	confectionary, oils
	stabilizer, sweetener	nonstandardized frozen desserts
	humectant, texturizing agent	dietetic fruits & drinks, shredded coconut, frozen desserts
Stearate		
magnesium, calcium	anti-caking agent	onion & garlic salts
potassium	defoaming agent	powdered mixes
sodium	emulsifier	prepared mixes
sulfate	alkali, yeast food	breads
Stannous chloride	antioxidant	canned asparagus
Succinic acid	acid	brewing industry
Sulfur dioxide	antioxidant anti-browning agent	wine, corn syrup, jelly dried fruit, beverages, soups
potassium bisulfate	antioxidant	ale, beer, wine, maraschino cherries
potassium metabisulfate	anti-browning agent	general
Tartaric acids & salts	acid, buffer	baking powder, dried egg whites, confectionery
potassium (cream of tartar)	acid, buffer	baking powder, dried egg whites, confectionery
sodium potassium	buffer	confections, jelly, cheese
Triethyl citrate	antioxidant	dried egg whites
Thiodipropionic acid	antioxidant	general food use
Tragacanth gum	thickener, stabilizer	jelly, icing, salad dressing

Home drying chart: vegetables

Vegetables	Preparation	Blanching (minutes) Method	Time	Drying (hours) Method	Time
Artichoke, globe	Cut hearts into ⅛ inch strips.	Heat in boiling solution (¾ cup water, 1 tbs lemon juice.)	6 -8	dehydrator* . . . oven* sun*	12 -16 4 - 7 10 -12
Asparagus	Wash thoroughly. Halve large tips.	Steam Water	4 -5 3½-4½	dehydrator oven sun	6 -10 3 - 4 8 -10
Beans, green	Wash thoroughly. Cut in short pieces or lengthwise.	Steam Water	2 -2½ 2	dehydrator oven sun	8 -14 3 - 6 8
Beets	Cook as usual. Cool; peel. Cut into shoestring strips ⅛ inch thick.	Already cooked; no further blanching required	—	dehydrator oven sun	10 -12 3 - 5 8 -10
Broccoli	Trim, cut as for serving. Wash thoroughly. Quarter stalks lengthwise.	Steam Water†	3 -3½ 2	dehydrator oven sun	12 -15 3 - 4½ 8 -10
Brussels sprouts	Cut in half lengthwise through stem.	Steam Water	6 -7 4½-5½	dehydrator oven sun	12 -18 4 - 5 9 -11
Cabbage	Remove outer leaves; quarter and core. Cut into strips ⅛ inch thick.	Steam until wilted Water	2½-3 1½-2	dehydrator oven sun	10 -12 1 - 3 6 - 7
Carrots	Use only crisp, tender carrots. Wash thoroughly. Cut off roots and tops; preferably peel, cut in slices or strips ⅛ inch thick.	Steam Water	3 -3½ 3½	dehydrator oven sun	10 -12 3½- 5 8
Cauliflower	Prepare as for serving.	Steam Water†	4 -5 3 -4	dehydrator oven sun	12 -15 4 - 6 8 -11
Celery	Trim stalks. Wash stalks and leaves thoroughly. Slice stalks.	Steam Water	2 2	dehydrator oven sun	10 -16 3 - 4 8
Corn on the cob	Husk, trim.	Steam until milk does not exude from kernel when cut Water	2 -2½ 1½	dehydrator . . . . oven. . . . . sun.	12 -15 4 - 6 8
Corn, cut	Prepare in the same manner as corn on the cob, except cut the kernels from the cob after blanching.			dehydrator oven sun	6 -10 2 - 3 6
Egg plant	Use the same directions as for summer squash.	Steam Water	3½ 3	dehydrator oven	12 -14 3½- 5
Okra	Wash, trim, slice crosswise in ⅛–¼ inch disks.	None	—	dehydrator oven sun	8 -10 4 - 6 8 -11
Onions	Wash, remove outer "paper shells." Remove tops and root ends, slice ⅛–¼ inch thick.	None	—	dehydrator oven sun	10 -20 3 - 6 8 -11
Parsley	Wash thoroughly. Separate clusters. Discard long or tough stems.	None	—	dehydrator oven sun	1 - 2 2 - 4 6 - 8
Peas	Shell.	Steam Water	3 2	dehydrator oven sun	8 -10 3 6 - 8
Peppers and pimentos	Wash, stem, core. Remove "partitions." Cut into disks about ⅜ by ⅜ inch.	None	—	dehydrator oven sun	8 -12 2½- 5 6 - 8
Potatoes	Wash, peel. Cut into shoestring strips ¼ inch thick, or cut in slices ⅛ inch thick.	Steam Water	6 -8 5 -6	dehydrator oven sun	8 -12 4 - 6 8 -11
Spinach and other greens (kale, chard, mustard)	Trim, wash very thoroughly.	Steam until thoroughly wilted Water	2 -2½ 1½	dehydrator oven sun	8 -10 2½-3½ 6 - 8

Vegetables	Preparation	Blanching (minutes) Method	Time	Drying (hours) Method	Time	
Squash:						
Banana	Wash, peel, slice in strips about ¼ inch thick.	Steam Water	2½-3 1	dehydrator oven sun	10 4 6	-16 - 5 - 8
Hubbard	Cut or break into pieces. Remove seeds and cavity pulp. Cut into 1 inch wide strips. Peel rind. Cut strips crosswise into pieces about ⅛ inch thick.	Steam Water	2½-3 1	dehydrator oven sun	10 4 6	-16 - 5 - 8
Summer	Wash, trim, cut into ¼ inch slices.	Steam Water	2½-3 1½	dehydrator oven sun	10 4 6	-12 - 6 - 8
Tomatoes, for stewing	Steam or dip in boiling water to loosen skins. Chill in cold water. Peel. Cut into sections about ¾ inch wide, or slice. Cut small pear or plum tomatoes in half.	Steam Water	3 1	dehydrator oven sun	10 6 8	-18 - 8 -10

*For oven and portable dehydrators, set temperatures at 140° F.
Sun drying requires temperatures at 98° to 100° F.
†Preferred method.

Fruit and vegetable canning yields

Generally, the following amounts of fresh fruit or tomatoes (as purchased or picked) make 1 quart of canned food: In 1 pound there are about 3 medium apples or pears; 4 medium peaches or tomatoes; 8 medium plums.

	Pounds
Fruit	
Apples	2½ to 3
Berries, except strawberries	1½ to 3 (1 to 2 quart boxes)
Cherries (canned unpitted)	2 to 2½
Peaches	2 to 3
Pears	2 to 3
Plums	1½ to 2½
Tomatoes	2½ to 3½
Vegetable	
Asparagus	2½ to 4½
Beans, lima, in pods	3 to 5
Beans, snap	1½ to 2½
Beets, without tops	2 to 3½
Carrots, without tops	2 to 3
Corn, sweet, in husks	3 to 6
Okra	1½
Peas, green, in pods	3 to 6
Pumpkin or winter squash	1½ to 3
Spinach and other greens	2 to 6
Squash, summer	2 to 4
Sweetpotatoes	2 to 3

Frozen yield from fresh fruit

Fruit	Fresh, as purchased or picked	Frozen
Apples	1 bu. (48 lb.)	32 to 40 pt.
	1 box (44 lb.)	29 to 35 pt.
	1 ¼ to 1½ lb.	1 pt.
Apricots	1 bu. (48 lb.)	60 to 72 pt.
	1 crate (22 lb.)	28 to 33 pt.
	⅔ to ⅘ lb.	1 pt
Berries*	1 crate (24 qt.)	32 to 36 pt.
	1⅓ to 1½ pt.	1 pt.
Cantaloupes	1 dozen (28 lb.)	22 pt.
	1 to 1¼ lb.	1 pt.
Cherries,	1 bu. (56 lb.)	36 to 44 pt.
sweet or sour	1¼ to 1½ lb.	1 pt.
Cranberries	1 box (25 lb.)	50 pt.
	1 peck (8 lb.)	16 pt.
	½ lb.	1 pt.
Currants	2 qt. (3 lb.)	4 pt.
	¾ lb.	1 pt.
Peaches	1 bu. (48 lb.)	32 to 48 pt.
	1 lug box (20 lb.)	13 to 20 pt.
	1 to 1½ lb.	1 pt.
Pears	1 bu. (50 lb.)	40 to 50 pt.
	1 western box (46 lb.)	37 to 46 pt.
	1 to 1¼ lb.	1 pt.
Pineapple	5 lb.	4 pt.
Plums and prunes	1 bu. (56 lb.)	38 to 56 pt.
	1 crate (20 lb.)	13 to 20 pt.
	1 to 1½ lb.	1 pt.
Raspberries	1 crate (24 pt.)	24 pt.
	1 pt.	1 pt.
Rhubarb	15 lb.	15 to 22 pt.
	⅔ to 1 lb.	1 pt.
Strawberries	1 crate (24 qt.)	38 pt.
	⅔ qt.	1 pt.

*Includes blackberries, blueberries, boysenberries, dewberries, elderberries, gooseberries, huckleberries, loganberries, and youngberries.

Frozen yield from fresh vegetables

Vegetable	Fresh, as purchased or picked	Frozen
Asparagus	1 crate (12 2-lb. bunches)	15 to 22 pt.
	1 to 1½ lb.	1 pt.
Beans, lima (in pods)	1 bu. (32 lb.)	12 to 16 pt.
	2 to 2½ lb.	1 pt.
Beans, snap, green, and wax	1 bu. (30 lb.)	30 to 45 pt.
	⅔ to 1 lb.	1 pt.
Beet greens	15 lb.	10 to 15 pt.
	1 to 1½ lb.	1 pt.
Beets (without tops)	1 bu. (52 lb.)	35 to 42 pt.
	1¼ to 1½ lb.	1 pt.
Broccoli	1 crate (25 lb.)	24 pt.
	1 lb.	1 pt.
Brussels sprouts	4 quart boxes	6 pt.
	1 lb.	1 pt.
Carrots (without tops)	1 bu. (50 lb.)	32 to 40 pt.
	1¼ to 1½ lb.	1 pt.
Cauliflower	2 medium heads	3 pt.
	1⅓ lb.	1 pt.
Chard	1 bu. (12 lb.)	8 to 12 pt.
	1 to 1½ lb.	1 pt.
Collards	1 bu. (12 lb.)	8 to 12 pt.
	1 to 1½ lb.	1 pt.
Corn, sweet (in husks)	1 bu. (35 lb.)	14 to 17 pt.
	2 to 2½ lb.	1 pt.
Kale	1 bu. (18 lb.)	12 to 18 pt.
	1 to 1½ lb.	1 pt.
Mustard greens	1 bu. (12 lb.)	8 to 12 pt.
	1 to 1½ lb.	1 pt.
Peas	1 bu. (30 lb.)	12 to 15 pt.
	2 to 2½ lb.	1 pt.
Peppers, sweet	⅔ lb. (3 peppers)	1 pt.
Pumpkin	3 lb.	2 pt.
Spinach	1 bu. (18 lb.)	12 to 18 pt.
	1 to 1½ lb.	1 pt.
Squash, summer	1 bu. (40. lb.)	32 to 40 pt.
	1 to 1¼ lb.	1 pt.
Squash, winter	3 lb.	2 pt.
Sweetpotatoes	⅔ lb.	1 pt.

Syrups for freezing and canning fruit

Freezing

Light (20 percent)	1 cup sugar + 4 cups water = 5 cups syrup
Medium (30 percent)	2 cups sugar + 4 cups water = 5⅓ cups syrup
Medium-Heavy (40 percent)	3 cups sugar + 4 cups water = 5½ cups syrup
Heavy (50 percent)	4¾ cups sugar + 4 cups water = 6½ cups syrup

Canning

Light	2 cups sugar + 4 cups water = 5 cups syrup
Medium	3 cups sugar + 4 cups water = 5½ cups syrup
Heavy	4¾ cups sugar + 4 cups water = 6½ cups syrup

Timetable for processing at high altitudes

Altitude	Increase in processing time if the time called for is— 20 minutes or less	More than 20 minutes
1,000 feet	1 minute	2 minutes
2,000 feet	2 minutes	4 minutes
3,000 feet	3 minutes	6 minutes
4,000 feet	4 minutes	8 minutes
5,000 feet	5 minutes	10 minutes
6,000 feet	6 minutes	12 minutes
7,000 feet	7 minutes	14 minutes
8,000 feet	8 minutes	16 minutes
9,000 feet	9 minutes	18 minutes
10,000 feet	10 minutes	20 minutes

Meal planning: restricted diets

Emergency meal plans

First day	Second day	Third day

No cooking facilities
Morning

Citrus fruit juice.*	Fruit juice.*	Grapefruit segments.*
Ready-to-eat cereal.	Corned beef hash.*	Ready-to-eat cereal.
Milk, cold coffee,† or tea.†	Crackers.	Vienna sausage.*
Crackers.	Spread.	Milk, cold coffee,† or tea.†
Peanut butter or other spread.	Milk, cold coffee,† or tea.†	

Noon

Spaghetti with meat sauce.*	Baked beans.*	Chile con carne with beans*
Green beans.*	Brown bread.*	Crackers.
Crackers.	Tomatoes.*	Fruit.*
Spread.	Fruit.*	Cookies.
Milk, cold coffee,† or tea.†	Milk, cold coffee,† or tea.†	Milk, cold coffee,† or tea.†

Between meals

Fruit-flavored drink or fruit drink.	Milk.	Tomato juice.

Night

Lunch meat.*	Pork and gravy.*	Sliced beef.*
Sweetpotatoes.*	Corn.*	Macaroni and cheese.*
Applesauce.*	Potatoes.*	Peas and carrots.*
Milk, cold coffee,† or tea.†	Instant pudding.	Crackers.
Candy.	Fruit juice.*	Milk, cold coffee,† or tea.†

Limited cooking facilities
Morning

Citrus fruit juice.*	Citrus fruit juice.*	Prunes.*
Ready-to-eat cereal.	Hot cereal (quick-cooking).	Ready-to-eat cereal.
Milk.	Milk.	Milk.
Hot coffee,† tea,† or cocoa.†	Hot coffee,† tea,† or cocoa.†	Crackers.
		Cheese.
		Hot coffee,† tea,† or cocoa.†

Diet and nutrition

First day	Second day	Third day
Noon		
Vegetable soup.*	Beef-and vegetable stew.*	Chile con carne with beans.*
Potato salad.*	Green beans.*	Tomatoes.*
Crackers.	Crackers.	Crackers.
Ham spread.*	Peanut butter.	Hot coffee,† tea,† or cocoa.†
Milk.	Milk.	
Candy bar.		
Between meals		
Fruit-flavored drink or fruit drink.	Tomato juice.*	Fruit-flavored drink or fruit drink.
Night		
Beef and gravy.*	Tuna fish,* cream of celery soup,* mixed sweet pickles*—combined in one dish.	Lunch meat.*
Noodles.*	Fruit.*	Hominy.*
Peas and carrots.*	Cookies.	Applesauce.*
Instant pudding.	Hot coffee,† tea,† or cocoa.†	Cookies.
Hot coffee,† tea,† or cocoa.†		Hot coffee,† tea,† or cocoa.†

*Canned.
†Instant.

Ingredient exchanges

Original ingredient	Substitute ingredients
1 whole egg, for baking or thickening	2 egg yolks
1 cup butter or margarine for baking	7/8 cup vegetable or animal shortening plus 1/2 teaspoon salt
1 ounce unsweetened chocolate	3 tablespoons cocoa plus 1 tablespoon fat
1 teaspoon double-acting baking powder	2 teaspoons quick-acting baking powder or 1/4 teaspoon baking soda plus 1/2 cup sour milk or buttermilk instead of 1/2 cup sweet milk
1 cup buttermilk or sour milk, for baking	1 cup fluid whole milk plus 1 tablespoon vinegar or lemon juice or 1 cup fluid whole milk plus 1 3/4 teaspoons cream of tartar
1 cup fluid whole milk	1/2 cup evaporated milk plus 1/2 cup water or 1 cup fluid nonfat dry or skim milk plus 2 1/2 teaspoons butter or margarine

57

Original ingredient	Substitute ingredients
1 cup fluid skim milk	1 cup reconstituted nonfat dry milk
1 tablespoon flour, for thickening	½ tablespoon cornstarch *or* 2 teaspoons quick-cooking tapioca
1 cup cake flour, for baking	⅞ cup all-purpose flour
1 cup catsup	1 8-ounce can tomato sauce plus ½ cup brown sugar and 2 tablespoons vinegar
1 cup cream	¾ cup milk plus ⅓ cup butter

Salt substitutes

Meat, fish, poultry

Beef	Bay leaf, dry mustard powder, green pepper, marjoram, fresh mushrooms, nutmeg, onion, pepper, sage, thyme.
Chicken	Green pepper, lemon juice, marjoram, fresh mushrooms, paprika, parsley, poultry seasoning, sage, thyme.
Fish	Bay leaf, curry powder, dry mustard powder, green pepper, lemon juice, marjoram, fresh mushrooms, paprika.
Lamb	Curry powder, garlic, mint, mint jelly, pineapple, rosemary.
Pork	Apple, applesauce, garlic, onion, sage.
Veal	Apricot, bay leaf, curry powder, ginger, marjoram, oregano.

Vegetables

Asparagus	Garlic, lemon juice, onion, vinegar.
Corn	Green pepper, pimento, fresh tomato.
Cucumbers	Chives, dill, garlic, vinegar.
Green Beans	Dill, lemon juice, marjoram, nutmeg, pimento.

Greens	Onion, pepper, vinegar.
Peas	Green pepper, mint, fresh mushrooms, onion, parsley.
Potatoes	Green pepper, mace, onion, paprika, parsley.
Rice	Chives, green pepper, onion, pimento, saffron.
Squash	Brown sugar, cinnamon, ginger, mace, nutmeg, onion.
Tomatoes	Basil, marjoram, onion, oregano.
Soups	A pinch of dry mustard powder in bean soup; allspice, a small amount of vinegar or a dash of sugar in vegetable soup; peppercorns in skim milk chowders; bay leaf and parsley in pea soup.

Salt and sodium conversions

Conversions	Formulas
Grams to milligrams	Multiply weight in grams by 1,000
Sodium into salt (NaCl) equivalent	Milligrams of sodium content ÷ .40 = milligrams of salt
Salt into sodium	Milligrams of salt × .40 = milligrams of sodium
Sodium in milligrams to sodium in milliequivalents*	Milligrams of sodium ÷ 23 (atomic weight of sodium) = milliequivalents of sodium
Milliequivalents of sodium to milligrams of sodium	Milliequivalents of sodium × 23 = milligrams of sodium

*Medical prescriptions are often given as milliequivalents (mEq).

Sodium content: fresh vs. processed foods

	Sodium content		Sodium content
Fresh foods		**Processed foods**	
Beef stew, home-made, 1 cup	91 mgs.	Beef stew, canned 1 cup	980 mgs.
Cheddar cheese, natural, 1 oz.	176 mgs.	Pasteurized, processed cheese, 1 oz.	406 mgs.
Corn, fresh, cooked 1 cup	trace	Corn, canned 1 cup	384 mgs.
Cucumber, whole 1 lg.	18 mgs.	Dill pickle, whole 1 large	1928 mgs.
Green beans, fresh, cooked, 1 cup	5 mgs.	Green beans, canned 1 cup	326 mgs.
Hamburger, lean 3 oz. (1 patty)	57 mgs.	Hot dog 1 hot dog	639 mgs.
Kidney beans, dry, cooked, 1 cup	4 mgs.	Kidney beans, canned 1 cup	844 mgs.
Lemon 1 wedge	1 mg.	Tartar sauce 1 tbsp	182 mgs.
Peas, cooked 1 cup	2 mgs.	Peas, canned 1 cup	493 mgs.
Potato, baked 1 med.	5 mgs.	Augratin potatoes 1 cup	1095 mgs.
Shrimp, raw 3 oz.	137 mgs.	Shrimp, canned 3 oz	1955 mgs.
Tomatoes, fresh, boiled 1 cup	10 mgs.	Tomatoes, canned, whole 1 cup	390 mgs.

SOURCE: U.S. Department of Agriculture, taken from THE HOUSEHOLD HANDBOOK, Meadowbrook Press

Meal preparation

Oven terms and temperatures

Recipe terms	Temperature range	Recipe types
Very cool oven	240° F/116° C	Stews, meringues
Cool oven	275° F/135° C 290° F/144° C	Casseroles, milk and egg dishes
Slow oven	325° F/163° C	Lamb and beef roasts
Moderate oven	350° F/177° C 375° F/190° C	Cookies, cakes, pies
Moderately hot oven	400° F/200° C	
Hot oven	425° F/218° C	Souffles, flan, sponge cake
Very hot oven	450° F/232° C 475° F/246° C	Fast roasts, bread, flaky pastry
Broil	500° F/269° C	Steaks, chops

Taken from SUPERWOMAN by Shirley Conran. Copyright © 1979 by Shirley Conran. Used by permission of Crown Publishers, Inc.

Microwave/oven temperature equivalents

Microwave Percentage of power	Oven Conventional settings
100	High
70	Medium high or roast
50	Medium or simmer
30	Medium low, low, or defrost
10	Low or warm

Recommended internal temperatures

Food	Temperature	Food	Temperature
Fresh beef		**Canned pork**	
Rare	140° F.	(fully cooked)	
Medium	160° F.	Ham	140° F.
Well done	170° F.		
		Poultry	
Fresh veal	170° F.	Chicken	165° to 170° F.
		Turkey	180° to 185° F.
Fresh lamb		Boneless	170° to 175° F.
Medium	160° F.	roasts	
Well done	170° F.	Stuffing	165° F.

Fresh pork		Operation	Temperature
Loin	170° F.		
Other roasts	185 ° F.	Home canning	240° F. to 260° F.
		Cooking	165° F. or higher
Cured Pork		Warm holding	140° F. or higher
(cook before eating)		Refrigeration	35° F. to 45° F.
Ham	160° F.	Frozen storage	0° F. or lower
Shoulder	170° F.		
Canadian bacon	160° F.		

Adopted from KEEPING FOOD SAFE by Hassell Bradley & Carole Sundberg. Copyright © 1975 by Hassell Bradley and Carole Sundberg. Reprinted by permission of Doubleday & Company, Inc.

Timetable for broiling meats

Kind and cut of meat	Approximate thickness (Inches)	Degree of doneness	Approximate total cooking time* (Minutes)
Beef steaks	1	Rare	10 to 15
Club, porterhouse, rib, sirloin, T-bone, tenderloin	1	Medium	15 to 20
	1	Well done	20 to 30
	1½	Rare	15 to 20
	1½	Medium	20 to 25
	1½	Well done	25 to 40
	2	Rare	25 to 35
	2	Medium	35 to 45
	2	Well done	45 to 55
Hamburgers	¾	Rare	8
	¾	Medium	12
	¾	Well done	14
Lamb chops	1	Medium	12
Loin, rib, shoulder	1	Well done	14
	1½	Medium	18
	1½	Well done	22
Cured ham slices	¾	Well done	13 to 14
Cook-before-eating	1	Well done	18 to 20

*Meat at refrigerator temperature at start of broiling.

Timetable for roasting meat and poultry

Kind and cut of meat or poultry	Ready-to-cook weight	Approximate roasting time at 325° F.	Kind and cut of meat or poultry	Ready-to-cook weight	Approximate roasting time at 325° F.
Beef			**Pork, fresh**		
Standing ribs:	*Pounds*	*Hours*	Loin, center cut	3 to 5	2 to 3⅓
Rare	6 to 8	2½ to 3	Shoulder, picnic	5 to 8	3 to 4
Medium	6 to 8	3 to 3½	Ham, whole	12 to 16	5½ to 6
Well done	6 to 8	3⅔ to 5	Ham, boneless, rolled	10 to 14	4⅔ to 5½
Rolled rump			Spareribs	3 to 4	2
Rare	5	2¼	**Pork, cured**		
Medium	5	3	Cook-before-eating:		
Well done	5	3¼	Ham, whole	10 to 14	3½ to 4¼
Sirloin tip:			Ham, half	5 to 7	2 to 2½
Rare	3	1½	Picnic shoulder	6	3½
Medium	3	2	Fully cooked:		
Well done	3	2¼	Ham, whole	12 to 16	3½ to 4
Veal			Ham, half	5 to 7	2
Leg	5 to 8	2½ to 3½	**Poultry***		
Loin	5	3	Chickens		
Shoulder	6	3½	Broilers, fryers,	1½ to 2½	1 to 2
Lamb			or roasters	2½ to 4½	2 to 3½
Leg (whole)	6 to 7	3¼ to 4	Ducks	4 to 6	2 to 3
Shoulder	3 to 6	2¼ to 3¼	Geese	6 to 8	3 to 3½
Rolled shoulder	3 to 5	2½ to 3		8 to 12	3½ to 4½
			Turkeys	6 to 8	3 to 3½
				8 to 12	3½ to 4½
				12 to 16	4½ to 5½
				16 to 20	5½ to 6½
				20 to 24	6½ to 7

*Unstuffed poultry may take slightly less time than stuffed poultry. Cooking time is based on chilled poultry or poultry that has just been thawed—temperature not above 40° F. Frozen unstuffed poultry will take longer. Do not use this roasting guide for frozen commercially stuffed poultry; follow package directions.

Timetable for cooking fish

Cooking method and market form	Approximate ready-to-cook weight or thickness	Cooking temperature	Approximate cooking time in minutes
Baking			
Dressed	3 pounds	350° F	45 to 60
Pan-dressed	3 pounds	350° F	25 to 30
Fillets or steaks	2 pounds	350° F	20 to 25
Portions	2 pounds	400° F	15 to 20
Sticks	2¼ pounds	400° F	15 to 20
Broiling			
Pan-dressed	3 pounds		10 to 16
Fillets or steaks	½ to 1 inch		10 to 15
Portions	⅜ to ½ inch		10 to 15
Sticks	⅜ to ½ inch		10 to 15
Charcoal broiling			
Pan-dressed	3 pounds	Moderate	10 to 16
Fillets or steaks	½ to 1 inch	Moderate	10 to 16
Portions	⅜ to ½ inch	Moderate	8 to 10
Sticks	⅜ to ½ inch	Moderate	8 to 10

Cooking method and market form	Approximate ready-to-cook weight or thickness	Cooking temperature	Approximate cooking time in minutes
Deep-fat frying			
Pan-dressed	3 pounds	350° F.	3 to 5
Fillets or steaks	½ to 1 inch	350° F.	3 to 5
Portions	⅜ to ½ inch	350° F.	3 to 5
Sticks	⅜ to ½ inch	350° F.	3 to 5
Oven-frying			
Pan-dressing	3 pounds	500° F.	15 to 20
Fillets or steaks	½ to 1 inch	500° F.	10 to 15
Pan-frying			
Pan-dressed	3 pounds	Moderate	8 to 10
Fillets or steaks	½ to 1 inch	Moderate	8 to 10
Portions	⅜ to ½ inch	Moderate	8 to 10
Sticks	⅜ to ½ inch	Moderate	8 to 10
Poaching			
Fillets or steaks	2 pounds	Simmer	5 to 10
Steaming			
Fillets or steaks	2 pounds	Boil	5 to 10

Timetable for cooking fresh vegetables

Vegetable	Boiling time (minutes)	Vegetable	Boiling time (minutes)
Asparagus, whole	10 to 13	Okra	12 to 14
Beans		Onions, mature	
Lima	25 to 27	Whole	11 to 15
Snap, 1-inch pieces	13 to 15	Quartered	10 to 14
Beets, whole	38 to 40	Parsnips	
Broccoli, heavy stalks, split	9 to 12	Whole	20 to 40
Brussels sprouts	15 to 17	Quartered	8 to 15
Cabbage		Peas	10 to 14
Shredded	6 to 8	Potatoes	
Wedges	10 to 13	Whole, medium size	25 to 29
Carrots		Quartered	15 to 17
Whole	20 to 22	Spinach	8 to 12
Sliced or diced	18 to 20	Squash	
Cauliflower		Acorn, quartered	18 to 20
Separated	8 to 12	Butternut, cubed	16 to 18
Whole	20 to 24	Yellow, crookneck, sliced	11 to 13
Celery, sliced	15 to 19	Zucchini, sliced	13 to 15
Collards	15 to 20	Sweet potatoes, whole	28 to 35
Corn		Turnips	
On cob	5 to 7	Cut up	10 to 12
Whole kernel	6 to 8	Whole	30 to 38
Kale	15 to 20		

Timetable for cooking frozen vegetables

Vegetable	Time to allow after water returns to boil (minutes)	Vegetable	Time to allow after water returns to boil (minutes)
Asparagus	5–10	Chard	8–10
Beans, lima		Corn	
Large type	6–10	Whole-kermel	3–5
Baby type	15–20	On-the-cob	3–4
Beans, snap, green, or wax		Kale	8–12
1-inch pieces	12–18	Kohlrabi	8–10
Julienne	5–10	Mustard greens	8–15
Beans, soybeans, green	10–20	Peas, green	5–10
Beet greens	6–12	Spinach	4–6
Broccoli	5–8	Squash, summer	10–12
Brussels sprouts	4–9	Turnip greens	15–20
Carrots	5–10	Turnips	8–12
Cauliflower	5–8		

Appropriate spices

	Allspice	Basil	Caraway seeds	Chives	Cloves	Curry powder	Dill	Garlic	Ginger	Marjoram	Onion powder	Oregano	Poppy seeds	Rosemary	Savory	Tarragon	Thyme	Tumeric
Pot roast or meat loaf	•							•		•							•	
Fish			•			•										•		
Poultry										•				•		•		
Soups				•					•									
Pastas													•		•			
Tomatoes		•										•						
Rice or bulgur	•					•					•							•
Cooked cabbage, broccoli			•			•				•								
Cooked carrots or beets			•		•													
Cooked beans or peas							•							•				

3   Home management

The key to effective home management may be as simple as learning to effectively keep home records. The third section of TABLES AND FORMULAS begins with a set of guidelines for establishing such a system. This is followed by a group of tables dealing with household finances: a basic budget form, a system for calculating net worth, a consumer credit check, and methods for determining interest rates.

The reader, continuing in Section 3, will find tables and formulas for both the tenant and homeowner. If you are buying a house or considering taking this step, you will profit from the "Real Estate Closing Checklist," which shows the procedure for closing a real estate transaction. A mortgage interest table will also help the prospective buyer calculate the interest charges on a new house.

The next area of "Home Management" deals with home energy, including alternate sources and methods of conservation. In this era of constantly climbing energy costs, these tables could be of real value. Car expenses occupy another portion of Section 3. After studying these tables, the reader should not only be able to keep detailed records of auto costs, but be able to save money as well.

"Home Management" continues with tables dealing with insurance, including workman's compensation laws as they exist in the 50 states. Also featured are methods of determining which insurance companies offer the best value for one's dollar and the many coverage formats available for household insurance. The section concludes with information for the prospective retiree and tax checklists and data.

The tables and formulas comprising "Home Management," in total, offer the reader an effective system of efficiently planning and managing the day-to-day details of his or her life.

Keeping records

Maintaining house records: a checklist

Records of your purchase and ownership of the house

☑ Receipts for money paid on or before the closing (loan disclosure statement)

☐ Your copy of the mortgage note or deed of trust

☐ Your copy of the deed

☐ Your warranties on the house (if any)

☐ FHA or VA related documents

Insurance records

☐ Copy of hazard or homeowner's insurance policy

☐ Mortgage, life, or flood insurance policies

☐ A list of your personal property in the home and its value (photographs of each room are helpful to have)

Maintenance, repairs, and home improvement records

☐ Utility bills and receipts

☐ Receipts for any repairs (including labor and materials)

☐ Warranties on any items in the house (equipment and appliances)

☐ Description of any improvements you have made to the house and their costs

Tax and mortgage payment records

☐ Receipts of all payments made to your mortgage lender (real estate taxes and mortgage interest payments are deductible from your income for federal income tax purposes)

☐ Other receipts for local taxes or assessments you have paid

Other records

☐ Homeowner's association dues paid

☐ Other payments you may have made for your home, such as condominium or cooperative association dues and maintenance expenses

Maintaining financial records: a checklist

☑ Past net worth statements

☐ Medical records
· children's immunization records
· receipts and cancelled checks for medical and dental bills
· prescription numbers

☐ Home management materials
- warranties, service contracts, and operating instructions
- current inventory of household items

☐ Wills and estate planning records
- an unsigned copy of the original will and a note giving the location of the original
- instructions regarding final services and the location of the burial plot
- names and addresses of lawyer and executor

☐ Insurance information
- copies or originals of all policies (life, medical, automobile, homeowner's, and personal property)
- names, phone numbers, and addresses of agents

☐ Credit information
- copies of all loan agreements, promissory notes, statements and receipts from each account

☐ Investment transaction records
- stock certificates and broker's confirmations of purchases and sales

☐ Cancelled checks and bank statements
- the past three years

☐ Miscellaneous proofs of purchase
- paid bill receipts

☐ Safe-deposit box folder
- list of all items stored in safe-deposit box
- location of safe-deposit key

☐ Tax records
- state, federal, and personal property tax forms (for at least three years)
- records of deductible business and professional expenses
- records of the interest paid on mortgage loans and others
- records of medical bills (once deducted)
- records of capital gains and losses
- records of casualty losses
- records of contributions
- bills of sale for large-ticket items, e.g., a car (After three years, this information should be refiled in dead storage for at least three more years, as you can be audited back to six years. After this time your records cannot be subpoenaed unless fraud is involved.)

Filing records

Home strongbox	Safe-deposit box
apartment lease	appraisals of jewelry, furs
canceled checks	automobile titles
charitable contribution records	birth certificates
credit card numbers	discharge papers
equipment, appliance records	government bonds
home-improvement records	household inventory
income tax records	marriage certificate
insurance policies	mortgage
medical records	property records
payroll check stubs	stock and bond certificates
receipts	wills (duplicate)
savings passbooks	
school records	
social security records	
wills	

Reprinted with permission from CHANGING TIMES Magazine, © 1979 Kiplinger Washington Editors, Inc., Dec 1979.

Replacing key documents

Item	Who to contact
Animal registration papers	Society of registry
Auto registration title cards	Department of motor vehicles
Bank books	Your bank, as soon as possible
Birth, death, marriage certificates	State bureau of records in the state of birth, death, or marriage
Citizenship papers	The U.S. Immigration and Naturalization Service
Credit cards	The issuing companies, as soon as possible
Divorce papers	Circuit court where decree was issued
Driver's license	Local department of motor vehicles
Income tax records	The Internal Revenue Service Center where filed or your accountant
Insurance policies	Your insurance agent
Medical records	Your doctor
Military discharge papers	Local Veterans Administration
Passports	Local passport office
Prepaid burial contracts	Issuing company
Social Security or Medicare cards	Local Social Security office
Stocks and bonds	Issuing company or your broker
Titles to deeds	Records department of city or county in which the property is located
Warranties	Issuing company

Household finances

A basic budget form

Income

Salary $\$\underline{\qquad}$

  Salary deductions

    Income taxes $\$\underline{\qquad}$

    Social security $\underline{\qquad}$

    Other salary deductions $\underline{\qquad}$

    Total salary deductions $\underline{\qquad}$

  Net salary $\underline{\qquad}$

Other income (interest, dividends, rent, etc.) $\underline{\qquad}$

Total spendable income $\qquad$ $\$\underline{\qquad}$

Fixed expenses

Home mortgage or rent $\$\underline{\qquad}$

Real estate tax $\underline{\qquad}$

Homeowner's insurance $\underline{\qquad}$

Life insurance $\underline{\qquad}$

Health insurance $\underline{\qquad}$

Automobile insurance $\underline{\qquad}$

Installment payments $\underline{\qquad}$

Other fixed expenses $\underline{\qquad}$

Total fixed expenses $\underline{\qquad}$

Day-to-day expenses

Food $\$\underline{\qquad}$

Clothing $\underline{\qquad}$

Other housekeeping expenses $\underline{\qquad}$

Utilities $\underline{\qquad}$

Home repair and maintenance $\underline{\qquad}$

Medical care $\underline{\qquad}$

Personal care $\underline{\qquad}$

Transportation $\underline{\qquad}$

Recreation and entertainment $\underline{\qquad}$

Education $\underline{\qquad}$

Gifts and contributions $\underline{\qquad}$

Other day-to-day expenses $\underline{\qquad}$

Total day-to-day expenses $\underline{\qquad}$

Savings $\underline{\qquad}$

Total budget $\$\underline{\qquad}$

Calculating net worth

Assets	Value
Amount you now have in savings account(s)	$
Cash on hand (in cash or checking account)	$
Stocks, bonds, life insurance policies (give current market value or actual cash value)	$
Real Estate you now own (give assessed market value or price paid)	$
Automobile(s) (give the book value for make, model, and year of the car)	$
Household furnishings (give the value of all items including furniture, silverware, carpets, paintings, T.V.'s, stereo, other appliances)	$
Jewelry, antiques, furs (give appraised value)	$
Other items of value (for example, boat, trailer, bike, etc.)	$
Amount of money owed to you (IOU's, tax refunds, etc.)	$
Other	$

Total assets $

Liabilities	
Mortgage	$
Notes, loans	$
Others	$

Total liabilities $

Net worth

Total assets minus total liabilities $

Consumer credit checklist

To use consumer credit wisely, make certain that—

☑ You know how much the use of credit costs.

☐ You have shopped around and chosen the best available terms.

☐ You need the item urgently enough to justify the credit cost.

☐ Your budget can stand the additional payment.

It will help you to understand how credit rates vary. To compare the cost of credit charged by different lenders and creditors—

☑ Use only the annual percentage rate.

☐ If interest rate is quoted on a monthly basis, multiply the monthly rate by 12 to get the annual percentage rate.

☐ Note how the finance charge is made. You will pay a lower finance charge if the monthly percentage rate is based on the unpaid balance rather than on the previous month's balance (before any payment is deducted).

Calculating interest charges

If the quoted rate is—	The buyer pays a true annual interest rate of—
½ of 1 percent per month	6 percent
¾ of 1 percent per month	9 percent
1 percent per month	12 percent
1¼ percent per month	15 percent
1½ percent per month	18 percent
1¾ percent per month	21 percent
2 percent per month	24 percent

Calculating total interest charges

The total interest charges on a loan can be calculated by using the following simple formula:

$$I = P \times r \times t$$

I represents the amount of interest charged. *P* is the principal, or amount borrowed. The letter *r* stands for the annual rate of interest, and *t* represents time, specifically the number of years or fractions of years.

Interest charges on a $1,000.00 loan

Rate	12 months	24 months	36 months	48 months	60 months
8%	$ 43.86	$ 85.45	$128.11	$171.82	$216.58
9%	49.42	96.43	144.79	194.48	245.50
10%	54.99	107.48	161.62	217.40	274.82
11%	60.58	118.59	178.59	240.59	304.55
12%	66.19	129.76	195.72	264.02	334.67
14%	77.45	152.31	230.39	311.67	396.10
16%	88.77	175.11	265.65	360.33	459.08
18%	100.16	198.18	301.49	410.00	523.61

From SYLVIA PORTER'S NEW MONEY BOOK FOR THE 80'S by Sylvia Porter. Copyright © 1975, 1979 by Sylvia Porter. Reprinted by permission of Doubleday & Company, Inc.

Housing

Housing expenses worksheet

Step 1 Figure out your regular monthly take-home (net) pay after deductions for taxes, social security, pension, union dues, etc. (include only what you can definitely count on).

	An Example	Your Estimate
Employment (after deductions)	$ 850	$
Social Security, disability/pension benefits, welfare payments, etc.	$ 0	$
Alimony, child support	$ 0	$
Interest on savings accounts	$ 15	$
Stock dividends, bond income, etc.	$ 0	$
Other income (such as, second job)	$ 135	$
Total (net) income	$ 1,000	$

Step 2 Figure out your regular monthly expenses (excluding rent and utilities).

Food (groceries, eating out, etc.)	$ 250	$
Clothes (new clothes, laundry, etc.)	$ 60	$
Personal care (cosmetics, hair care, personal hygiene)	$ 25	$
Medical/dental bills (plus prescriptions)	$ 35	$
Home furnishings and expenses	$ 20	$
Recreation (movies, vacation)	$ 30	$
Gifts (birthdays, holidays)	$ 25	$
Car expenses (auto loan, insurance, gas, oil, maintenance, etc.)	$ 110	$
Life and health insurance	$ 50	$
Child care expenses	$ 15	$
Installment loans (charge accounts, credit cards)	$ 30	$
Regular savings	$ 30	$
All Other Miscellaneous Expenses	$ 20	$
Total (non-housing) expenses	$ 700	$

Step 3 Subtract the total in Step 1 from the total in Step 2 to get the amount available for housing expenses

Total available for housing	$ 300	$

Step 4 Take ⅔ of total available for housing (step 3) to estimate your monthly mortgage payment

⅔ × $ _300_ = $ _200_ $ _____

Step 5 Multiply this figure by 12 to get your annual mortgage payment

12 × $ _200_ = $ _2,400_ $ _____

Step 6 Multiply this figure by 10 to estimate the size of a loan you can support

10 × $2,400 = (Loan Amount) $ _24,000_ $ _____

Step 7 Add the amount you have saved for a down payment (but set aside enough for closing costs and move-in expenses)

Down payment $ _3,000_ $ _____

This is the approximate amount you can afford to pay for a house. $ _27,000_ $ _____

Test the rules of thumb: 2 − 2½ × annual take-home (net) pay in Step 1

An example   2 × $12,000 = $24,000
                   2½ × $12,000 = $30,000

Your estimate   2 × $_____ = $_____
                   2½ × $_____ = $_____

Tenant protections, by state

Tenant protections change constantly. Tenants should, thus, check with tenant groups, housing authorities, legal aid societies, or private attorneys to see what tenant protections exist in their localities. States not included in the table offer none of the listed protections.

	Retaliatory eviction prohibited	Security deposit law	Tenant may deduct repairs from rent	Warranty of habitability
Alaska	Yes	Yes	Yes	Yes*
Arizona	Yes	Yes	Yes	Yes*
California	Yes	Yes	Yes	Yes*
Colorado	No	Yes	Yes	No
Connecticut	Yes	Yes	No	Yes*
Delaware	Yes	Yes	Yes	Yes*
District of Columbia	Yes	Yes	No	Yes*
Florida	Yes[A]	Yes	No	Yes*
Georgia	No	Yes	No	Yes
Hawaii	Yes	Yes	Yes	Yes*
Idaho	No	Yes	No	Yes*
Illinois	Yes	Yes	No	Yes

	Retaliatory eviction prohibited	Security deposit law	Tenant may deduct repairs from rent	Warranty of habitability
Iowa	Yes	Yes	No	Yes
Kansas	Yes	Yes	No	Yes
Kentucky[B]	Yes	Yes	Yes	Yes*
Louisiana	No	Yes	Yes	No
Maine	Yes	Yes	No	Yes*
Maryland	Yes	Yes	No	Yes*
Massachusetts	Yes	Yes	Yes	Yes*
Michigan	Yes	Yes	No	Yes*
Minnesota	Yes	Yes	No	Yes*
Missouri	No	No	No	Yes
Montana	No	No	Yes	Yes*
Nebraska	Yes	Yes	Yes[C]	Yes*
Nevada	Yes	Yes	Yes	Yes*
New Hampshire	Yes	Yes	No	Yes
New Jersey	Yes	Yes	Yes	Yes
New Mexico	Yes	Yes	No	Yes*
New York	No	Yes	No	Yes*
North Carolina	No	Yes	No	Yes*
North Dakota	No	Yes	Yes	Yes*
Ohio	Yes	Yes	No	Yes*
Oklahoma	No	Yes	Yes	Yes*
Oregon	Yes	Yes	Yes	Yes*
Pennsylvania	No[D]	Yes	No	Yes
Puerto Rico	No	No	No	Yes*
Rhode Island	Yes	Yes	No	Yes*
South Dakota	No	Yes	Yes	Yes*
Tennessee[E]	Yes	Yes	Yes	Yes*
Texas	Yes	Yes	Yes	Yes
Vermont	No	No	No	Yes[F]
Virginia	Yes	Yes	No	Yes*
Washington	Yes	Yes	Yes	Yes*
West Virginia	No	No	No	Yes*
Wisconsin	Yes	Yes	No	Yes

*By statute.
A. Tenant protected not by state law but by opinion of attorney general.
B. Law applies only to Lexington and Louisville.
C. Limited to utilities and essential services.
D. Except in Philadelphia.
E. Limited to dwellings in counties having a population of more than 200,000.
F. Recognized by common law.

GUIDE TO CONSUMER SERVICES, Revised Edition by The Editors of Consumer Report Books. Copyright © 1974, 1975, 1976, 1977, 1978, 1979 by Consumers Union of United States, Inc., Mount Vernon, New York 10550. By permission of Little, Brown and Company.

House inventory: exterior checklist

☑ **Foundation:** Check for holes, cracks, unevenness.

☐ **Brickwork:** Look for cracks; loose or missing mortar.

☐ **Siding** (clapboards, shingles, etc.): Look for loose or missing pieces, lifting, or warping.

☐ **Gutters and Downspouts:** Check for missing sections; gaps or holes in joints; are there signs of leaks?

☐ **Chimney:** Look for tilting; loose or missing bricks.

☐ **Paint:** Look for peeling, chipping, blistering, etc.

☐ **Entrance Porch:** Examine steps, handrails, posts, etc., for loose or unsafe features.

☐ **Windows/Screens:** Look for cracked or broken glass; holes in screens.

☐ **Storm Windows** (northern climates): Are they complete? Are they secure and properly caulked?

☐ **Roof:** Look for worn or bald spots; ask how old and if under warranty or not.

☐ **Walls and Fences:** Look for holes, loose or missing sections, rotted posts.

☐ **Garage** (if separate from house): check doors, roof, siding, windows.

☐ **Driveway and Sidewalks:** Look for holes and cracks.

☐ **Grounds/Landscaping:** Locate property line; are trees, shrubbery and grass in good shape?

☐ **Proper drainage:** Will rain (or snow) flow *away* from the house? Are there any problems with leaching fields or septic tanks?

House inventory: interior checklist

☑ **Structure of the house:** Does the house feel solid? (Jump up and down on the floors). Check support posts and floor supports in basement; look for looseness, bending, rot or termites.

☐ **Floors:** Check for levelness, bowing, movement when you walk on them.

☐ **Stairs:** Look for loose treads; loose handrails.

☐ **Plumbing System:** Check water pipes and sewer lines for leaking or rusting; flush all toilets; turn on faucets to test the water pressure; look for clogged or sluggish drains; dripping faucets.

☐ **Windows:** Check for broken sash cords; loose frames. locks.

☐ **Kitchen:** What appliances are included (stove, refrigerator, dishwasher, garbage disposal)? Check for age, workability. Are there enough shelves and counter space? Are there enough electrical outlets? Are there leaks under the sink?

☐ **Bathrooms:** Are there enough for your family? Check for cracks in tiles; signs of leaks; how long it takes to get hot water; proper ventilation (window or fan?).

☐ **Living Room/Dining Room:** Are they large enough? Is there a fireplace? If so, does the damper work; has the chimney been cleaned out recently?

☐ **Doors:** Do they close properly? Are there good locks?

76

☐ **Heating System:** Find out what type of heat (warm air, hot water, electrical or steam): what type of fuel is used? How much does it cost to heat? (get last year's fuel bills); find out when system was last serviced.

☐ **Hot Water Heater:** Check for signs of leaking or rusting. What is the capacity or "recovery rate?" (Should be a minimum of 30 gallons for family of 4; more for larger families.) How old is it?

☐ **Electrical System:** Look at the "service box." Are there fuses or circuit breakers? Is it old or new? Look for exposed wires and signs of wear.

☐ **Cooling/Air Conditioning:** What kind of cooling is there? What is the age and condition? Is the unit under warranty? How much did it cost to use last year?

☐ **General Layout:** Are the rooms conveniently located? What are the "traffic patterns?"

☐ **Bedrooms:** Are there enough for your family? Are they large enough? Does each have a window to the outside? Does each have a closet large enough for your needs?

☐ **Storage Space:** Are there enough closets in the house? Are there other rooms you can use to store things?

☐ **Walls/Ceilings:** Check for major cracks; loose or falling plaster; signs of leaks or stains.

☐ **Basement** (if present): Check for signs of leaks, dampness or flooding; make sure there's enough lighting.

☐ **Attic** (if accessible): Look for signs of roof leaks; check insulation (how much? what type?); are there signs of squirrels or other rodents?

Mortgage principle and interest table*

Interest rate	9.5%			12.5%			15.5%		
Term	20 Years	25 Years	30 Years	20 Years	25 Years	30 Years	20 Years	25 Years	30 Years
Amount									
11000	102.54	96.11	92.50	124.98	119.94	117.40	148.98	145.18	143.50
12000	111.86	104.85	100.91	136.34	130.85	128.08	162.47	158.37	156.55
13000	121.18	113.59	109.32	147.70	141.75	138.75	176.01	171.57	169.59
14000	130.50	122.32	117.72	159.06	152.65	149.42	189.55	184.77	182.64
15000	139.82	131.06	126.13	170.43	163.56	160.09	203.09	197.97	195.68
16000	149.15	139.80	134.54	181.79	174.46	170.77	216.63	211.16	208.73
17000	158.47	148.53	142.95	193.15	185.37	181.44	230.16	224.36	221.77
18000	167.79	157.27	151.36	204.51	196.27	192.11	243.70	237.56	234.82
19000	171.11	166.01	159.77	215.87	207.17	202.78	257.24	250.76	247.86
20000	186.43	174.74	168.18	227.23	218.08	213.46	270.78	263.95	260.91

Mortgage interest table—*continued*

Interest rate Term	9.5%			12.5%			15.5%		
	20 Years	25 Years	30 Years	20 Years	25 Years	30 Years	20 Years	25 Years	30 Years
21000	195.75	183.48	176.58	238.59	228.98	224.13	284.32	277.15	273.95
22000	205.07	192.22	184.99	249.96	239.88	234.80	297.86	290.35	287.00
23000	214.40	200.96	193.40	261.32	250.79	245.47	311.40	303.55	300.04
24000	223.72	209.69	201.81	272.68	261.69	256.15	324.94	316.74	313.09
25000	233.04	218.43	210.22	284.04	272.59	266.82	338.48	329.94	326.13
26000	242.36	227.17	218.63	295.40	283.50	277.49	352.01	343.14	339.18
27000	251.68	235.90	227.04	306.76	294.40	288.16	365.55	356.34	352.22
28000	261.00	244.64	235.44	318.12	305.30	298.84	379.09	369.53	365.27
29000	270.32	253.38	243.85	329.49	316.21	309.51	392.63	382.73	378.31
30000	279.64	262.11	252.26	340.85	327.11	320.18	406.17	395.93	391.36
31000	288.97	270.85	260.67	352.21	338.01	330.85	419.71	409.13	404.41
32000	298.29	279.59	269.08	363.57	348.92	341.53	433.25	422.32	417.45
33000	307.61	288.32	277.49	374.93	359.82	352.20	446.79	435.52	430.50
34000	316.93	297.06	285.90	386.29	370.73	362.87	460.32	448.72	443.54
35000	326.25	305.80	294.30	397.65	381.63	373.55	473.86	461.92	456.59
40000	372.86	349.48	336.35	454.46	436.15	426.91	541.56	527.90	521.81
45000	419.46	393.17	378.39	511.27	490.66	480.27	609.25	593.89	587.04
50000	466.07	436.85	420.43	568.08	545.18	533.63	676.95	659.88	652.26
55000	512.68	480.54	462.47	624.88	599.70	587.00	744.64	725.86	717.49
60000	559.28	524.22	504.52	681.69	654.22	640.36	812.33	791.85	782.72
65000	605.89	567.91	546.56	738.50	708.74	693.72	880.03	857.84	847.94
70000	652.50	611.59	588.60	795.30	763.25	747.09	947.72	923.83	913.17
75000	699.10	655.28	630.65	852.11	817.77	800.45	1015.42	989.81	978.39
80000	745.71	698.96	672.69	908.92	872.29	853.81	1083.11	1055.80	1043.62
100000	932.14	873.70	840.86	1136.15	1090.36	1067.26	1353.89	1319.75	1304.52

*These figures do not include the additional costs usually included in a monthly mortgage payment: real estate taxes, hazard insurance, mortgage insurance, etc.

Real estate closing checklist

☑ Are all necessary inspections done? (Bring inspection reports with you to the closing.)

☐ Are all required repairs complete? (Bring certificate of completion to the closing.)

☐ Do you have a paid insurance policy or binder in effect the day of the closing?

☐ Did you give your old landlord notice?

☐ Have you made a final inspection of the house?

☐ Have you confirmed with the seller the move-out date?

☐ Have you confirmed with your mover the move-in date?

☐ Have you confirmed with your mover the time of pick-up and delivery?

☐ Have you confirmed with your mover the cost of the move?

☐ Do you have enough money for moving?

☐ Have you obtained from the lender or escrow agent the exact amount of money you will need for closing? (Ask about prepayable and other costs that did not appear on your RESPA statement.)

☐ Do you have a certified check for that amount?

☐ Do you have additional cash "just in case?"

☐ Have you confirmed with your lawyer or escrow agent the *time, date,* and *place* of the closing?

☐ Do you have receipts for those items you have already paid for on the house?

Moving checklist

Have you . . .

☑ Checked the condition of your new house to make sure all the seller's things are moved out and that it is swept and free from all trash (in the basement, attic, and yard)?

☐ Given your landlord plenty of notice?

☐ Cleaned your apartment and had the landlord inspect it?

☐ Returned your key to the landlord?

☐ Arranged to get your security deposit back?

☐ Notified all utility companies to shut off your present service and turn on service at the new address?

☐ Notified your employer, driver's license bureau, credit card companies, magazine companies, etc. of your move?

☐ Filled out "change of address" forms at Post Office?

☐ Notified your children's school or day care center?

☐ Made arrangements for your children *during* the move?

☐ Checked with the moving company about the date of the move, time of pickup and delivery, and *cost* of the move (in a written estimate)?

☐ Checked with the mover to make sure all your items will be insured?

☐ Checked with the rental company (if you plan to rent a truck or van) about the date and *cost* of the rental?

☐ Arranged with family or friends to help you with the move?

☐ Stocked up on plenty of boxes, cartons, rope, tape, and newspapers?

☐ Made a *list of items to be moved* and marked the contents on the boxes?

☐ Made a list of what items should be moved first (food, dishes, clothing, rugs) and where they should go in your new house?

☐ Made sure you have *all the keys* to your new house and that they work properly?

Home warranty plans

Major provisions	Home owner's warranty (NAHB)	Home protection programs (NAR)	Federal Housing Administration
Plan coverage	Covers only operating failures: 1st year—faulty workmanship or materials. 2nd year—heating, plumbing, electrical & air conditioning systems; structural soundness. 3rd–10th years—major structural defects. Plan covers new homes.	Covers only operating failures: Heating, plumbing, electrical & air conditioning systems; structural soundness of exterior & interior walls, including floors & ceilings. Plan covers resale homes.	Covers faulty workmanship or materials Plan covers new homes.
Length of coverage	10-year policy	Certified's coverage is for one year. Soundhome's coverage is for 2 years.	One year
Warranty exclusions	Loss due to fire, flood, other acts of God, normal shrinkage, buyer neglect.	Coverage limited to inspected & approved items. Exterior structures (garage)	Loss due to fire, flood, other acts of God, normal shrinkage, buyer neglect
Policy transferable	Yes, within 10 year period.	Yes, within the period of contract.	Yes, within the one-year period.
Deductible	None	$100 per element per occurrence.	None
Cost	$2 per thousand with a minimum of $50	Premium set exclusively by participating companies, usually about $200.	No cost
Covers condominiums	Yes, with some provisions.	Not required. One program does; two do not.	Yes

Major provisions	Home owner's warranty (NAHB)	Home protection programs (NAR)	Federal Housing Administration
Includes termite inspection	No	No	No
Insulation requirements	House must meet either FHA or local warranty council standards.	Not included in inspection	House must meet FHA requirements.
Program includes uniform complaint resolution mechanism	Yes, conciliation and arbitration are available at no charge.	No	No
Inspection arrangements	Where adequate building codes & acceptable inspections by FHA, Veterans Administration, or the local municipality exist, local councils' inspections are not necessary. Otherwise, the local warranty council is responsible for inspection.	NAR does not select inspectors; only approved companies engage professional engineers to perform the necessary inspections.	FHA's field staff conducts inspections.

Home energy

Home energy costs: household appliances

Appliance	Average wattage	Av. hours per year	KWH hours per year	Av. cost* per year
Air Cleaner	50	4320	216	$ 12.96
Air Conditioner	566	887	1398	83.34
Blanket	177	831	147	8.42
Blender	386	39	15	.90
Broiler	1436	69	100	6.00
Clock	2	8500	17	1.02
Clothes Dryer	4856	204	993	59.58
Coffeemaker	894	119	106	6.36
Dehumidifier	257	1467	377	22.62
Dishwasher	1201	302	363	21.78
Fan, Attic	370	786	291	17.46
Fan, Circulating	88	489	43	2.58
Fan, Window	200	850	170	10.20
Freezer, 15 cu. ft.	440	4002	1761	105.66
Freezer, Frostless, 15 cu. ft.	440	4002	1761	105.66
Frying pan	1196	157	188	11.28
Hair dryer	381	37	14	1.04
Heater, Portable	1322	133	176	10.56
Heating pad	65	154	10	.60
Hot plate	1257	72	90	5.40
Humidifier	177	921	163	9.78
Iron, Hand	1008	143	144	8.64
Mixer	127	102	13	.78
Oven, Microwave	1500	200	300	18.00
Oven, Self-Cleaning	4800	239	1146	68.76
Radio	71	1211	86	5.16
Radio/Record player	109	1000	109	6.54
Range	8200	128	1175	70.50
Refrigerator, 12 cu. ft.	241	3021	728	43.68

Appliance	Average wattage	Av. hours per year	KWH hours per year	Av. cost* per year
Refrigerator, Frostless, 12 cu. ft.	321	31	1217	73.02
Refrigerator/Freezer, 14 cu. ft.	326	3488	1137	68.22
Refrigerator/Freezer, frostless, 14 cu. ft.	615	2974	1829	109.74
Roaster	1333	154	205	12.30
Sewing machine	75	147	11	.66
Shaver	14	129	2	.12
Sun lamp	279	57	16	.96
Toaster	1146	34	39	2.34
Toothbrush	7	7	1	.06
Trash compacter	400	125	50	3.00
TV, B&W	237	1527	362	21.72
TV, Color	332	1512	502	30.12
Vacuum cleaner	630	73	46	2.76
Waffle iron	1116	20	22	1.32
Washing Machine, automatic	521	198	103	6.18
Washing Machine, nonautomatic	286	266	76	4.58
Waste disposer	445	67	30	1.80
Water heater	2475	1705	4219	253.14
Water heater, quick recovery	4474	1075	4811	288.66

*At 6 cents per KWH (kilowatts per hour).

Common firewood ratings

	Relative amount of heat	Easy to ignite	Easy to split	Does it have heavy smoke?	Does it pop or throw sparks?	General rating and remarks
Hardwood trees						
Apple, ash, beech, birch, dogwood, hard maple, hickory, locust, mesquite, oaks, Pacific madrone, pecan	High	No	Medium	Little	Yes	Excellent
Alder, cherry, soft maple, walnut	Medium	Medium	Yes	Little	Little	Good
Elm, gum, sycamore	Medium	Medium	No	Medium	Little	Fair—contains too much water when green
Aspen, basswood, cottonwood, yellow-poplar	Low	Yes	Yes	Medium	Little	Fair—but good for kindling
Softwood trees						
Douglas-fir, southern yellow pine	Medium	Yes	Yes	Yes	Little	Good but smoky
Cypress, redwood	Low	Yes	Yes	Medium	Little	Fair
Eastern redcedar, western redcedar, white cedar	Low	Yes	Yes	Medium	Yes	Fair—excellent for kindling
Eastern white pine, ponderosa pine, sugar pine, western white pine, true firs	Low	Yes	Yes	Medium	Little	Fair—good kindling
Larch, tamarack	Medium	Yes	Yes	Yes	Yes	Fair
Spruce	Low	Yes	Yes	Medium	Yes	Fair—but good for kindling when dry

Home energy cost cutters

Direct energy	Indirect energy
Transportation	
Number and length of trips, including vacations	Need for one or more cars
Type of transportation, i.e., public vs. private, air vs. rail	Need for recreational vehicle
Sharing of private transportation	Cost of manufacture of vehicle
Efficiency as miles per gallon	Lifespan of vehicle
Housing	
Temperature of space	Type of dwelling, i.e., single vs. multiple
Type of heating fuel	Size of home
Size of home/number of residences	Type of fuel and equipment
Number and location of windows and doors	Furnishings
Insulation, caulking, storm windows	Number of bathrooms and kitchen facilities
Household activities	
Practices related to cooking and refrigerating	Number of appliances
Appliance efficiency	Amount of home production
Cleanliness standards for clothing and person	Amount and type of household goods purchased
Water heat efficiency	Degree of processing and packaging
Convenience features of appliances	
Size of appliances vs. use of capacity	

Home energy sources

Finite	Infinite	
Natural gas	Wind	Plutonium
Oil	Waves	Wood
Oil shale	Tides	Animal muscle (manpower)
Tar sands	Sun	Hydroelectric
Coal	Methanol (distillates of wood)	Geothermal water
Uranium	Ethanol (distillates of grain)	
Geopressurized methane	Methane (from animal wastes)	

Reprinted by permission of Grosset & Dunlap, Inc. from THE HOMEBUYER'S GUIDE FOR THE 80'S, copyright © 1980 by Richard W. O'Neill.

Home heating cost ratios

Energy system or source	Heat unit	BTU/heat unit	Assumed useful heat
Natural gas	Therm	100,000	0.6
No. 2 fuel oil	Gallon	138,000	0.50
Electricity			
Direct resistance	Kilowatt	3,413	1.41
Electric furnace	Kilowatt	3,413	.9
Heat pump	Kilowatt	3,413	varies 1.3–1.8

Reprinted by permission of Grosset & Dunlap, Inc. from THE HOMEBUYER'S GUIDE FOR THE 80'S, copyright © 1980 by Richard W. O'Neill.

Transportation

Calculating annual automobile costs

1. Actual price paid, including trade-in allowance $ _____
2. Interest on car loan (e.g., three years' total ÷ 3) $ _____
3. Taxes and fees
   - Sales tax ÷ 3 $ _____
   - Excise/Property tax (average bill) $ _____
   - Registration $ _____
   - Title fee ÷ 3 $ _____
   - License (divide total fee by number of years valid) $ _____
   - Inspections $ _____

Total $ _____

4. Depreciation (Take the following percentage of item 1: full-size car 20%; intermediate 18%; compact 17%; subcompact 15%) $ _____
5. Insurance (total annual premium) $ _____
6. Total gasoline cost (Determine miles per gallon, divide into total annual miles, then multiply by the average per gallon cost) $ _____
7. Maintenance
   - Tuneups $ _____
   - Oil, filters, lubes $ _____
   - Tires $ _____
   - Other $ _____

Total $ _____

Yearly total $ _____

Cost per mile (Divide yearly total by annual number of miles driven) $ _____

Calculating annual driving costs

	Yearly totals

Fixed costs
1. Depreciation (divide by number of years of ownership) $ _____
2. Insurance $ _____
3. Taxes $ _____
4. License & registration $ _____
5. Finance charge $ _____

Total fixed costs $ _____

Variable costs
6. Gas & oil per mile $ _____
7. Number of miles driven $ _____
8. Cost per year (multiply miles driven by gas & oil per mile) $ _____
9. Maintenance (use your own figures multiplied by miles driven) $ _____
10. Tires (see note for maintenance) $ _____

Total variable costs $ _____

Other costs (Car wash, repairs, accessories, etc.) $ _____

Total driving costs per year $ _____

Cost per mile (divide yearly total by total miles driven) $ _____

Reprinted with the permission of the American Automobile Association from YOUR DRIVING COSTS, copyright © 1983.

Factors affecting automobile mileage

	Effects of speed, air conditioning and tuneup on gasoline mileage				
	30 MPH	40 MPH	50 MPH	60 MPH	70 MPH
Effect of turning a/c off:					
Mpg with a/c on	18.14	17.51	16.42	15.00	13.17
Mpg with a/c off	20.05	19.71	18.29	16.23	14.18
Increase in mpg with a/c off	10.53%	12.56%	11.39%	8.33%	7.67%
Effect of tuneup:					
Mpg before tuneup	19.30	18.89	17.29	15.67	13.32
Mpg after tuneup	21.33	21.33	18.94	17.40	15.36
Increase in mpg after tuneup	10.52%	12.92%	9.54%	11.04%	15.32%

Calculating gas mileage

Have gas put in the tank until it is exactly full at the filler neck. At the same time, record the mileage reading on the dashboard odometer.

Original odometer reading	21864

Drive until the tank is almost empty; a calculation based on fewer miles or gallons is less accurate. Then have the tank refilled to the same level on the filler neck and write down the gas pump reading in gallons and the new odometer reading in miles.

Gallons of gas	$13\frac{2}{10}$
New odometer reading	22014

Subtract the original odometer reading from the new one to obtain the miles traveled between gasoline fills.

New odometer reading	22014
− Original odometer reading	21864
= Miles traveled	150

Divide the miles traveled by the gallons required to refill the tank. The answer is the miles the car traveled on each gallon of gas or the gasoline mileage.

Miles traveled	150
÷ Gallons of gas	$13\frac{2}{10}$
= Miles per gallon	$11\frac{3}{10}$

Carpool savings

Daily commute (one way)	Item	Sub-compact	Compact	Standard
	Cost of driving to work alone:			
	Gasoline and oil	$ 163	$ 224	$ 299
	Maintenance and repair	130	145	163
	Parking	191	191	191
	Insurance	280	297	319
	Depreciation	144	188	327
10 Miles	Total	$ 908	$1045	$1299
	Savings per person in a:			
	2-person carpool	$ 381	$ 439	$ 646
	3-person carpool	490	564	701
	4-person carpool	544	627	779
	5-person carpool	572	658	784
	Cost of driving to work alone:			
	Gasoline and oil	$ 328	$ 448	$ 595
	Maintenance and repair	257	290	347
	Parking	191	191	191
	Insurance	280	297	319
	Depreciation	289	374	664
20 Miles	Total	$1345	$1600	$2116
	Savings per person in a:			
	2-person carpool	$ 605	$ 720	$ 952
	3-person carpool	753	896	1185
	4-person carpool	874	1072	1375
	5-person carpool	928	1104	1460

Calculating van pool savings

Calculate the monthly fixed cost of a purchased vehicle

1. Cost of the van $10,000
   Less salvage value (after 4 years)   3,300
   Equals depreciable value $ 6,700 or $140/month

2. Add other annual expenses
   License, registration, taxes $ 120
   Insurance   +   460
   Equals other fixed expenses $ 580 or + $ 48/month

3. Monthly fixed cost (items 1 plus 2 above) $188 month

4. Add optional maintenance contract   + $ 45/month
   Total monthly fixed cost   **$233/month**

Calculate passenger fares

1. Start with each van's daily round trip distance   50 miles

2. Multiply this by your average number of work-
   days in a month   × 21 = 1,050 miles

3. Multiply this by your per mile operating cost   × 0.24 = $225/month

4. Add the van's monthly fixed cost (est.) $413/month

5. Divide this cost by your breakeven number of $ 46/month
   passengers

Small car economy

Figures for low-cost and high-cost areas apply to small towns or rural locations and to large metropolitan areas, respectively.

	Low-cost area		High-cost area	
	Per day	Per mile	Per day	Per mile
Subcompact (4 cyl)	$5.11	7.00¢	$6.40	7.25¢
Compact (6 cyl)	$5.89	8.15¢	$7.51	8.45¢
Intermediate (6 cyl)	$6.44	8.90¢	$7.93	9.20¢
Standard (8 cyl)	$6.81	10.20¢	$8.36	10.60¢

"Per day" costs include $100 deductible comprehensive, $250 deductible collision, $100/300/M public liability, $50M property damage, state taxes, registration fees, depreciation, and finance charge. All insurance is based on a pleasure use category where the vehicle is driven less than 10 miles to or from work and there is no youthful operator.

"Per mile" costs include gas, oil, maintenance, and tires.

Based on 15,000 miles annually, total costs are:

	Low-cost area	High-cost area
Subcompact	$2,915	$3,424
Compact	$3,372	$4,009
Intermediate	$3,686	$4,274
Standard	$4,016	$4,641
Thus, the per-mile costs are:		
Subcompact	19.4¢	22.8¢
Compact	22.5¢	26.7¢
Intermediate	24.6¢	28.5¢
Standard	26.8¢	30.9¢

Reprinted with the permission of the American Automobile Association from YOUR DRIVING COSTS, copyright © 1983.

Insurance

Health insurance checklist

☑ What is the company's loss ratio? (Remember, the higher, the better.)

☐ What kinds of coverage does the policy provide?

☐ What, if any, is the waiting period before new health problems are covered?

☐ What kinds of benefits are offered? (Service benefits or full coverage are better than indemnity benefits that pay up to specified dollar amounts.)

☐ Do the indemnity benefits, if any, cover most of the typical daily hospital costs in your area?

☐ Does the policy have exclusions against coverage of pre-existing conditions? Do they specify exclusions of more than one year?

☐ How does *Best's Insurance Reports* rate the insurer?

☐ With family coverage, would you have automatic coverage of infants from date of birth?

☐ Is the policy cancelable, and if so, when and under what circumstances?

☐ Is the company noted for fair, efficient, courteous claim service?

☐ Could your premiums be raised? If so, under what circumstances?

☐ Is it a mail-order policy? (If so, beware.)

From GETTING YOUR MONEY'S WORTH by Herbert S. Denenberg. Copyright © 1974. Reproduced by permission of Public Affairs Press.

Health insurance companies compared*

50 largest insurers, in order	Claims paid as % of premiums	
	On group and individual policies(†)	On individual guar. renew. policies(**)
Mutual of Omaha Insurance Company	75.9%	60.2%
Combined Insurance Company of America	43.4	66.7
Prudential Insurance of America	79.9	67.2
Bankers Life and Casualty Co.	60.5	54.5
American Family Life Assurance	48.9	48.8
U.S. Letter Carriers Mutual	94.5	—
Metropolitan Life Insurance Company	72.6	62.8
National Home Life Assurance	53.3	54.5
Continental Assurance Company	79.8	82.4
Physicians Mutual Insurance Company	62.2	62.5
United Insurance Company of America	45.3	25.2
Pennsylvania Life Insurance Company	48.7	29.9
Paul Revere Life Insurance Company	70.6	139.2
Aetna Casualty and Surety	67.8	59.5
New York Life Insurance Company	73.0	56.2
Washington National Insurance	73.7	62.1
Provident Life and Accident	82.6	74.9
State Farm Mutual Auto	58.1	74.8
Colonial Life and Accident	44.3	51.6
Independent Life and Accident	41.8	24.0
Reserve Life Insurance Company	57.4	52.5
Liberty National Life Insurance	48.1	39.0
National Life and Accident	57.0	33.8
United American Insurance Company	62.4	62.9
Travelers Indemnity of Rhode Island	84.4	101.6
Union Fidelity Life Insurance	44.8	46.4
Monarch Life Insurance Company	69.6	72.3
Time Insurance Company	65.1	64.5
Equitable Life Assurance Society	83.3	57.9
Travelers Insurance Company	88.3	57.8
American Family Mutual	68.1	78.3
American Republic Insurance	54.4	52.2
Inter-Ocean Insurance Company	52.2	52.2
Guarantee Trust Life Insurance	59.3	52.6
Bankers Multiple Life Insurance	60.9	60.1
Globe Life and Accident	52.0	48.8
Union Bankers Insurance Company	55.8	53.0
American Health and Life	62.1	62.8
Lone Star Life Insurance Company	55.1	49.9
Lincoln National Life	85.7	68.9
Alexander Hamilton Insurance Company	72.5	10.7
Massachusetts Indemnity and Life	42.4	41.3
American National Insurance Company	72.2	74.6
Occidental Life Insurance, California	90.2	84.4
Certified Life Insurance Company, California	49.6	47.5
Ford Life Insurance Company	66.7	—
Cudis Insurance Society Incorporated	58.2	—
Beneficial Standard Life	46.6	46.7
Federal Home Life Insurance Company	67.8	50.2
Connecticut General Life	88.5	72.0

*Comparison based upon proportion of premiums returned via claims to policyholders.
†Claims paid divided by earned premium for individual and group policies.
**Claims paid plus expenses divided by net premium for individual guaranteed renewable policies only.

Loss ratios, medigap policies

Company	Loss ratio	Company	Loss ratio
Mutual Protective Ins.	22%	All American Casualty	53%
Medico Life	25%	CNA	55%
New York Life	29%	Bankers Life and Casualty	57%
American United Life	29%	Guarantee Reserve Life	57%
National Casualty Co.	30%	American National	58%
American Progressive	33%	American Variable Annuity	63%
National Security Ins.	35%	Chesapeake Life	65%
Reliable Ins. Co.	36%	Guardian	66%
Constitution Life	37%	Rural Mutual	69%
Old American	38%	Mutual Benefit Life	70%
Pioneer Life cf Illinois	39%	Banker's (Iowa)	75%
Pacific Mutual	40%	Home Life	77%
Liberty National Life	40%	Nationwide	78%
Businessmen's Assurance	43%	Durhan Life	79%
American Exchange Life	44%	Life of Virginia	82%
Commercial State Life	47%	Metropolitan	83%
Union Bankers	48%	National Life and Accident	85%
Country Life	49%	Blue Cross/Blue Shield	91%
Aid to Lutherans	50%		

Homeowner's insurance: coverage formats

	Coverage A	Coverage B	Coverage C	Coverage D	Additional coverage
Policy Type	Amount on house and attached structures	Amount on detached structures	Amount on personal property	Loss of use, additional living expense	Amount on tree, shrubs, plants
Basic (HO-1*)	Up to 100% of replacement cost	10% of amount on house	50% of amount on house	10% of amount on house	5% of amount on house; $500 maximum per item
Broad (HO-2*)	Up to 100% of replacement cost	10% of amount on house	50% of amount on house	20% of amount on house	5% of amount on house; $500 maximum per item
Special (HO-3*)	Up to 100% of replacement cost	10% of amount on house	50% of amount on house	20% of amount on house	5% of amount on house; $500 maximum per item
Example:	$50,000 on house	$5,000 garage	$25,000 furniture, etc.	$10,000 for rent, food, etc.	$2500 or $500 per item
Renters (HO-4*)	Covers additions and alterations only, up to 10% of amount on personal property	(Not Applicable)	$4,000 Minimum	20% of amount on personal property	16% of amount on personal property; $500 maximum per item
Example:	$1,500 wallpaper roomdivider, etc.	Not your responsibility	$15,000	$3,000	$1500 balcony, plants, etc.
Comprehensive (HO-5*)	Up to 100% of replacement cost	10% of amount on house	50% of amount on house	20% of amount on house	5% of amount on house; $500 maximum per item
Condominium (HO-6*)	$1,000 on additions and alterations	(Not Applicable)	$4,000 Minimum	40% of amount on personal property	10% of amount on personal property; $500 maximum per item

*HO-1 through HO-6 are the standard insurance references to policy types. Check the first page of your policy to determine which HO coverage you hold.

Reprinted from *Fire in Your Home* Copyright © 1978 National Fire Protection Association, Quincy, Massachusetts. 02269 Reprinted by Permission.

Unemployment benefits by state

State	Weekly benefits			Duration of benefits (weeks)	
	Average payment	Legal minimum	Legal maximum	Legal range	1982 average
Alabama	$ 77.00	$15.00	$ 90.00	11-26	11.1
Alaska	129.00	34.00-58.00	156.00-228.00	16-26	15.5
Arizona	86.00	40.00	115.00	12-26	13.1
Arkansas	92.00	31.00	136.00	10-26	12.2
California	92.00	30.00	166.00	12-26	16.2
Colorado	122.00	25.00	190.00	7-26	11.7
Connecticut	111.00	15.00-22.00	156.00-206.00	26-26	11.8
Delaware	106.00	20.00	150.00	18-26	14.3
D.C.	131.00	13.00-14.00	206.00	17-34	20.5
Florida	81.00	10.00	125.00	10-26	11.8
Georgia	83.00	27.00	115.00	4-26	9.2
Hawaii	118.00	5.00	178.00	26-26	14.0
Idaho	105.00	36.00	159.00	10-26	12.6
Illinois	133.00	51.00	168.00-224.00	26-26	18.4
Indiana	91.00	40.00	84.00-141.00	9-26	11.5
Iowa	122.00	17.00-21.00	158.00-190.00	15-26	13.2
Kansas	102.00	40.00	163.00	10-26	13.7
Kentucky	106.00	22.00	140.00	22-26	14.2
Louisiana	121.00	10.00	205.00	12-28	16.0
Maine	94.00	22.00-27.00	124.00-186.00	7-26	12.7
Maryland	102.00	25.00-28.00	153.00	26-26	14.0
Massachusetts	105.00	14.00-21.00	172.00-258.00	9-30	14.8
Michigan	128.00	41.00-44.00	197.00	13-26	13.8
Minnesota	126.00	30.00	191.00	11-26	14.8
Mississippi	73.00	30.00	105.00	13-26	12.4
Missouri	91.00	14.00	105.00	10-26	13.1
Montana	111.00	39.00	158.00	8-26	13.2
Nebraska	95.00	12.00	106.00	17-26	12.0
Nevada	107.00	16.00	149.00	11-26	13.8
New Hampshire	86.00	26.00	132.00	26-26	8.7
New Jersey	106.00	20.00	158.00	15-26	14.9
New Mexico	90.00	29.00	142.00	19-26	15.5
New York	94.00	25.00	125.00	26-26	19.0
North Carolina	92.00	15.00	166.00	13-26	9.6
North Dakota	114.00	47.00	175.00	12-26	14.6
Ohio	128.00	10.00	158.00-250.00	20-26	14.7
Oklahoma	114.00	16.00	197.00	20-26	10.8
Oregon	107.00	44.00	175.00	8-26	14.2
Pennsylvania	126.00	35.00-40.00	205.00-213.00	26-30	16.6
Rhode Island	99.00	37.00-42.00	154.00-174.00	12-26	14.2
South Carolina	85.00	21.00	118.00	14-26	12.1
South Dakota	104.00	28.00	129.00	18-26	12.2
Tennessee	82.00	20.00	110.00	13-26	12.9
Texas	100.00	27.00	168.00	14-26	13.0
Utah	115.00	10.00	166.00	10-26	14.5
Vermont	97.00	18.00	146.00	26-26	13.7
Virginia	98.00	44.00	138.00	12-26	11.0
Washington	119.00	49.00	178.00	16-30	15.8
West Virginia	110.00	18.00	211.00	28-28	15.7
Wisconsin	123.00	37.00	196.00	1-34	14.2
Wyoming	121.00	24.00	180.00	12-26	12.3

Worker's compensation benefits, by state (1982)

State	Maximum weekly benefits if injuries are			Waiting period (Number of days)		
	(1983) Temporary	Permanent	Fatal (Spouse and children)	No benefit payment for first	Unless time off exceeds	Maximum burial allowance
Alabama	$174.00	$161.00	$161.00	3	21	$1000.00
Alaska	942.00	942.00	942.00	3	28	1000.00
Arizona	203.64	203.64	203.64	7	14	1000.00

State	Maximum weekly benefits if injuries are			Waiting period (Number of days)		
	(1983) Temporary	Permanent	Fatal (Spouse and children)	No benefit payment for first	Unless time off exceeds	Maximum burial allowance
Arkansas	154.00	140.00	140.00	7	14	750.00
California	175.00	175.00	175.00	3	21	1500.00
Colorado	283.71	261.80	261.80	3	14	1000.00
Connecticut	326.00 + $10.00 a child	310.00-465.00	310.00	3	7	1500.00
Delaware	208.45	194.81	292.22	3	7	700.00
Dist. of Colum.	524.54	396.78	396.78	3	14	1000.00
Florida	253.00	253.00	253.00	7	14	1000.00
Georgia	135.00	115.00	115.00	7	28	750.00
Hawaii	252.00	252.00	252.00	2	5	1500.00
Idaho	217.80-302.50	217.80-302.50	145.20	5	14	1500.00
Illinois	426.44	403.12	403.12	3	14	1750.00
Indiana	140.00	140.00	140.00	7	21	1500.00
Iowa	542.00	501.00	501.00	3	14	1000.00
Kansas	204.00	187.00	187.00	7	21	2000.00
Kentucky	254.33	254.33	190.75	7	14	1500.00
Louisiana	204.00	183.00	183.00	7	42	3000.00
Maine	396.48	367.25	367.25	3	14	1000.00
Maryland	267.00	267.00	267.00	3	14	1200.00
Massachusetts	297.85 + $6.00 a dependent	269.93	110.00 plus 6.00 per child	5	6	2000.00
Michigan	307.00	307.00	307.00	7	14	1500.00
Minnesota	290.00	267.00	267.00	3	10	1000.00
Mississippi	112.00	112.00	112.00	5	14	1000.00
Missouri	189.49	174.00	174.00	3	14	2000.00
Montana	262.00	241.00	241.00	5	5	1400.00
Nebraska	180.00	180.00	180.00	7	42	2000.00
Nevada	297.21	269.99	269.99	5	5	2500.00
New Hampshire	256.00	234.00	234.00	3	7	1200.00
New Jersey*	217.00	217.00	217.00	7	8	2000.00
New Mexico	246.44	246.44	246.44	7	28	1500.00
New York	215.00	215.00	215.00	7	14	1250.00
North Carolina	228.00	228.00	228.00	7	28	1000.00
North Dakota	261.00 + $5.00 a child	233.00 + dependents	100.00 plus 7.00 per child	5	5	2000.00
Ohio	298.00	298.00	298.00	7	14	1200.00
Oklahoma	196.00	175.00	175.00	3	3	1000.00
Oregon	304.60	286.88-311.88	236.88	3	14	3000.00
Pennsylvania	284.00	284.00	284.00	7	14	1500.00
Rhode Island	257.00 + $6.00 a dependent	238.00-285.60	285.60	3	14	1800.00
South Carolina*	235.00	235.00	235.00	7	14	400.00
South Dakota	227.00	208.00	100% of SAWW† plus $50.00 per child	7	8	2000.00
Tennessee	136.00	126.00	126.00	7	14	1250.00
Texas*	182.00	154.00	154.00	7	28	1250.00
Utah	284.00 + $5.00 a dependent	218.00	218.00	3	14	1000.00
Vermont	243.00	225.60-337.50	225.00	3	4	1000.00
Virginia	253.00	231.00	231.00	7	21	2000.00
Washington	243.00	223.11	223.11	3	14	1000.00
West Virginia	301.00	276.29	276.29	3	7	1500.00
Wisconsin	269.00	269.00	260.00	3	7	1000.00
Wyoming	434.42	277.12 + dependent	66⅔% of SAMW** plus $60.00 per child	3	8	1100.00

*Compensation laws are not compulsory in these states †SAMW (states average weekly wage)
**SAWW (state's average monthly wage)

Retirement planning

Retirement opportunity roster

ACTION, 806 Connecticut Ave. N.W., Washington, D.C. 20525
· Foster Grandparent Program
· Retired Senior Volunteer Program (RSVP)
· Volunteers in Service to America (VISTA)
· Peace Corps
· Senior Companion Program

U.S. Department of Commerce, Bureau of the Census, Washington, D.C. 20233
· Census interviews

U.S. Department of Education, Washington, D.C. 20202
· Teacher Corps

Small Business Administration, 1441 L Street N.W., Washington, D.C. 20416
· Service Corps of Retired Executives (SCORE)

U.S. Department of Labor, Washington, D.C. 20212
· Senior Community Service Employment Program (SCSEP)
· Comprehensive Employment and Training Act (CETA)

Retirement investments calculator

If you need this amount total extra money for retirement	And it will be _____ years before retirement				
	5	10	15	20	25
	You should save this amount each month—				
	In an investment yielding a 6% rate of return				
$ 5,000	$74.40	$ 31.57	$ 17.88	$11.32	$ 7.59
$10,000	148.81	63.13	35.77	22.64	15.18
$15,000	223.21	94.70	53.65	33.97	22.77
$20,000	297.62	126.26	71.53	45.29	30.36
$25,000	372.02	157.83	89.41	56.61	37.95
$30,000	444.05	189.68	107.39	67.95	45.57
	In an investment yielding a 9% rate of return				
$ 5,000	$ 69.68	$ 27.43	$14.19	$ 8.14	$ 4.92
$10,000	139.35	54.86	28.38	16.29	9.84
$15,000	209.03	82.29	42.57	24.43	14.76
$20,000	278.71	109.72	56.77	32.58	19.68
$25,000	348.38	137.15	70.96	40.72	24.60
$30,000	418.06	164.58	85.15	48.86	29.52

Social security benefits

Year you reach 62, die, or become disabled	Amount of work credit you need to be fully insured	Year you reach 62, die, or become disabled	Amount of work credit you need to be fully insured
1975	6	1981	7½
1976	6¼	1983	8
1977	6½	1987	9
1978	6¾	1991 or later	10
1979	7		

Who will get monthly payments?	Insured status you must have
You, as a retired worker, and your wife and children, and in some cases your former wife or surviving former wife	Fully insured
Your husband age 60 or older	Fully insured
Widow 60 or older, or disabled widow, 50 or older, and in some cases your wife or surviving former wife	Fully insured
Widow of any age if caring for child who is less than 18 or disabled and entitled to benefits, and in some cases your former wife or surviving former wife	Fully or currently insured
A widower of any age caring for a child who is less than 18 or disabled and entitled to benefits	Fully or currently insured
Dependent child	Fully or currently insured
Widower 60 or older, or disabled widower, 50 or older	Fully insured
Dependent parent 62 or older	Fully insured
Lump-sum death payment	Fully or currently insured
You and your dependents if you are disabled	Fully insured and meet work requirements

From YOUR RIGHTS TO SOCIAL SECURITY BENEFITS by David Andrews, © 1981 by Andrews Publishing Co. Reprinted by permission of Facts on File Publications, 460 Park Avenue South, NY NY 10016

Taxes

Do you need assistance preparing a tax return?

	Yes	No

Your qualifications

1. Do you find reading tax rules and instructions extremely arduous?
2. Do you lack the 10 to 30 hours needed to prepare a simple to moderately complicated return?
3. Do you question your competence to do a satisfactory preparation?
4. Will you have sleepless nights worrying whether your return was correct?

Your tax return

1. Has your filing status changed?
2. Has your current year's income increased substantially?
3. Do you anticipate a lengthy list of itemized deductions?
4. Will you have to file numerous supporting forms: sick pay, capital gains, business expenses?
5. Do you have major financial transactions with extensive tax ramifications: a move to a new job, sale of your house, a complicated capital gain or loss, an opportunity to use income averaging?
6. Did you use outside assistance last year?

STRATEGY FOR PERSONAL FINANCE by Larry R. Lang and Thomas H. Gillespie. Copyright © 1977. Reprinted by permission of McGraw-Hill Book Company.

IRS information sources

Alabama—Caller No. 848, Atlanta, GA   30370

Alaska—P.O. Box 12626, Fresno, CA   93778

Arizona—P.O. Box 12626, Fresno, CA   93778

Arkansas—P.O. Box 2924, Austin, TX   78769

California—P.O. Box 12626, Fresno, CA   93778

Colorado—P.O. Box 2924, Austin, TX   78769

Connecticut—P.O. Box 1040, Methuen, MA   01844

Delaware—P.O. Box 25866, Richmond, VA   23260

District of Columbia—P.O. Box 25866, Richmond, VA   23260

Florida—Caller No. 848, Atlanta, GA   30370

Georgia—Caller No. 848, Atlanta, GA   30370

Hawaii—P.O. Box 12626, Fresno, CA   93778

Idaho—P.O. Box 12626, Fresno, CA   93778

Illinois—6000 Manchester Trafficway Terrace, Kansas City, MO   64130

Indiana—P.O. Box 636, Florence, KY   41042

Iowa—6000 Manchester Trafficway Terrace, Kansas City, MO   64130

Kansas—P.O. Box 2924, Austin, TX   78769

Kentucky—P.O. Box 636, Florence, KY   41042

Louisiana—P.O. Box 2924, Austin, TX   78769

Maine—P.O. Box 1040, Methuen, MA   01844

Maryland—P.O. Box 25866, Richmond, VA   23260

Massachusetts—P.O. Box 1040, Methuen, MA   01844

Michigan—P.O. Box 636, Florence, KY   41042

Minnesota—6000 Manchester Trafficway Terrace, Kansas City, MO   64130

Mississippi—Caller No. 848, Atlanta, GA   30370

Missouri—6000 Manchester Trafficway Terrace, Kansas City, MO   64130

Montana—P.O. Box 12626, Fresno, CA   93778

Nebraska—6000 Manchester Trafficway Terrace, Kansas City, MO   64130

Nevada—P.O. Box 12626, Fresno, CA   93778

New Hampshire—P.O. Box 1040, Methuen, MA   01844

New Jersey—P.O. Box 25866, Richmond, VA   23260

New Mexico—P.O. Box 2924, Austin, TX   78769

New York—

  Western New York: P.O. Box 240, Buffalo, NY   14201

  Eastern New York (including NY City): P.O. Box 1040, Methuen, MA   01844

North Carolina—Caller No. 848, Atlanta, GA   30370

North Dakota—6000 Manchester Trafficway Terrace, Kansas City, MO   64130

Ohio—P.O. Box 636, Florence, KY   41042

Oklahoma—P.O. Box 2924, Austin, TX   78769

Oregon—P.O. Box 12626, Fresno, CA   93778

Pennsylvania—P.O. Box 25866, Richmond, VA   23260

Rhode Island—P.O. Box 1040, Methuen, MA   01844

South Carolina—Caller No. 848, Atlanta, GA   30370

South Dakota—6000 Manchester Trafficway Terrace, Kansas City, MO   64130

Tennessee—Caller No. 848, Atlanta, GA   30370

Texas—P.O. Box 2924, Austin, TX   78769

Utah—P.O. Box 12626, Fresno, CA   93778

Vermont—P.O. Box 1040, Methuen, MA   01844

Virginia—P.O. Box 25866, Richmond, VA   23260

Washington—P.O. Box 12626, Fresno, CA   93778

West Virginia—P.O. Box 636, Florence, KY   41042

Wisconsin—6000 Manchester Trafficway Terrace, Kansas City, MO   64130

Wyoming—P.O. Box 2924, Austin, TX   78769

Foreign Addresses—Taxpayers with mailing addresses in foreign countries should send their requests for forms and publications to: Director, Foreign Operations District, Internal Revenue Service, Washington, DC   20225

Puerto Rico—Director's Representative, U.S. Internal Revenue Service, Federal Office Building, Chardon Street, Hato Rey, PR   00918

Virgin Islands—Department of Finance, Tax Division, Charlotte Amalie, St. Thomas, VI   00801

4 The home handyman

The tables and formulas in the "Home Handyman" section have been carefully chosen, with an eye toward making life both cleaner and simpler. The information contained in the chapter, for the most part, takes a problem-solving, practical approach to the business of maintaining or improving the house. The do-it-yourself enthusiast will find much of the information invaluable.

Section 4 begins with a listing of basic tools necessary for the maintenance and upkeep of a house. A handyman's toolbox checklist appears side by side with a listing of rules for proper tool use.

The next area examined is house cleaning. Included are lists of equipment and cleaning or cleansing agents basic to good housekeeping. Recipes for home-made furniture polish and varnish stripper are followed by the myriad uses of vinegar and baking soda.

Listed under "painting" are charts showing how to select appropriate types of both interior and exterior paints. Also included is a fascinating table that gives the reflective values of basic paint colors, an extraordinary aid in choosing colors to both brighten the dark interior and tone down the glare of spaces with too much sunlight.

Home security is given full attention. The subsection provides the reader with a virtually complete guide to maintaining a safe environment. The tables range from a home security checklist to an electrical appliance safety chart.

Section 4, "The Home Handyman," concludes with methods for bringing home energy efficiency up to acceptable standards. The types and appropriate uses for insulation are examined as well as R-value. A weatherstripping selector guides the reader toward the kind of materials most useful and efficient.

Tools

Toolbox checklist

☑ 3 screwdrivers (with $\frac{3}{16}''$, $\frac{1}{4}''$ and $\frac{5}{16}''$ blades)	☐ 1 hacksaw
☐ 2 Phillips screwdrivers (a #1 and a #2)	☐ 1 center punch ($\frac{3}{8}''$-by-4")
	☐ 1 electric drill (with 5–7 drill bits up to $\frac{1}{4}''$ in diameter)
☐ 1 claw hammer (12- or 13-oz.)	☐ sandpaper (various grades)

☐ 1 pliers (7″)

☐ 1 vise-grip pliers

☐ 1 needlenose pliers

☐ 1 adjustable wrench (10″ or larger)

☐ 1 level (6–12″)

☐ 1 steel square (8″-by-12″)

☐ 1 cross-cut handsaw (with 8–10 teeth points per inch)

☐ 1 tape measure (12′)

☐ 1–2 putty knives (2 widths)

☐ 4–5 wood chisels (from ¼″–1″ wide)

☐ 1 rubber drain plunger

☐ C–clamps

☐ masking and black electrical tape

☐ white polyvinyl glue

☐ 1 can light machine or household oil

☐ nails, screws

Tool tips

Hammer
A medium weight (12-13 ounce) claw hammer is good for general purposes.
· Hold a hammer near the end of the handle for more hitting power. To start a nail, hold it in place and tap it gently a few times until it is firmly set. Hit it straight in.
· To avoid hammer marks on the wood, use a nail set or another nail to drive a nail the last one-eighth inch into the wood.
· To remove a nail use claw end of hammer. Place a small block of wood under the head of the hammer to avoid marking the wood.

Screwdriver
You need two types of screwdrivers for household repairs:
straight blade and Phillips. Both come in various sizes. The blade of the screwdriver should fit the slot in the screw.
· When using the screwdriver, push against the head of the screw as you turn it.
· It's easier to put a screw into wood if you make a hole first with a nail or drill. Rub wax or soap on the screw threads to make it go in easier.

Pliers
A slip joint pliers can be used for many jobs around the house.
· Use pliers to hold a nut while you turn a bolt with a screwdriver.
· Use it to remove nails or brads. Pull the nail out at the same angle it was driven in. Use small blocks under the pliers if you need leverage.
· Use it to bend or cut wire or to straighten a bent nail.
· Use it to turn nuts. Wrap tape or cloth around the nut to avoid scratching it.
An adjustable wrench is adjustable to fit different sizes of nuts. If a nut is hard to loosen, apply a few drops of penetrating oil or kerosene. Let it soak a couple of hours or overnight. If the wrench has a tendency to slip off, try turning it over.

Handsaw

A handsaw with about 10 teeth to the inch is good for most household work. Mark where you want to cut. Pull the saw back and forth several times to start a groove. Let the weight of the saw do the cutting at first. If you are sawing a board, it will be easier if you support it and hold it firmly near where you're cutting.

Nail sizes

	Length in inches	in millimeters		Length in inches	in millimeters
2 d (penny)	1″	25.00 mm	12 d	3¼″	81.25 mm
3 d	1¼″	31.25 mm	16 d	3½″	87.50 mm
4 d	1½″	37.50 mm	20 d	4″	100.00 mm
5 d	1¾″	43.75 mm	30 d	4½″	112.50 mm
6 d	2″	50.00 mm	40 d	5″	125.00 mm
8 d	2½″	62.50 mm	50 d	5½″	137.50 mm
10 d	3″	75.00 mm	60 d		150.00 mm

Choosing the right adhesive

Key to chart:
C—Cellulose cement
E—Epoxy glue
F—Fabric glue
P—Plastic-mending adhesive
R—Rubber cement
Re—Resorcinol glue
W—White glue

	Ceramics (china, earthenware, etc.)	Cork	Felt	Glass	Leather	Metal	Plastics	Rubber	Stone	Wood
Ceramics (china, earthenware, etc.)	C or E									
Cork	R	R								
Felt	R	R	F							
Glass	C or E	R	R	C or E						
Leather	R	R	R	R	R					
Metal	C or E	R	R	C or E	R	E				
Plastics	P	R	R	C	R	P	P			
Rubber	R	R	R	R	R	R	R	R		
Stone	E	R	R	E	R	E	C	R	E	
Wood	C or E	R	W	C	R	C or E	E or P	R	E	W or Re

98

House cleaning

Cleaning tools

Tools for dusting	Tools for scrubbing
broom	art gum eraser (optional)
carpet sweeper (optional)	pail
dust mop (optional)	paper towels (optional)
dustpan and brush	rags
feather duster (optional)	rubber gloves
rags	scouring pads (copper, nylon, plastic, steel wool)
step stool	sponges (optional)
vacuum cleaner and attachments	wet mop (optional)

Cleaning agents

Agent	Uses	State
Abrasive cleaner (scouring powder)	adds abrasive rubbing action for cleaning surfaces where chemical means not sufficient	powder
Ammonia	cleaning glass	liquid
Baking soda, cream of tartar, vinegar, salt	miscellaneous jobs—see chapter on how to clean	
Dishwasher detergent	washing dishes in dishwasher	granular
Drain cleaner	keeping drains clear	granular liquid
General household cleaner	all washable surfaces; cleaning abilities differ in concentration or strength of solution	granular liquid spray (needs no diluting)
Metal polishes	cleaning and polishing metals	liquid, paste
Mild detergent	dishes, cleaning upholstery, other delicate cleaning jobs as noted	granular liquid
Mild soap	interchangeable with above except for ecological reasons	bar granular
Oven cleaner	cleaning ovens	liquid spray
Reinforced soaps and detergents	for laundering clothes	granular
Toilet bowl cleaner	cleaning toilet bowls	granular liquid
Wallpaper cleaner	cleaning dirt off unwashable wallpaper	gum paste
Waxes and polishes	Waxing and polishing floors and furniture	liquid paste spray

Vinegar: household uses

Use	Amount	What to do
Kitchen		
Cutting grease	A few drops of white vinegar	When washing an item that is greasy or smelly, add white vinegar to the cleaning water to cut down on the grease and remove the odor.
Removing stains	Equal mixture of salt and white vinegar	Salt and white vinegar will clean coffee and tea stains from china cups.
Cleaning glassware	½ cup white vinegar to 1 gal. water	White vinegar added to rinse water will eliminate dull soap film from glassware and make it shine.
Freshening lunch boxes	Small amount of white vinegar	Dampen a piece of fresh bread with white vinegar and put it in the lunch box overnight.
Cleaning stainless steel	Small amount of white vinegar	Remove spots on your stainless-steel kitchen equipment by rubbing them with a cloth dampened with white vinegar.

Use	Amount	What to do
Loosening tough stains	¼ cup white vinegar to 2 cups water	To loosen hard-to-clean stains in glass, aluminum or porcelain pots or pans, boil white vinegar with water in pan. Wash in hot, soapy water.
Soaking pots and pans	Full-strength white vinegar	Soak normal food-stained pots and pans in white vinegar for 30 min. Rinse in hot, soapy water.
Eliminating cooking odors	1 tbsp. white vinegar to 1 cup water	Boil white vinegar in water to eliminate unpleasant cooking odors.
Handling onions	Small amount of white vinegar	Rub a little white vinegar on your fingers before and after slicing onions to remove the odor of onions quickly.
Cleaning jars	Small amount of white vinegar	Rinse the peanut butter and mayonnaise jars you save with white vinegar to eliminate the odor of the former contents.

Laundry

Use	Amount	What to do
Rinsing clothes	1 cup white vinegar	Put a little white vinegar in your last rinse water to make sure your clothes get a thorough rinse.
Fluffing blankets	2 cups white vinegar	Add white vinegar to a washer tub of water to make a good rinse for both cotton and wool blankets.
Removing deodorant stains	Small amount of white vinegar	Get rid of stains left by deodorants and antiperspirants on washables by lightly rubbing with white vinegar. Then launder as usual.

General

Use	Amount	What to do
Cleaning electric irons	Equal amounts of white or cider vinegar and salt	Remove dark or burned stains from an electric iron by rubbing with white or cider vinegar and salt, heated first in a small aluminum pan. Polish in the same way you do silver.
Rubbing varnished wood	1 tsp. white vinegar to 1 qt. lukewarm water	Renew the luster of varnished surfaces by rubbing them with a soft, lintless cloth wrung out from a solution of white vinegar in lukewarm water. When rubbing, follow the grain of the wood. Finish the job by wiping the surface with a soft, dry cloth.
Eliminating tobacco odors	Small bowl of white vinegar	Eliminate odors in smoke-filled rooms during and after a party by placing a small bowl of white vinegar in the room.
Removing fruit stains	Small amount of white vinegar	Remove fruit stains from your hands by rubbing them with a little white vinegar; then wipe with a cloth.
Eliminating paint odors	Small bowl of white vinegar	Absorb the odor of fresh paint by putting a small dish of white vinegar in the room.
Removing decals	Several applications of white vinegar	Remove old decals by simply painting them with several coats of white vinegar. Give the vinegar time to soak in. After several minutes, the decals should wash off easily.

SOURCE: The Vinegar Institute, taken from THE HOUSEHOLD HANDBOOK, Meadowbrook Press

How to make furniture polish, varnish remover

Furniture polish

Melt 1 tablespoon of carnauba wax in the top of a double boiler. Add 1 pint of mineral oil to the melted wax and stir until completely blended. If you want the polish to smell like lemon, add a few drops of lemon oil and stir well. Pour into a clean jar and cover tightly.

Varnish remover

Measure 5⅓ cups of acetone, 5⅓ cups of benzene, and 5⅓ cups of wood alcohol into a gallon container. Cap the container tightly and shake the contents to mix them thoroughly.

DO IT YOURSELF AND SAVE MONEY by the Editors of CONSUMER GUIDE®, published by Harper & Row, New York.

Cleaning cookware

Type of material	How to clean
Stainless steel	Wash by hand in hot, sudsy water or in dishwasher. Rinse and buff dry to remove water spots. Rub burned-on foods with baking soda or a paste made of ammonia, water, and a mild, nonchlorinated scouring powder.
Aluminum	Hand washing is preferable; or wash in dishwasher, but turn it off before the drying cycle begins. To remove stains and discolorations, boil a solution of 2–3 tbsp. of cream of tartar, lemon juice, or vinegar added to 1 qt. of water in the utensil for 5–10 min.; then lightly scour with a soap-filled pad.
Cast iron	Wash in hot, soapy water; rinse and dry immediately. Never use strong detergents or scouring powders. Never store with lid on. Remove rust with steel wool. To season, coat with unsalted oil or shortening, heat in moderate oven for 2 hours.
Porcelain on metal	Wash with a sponge or cloth in warm, sudsy water or in the dishwasher (check manufacturer's instructions first). Remove burned-on foods or stains by soaking the utensil or by using a nonabrasive cleansing powder and scrubber (such as a nylon net scrubber).
Copper	Polish copper with various commercial copper cleaners. Or use a mixture of flour, salt, lemon juice and ammonia, or a mixture of flour and vinegar, to clean. After cleaning, wash in sudsy water, rinse, and polish with a soft, clean cloth.
Tin	Remove burned-on foods by boiling a solution of 1 qt. water and 2 tsp. baking soda in the utensil.
Pewter	Rub with a paste made from denatured alcohol and whiting, a fine abrasive powder available in hardware stores. Let the paste dry on the metal, then wash, rinse, and buff dry with soft cloth.
Silver	Prepare a paste of whiting (an abrasive powder available in hardware stores) and household ammonia or alcohol. Apply paste with a damp cloth, wash, rinse, and wipe dry. A soft brush, like a mascara brush, is helpful for cleaning small crevices.
Glass	Wash in warm, sudsy water or in dishwasher. To remove burned-on foods, pre-soak in sudsy water with a little baking soda added; scrub with nonabrasive scrubber. To remove coffee and tea stains, soak in a solution of 2 tbsp. liquid chlorine bleach per 1 cup of water.
Nonstick finish	Let the utensil cool after each use; then wash in hot, sudsy water, rinse and dry. Avoid abrasive cleansers or pads. After washing in dishwasher, wipe lightly with cooking oil. To remove stains, simmer a mixture of 1 tbsp. liquid bleach, 1 tbsp. vinegar, and 1 cup water for 5–10 min. in the utensil: wash. rinse and dry.

SOURCE: Metal Cookware Manufacturers Association; New York State Cooperative Extension, taken from THE HOUSEHOLD HANDBOOK, Meadowbrook Press

Baking soda: household uses

- **Paste:** Mix 3 parts baking soda to 1 part water.
- **Solution:** Dissolve 4 tbsp. baking soda in 1 qt. of water.
- **Dry:** Sprinkle baking soda straight from the box.

Use	Amount	What to do
Kitchen		
Deodorizing refrigerator	1 box (1 lb.) every other month	Tear off the top of the box, and place open in the back of the refrigerator in a shelf on the door.
Deodorizing dishwasher	1 small handful daily	Save water and energy by running dishwasher only after the evening meal. Once in the morning, before adding soiled dishes, sprinkle baking soda over the bottom of machine. It will absorb odors all day.
Freshening drains, garbage disposal	1 box (previously used in refrigerator)	When a fresh box of baking soda goes into the refrigerator, recycle the contents of the old box down the drains to keep them sweet and fresh-smelling.
Soaking cooking utensils	Solution	Let pots and pans soak in hot or warm solution; then wash. Baking soda cleans glass, porcelain, enamel and metal cookware without scratching.
Scouring burned or baked-on foods	Sprinkle dry as needed/paste	Scrub with baking soda sprinkled on a plastic scouring pad; rinse and dry. Or let warm paste soak on burned area; keep wet, then scrub as needed.

Use	Amount	What to do
Shining silver flatware/serving pieces	Paste	Mix paste in small bowl and apply with a damp sponge or soft cloth. Rub until clean; rinse and buff to a shiny gloss.
Sweetening and removing stains from coffee and teapot	Solution/dry	Wash in solution to remove build-up of coffee oils and tea stains for better tasting brew. To remove stained areas, shake baking soda on damp cloth or sponge. Rub until clean; rinse and dry.
Freshing coolers, plastic food containers	Solution	Shake solution in bottle, or sponge out interior, and rinse with clear water to sweeten and clean.

Bathroom

Cleaning fiberglass shower stalls	Dry	Sprinkle on damp sponge and gently scour to clean, deodorize, and help remove mildew. Baking soda will not scratch the surface.
Cleaning bathtubs, toilets, tile, chrome	Dry/paste	Shake on damp sponge and rub soiled areas until clean; rinse and buff dry. For textured surfaces, apply paste and allow to set a few minutes. Sponge rinse and clean.

General

Deodorizing cat litter	1 part baking soda to 3 parts litter	Cover bottom of litter pan with 1 part baking soda; then cover baking soda with 3 parts litter to absorb odors for up to a week. Litter won't need replacing as often.
Improving septic system	1 cup per week	Baking soda poured down a toilet or any household drain in the recommended amount makes the average tank of 300–750 gallons work better.
Putting out fire	Dry	Toss handfuls at the base of flames in the event of grease, oil, or electrical fires. Do not use to put out flames in deep-fat fryers, since this could cause the grease to spatter and the fire to spread.
Deodorizing carpet, rug	Dry	Test for color-fastness in an inconspicuous area. Sprinkle baking soda dry from the box; allow to set overnight, then vacuum.
Freshening laundry	⅓ cup	Add baking soda to wash or rinse cycle. Clothes will be sweeter and cleaner smelling.

SOURCE: ARM & HAMMER Division of Church & Dwight Co., Inc., taken from THE HOUSE-HOLD HANDBOOK, Meadowbrook Press

Laundering

Stain remover checklist

☑	Blotting materials (paper towels, facial tissues, paper napkins, bath towels, white sheets, soft cloth)	☐	Chlorine bleach
		☐	Drycleaning fluid (Carbona, Energine, K2r)
☐	Ammonia	☐	Lemon juice
☐	Bar soap	☐	Liquid hand dishwashing detergent
☐	Rubbing alcohol		

SOURCE: Dress Better For Less by Vicki Audette, taken from THE HOUSEHOLD HANDBOOK, Meadowbrook Press

Treatments for common stains

Professional dry cleaning is the best way to remove most large, stubborn stains. Certain small stains may be removed at home by either *dry* or *wet* treatment. Dry treatment involves the use of commercial dry-cleaning solvents that do not contain water. Wet treatment involves water. Some stains require both treatments. Stains should be removed promptly so they do not become permanent. The chart below lists some common stains and tells how to remove them.

Dry treatment

Ballpoint ink	Mascara
Candle wax	Motor oil
Carbon paper	Road tar
Cooking grease and oil	Rouge
Foundation makeup	Rubber-base adhesive
	Printing ink

1. Place a towel under the stained area.
2. Apply a dry-cleaning substance to the stain.
3. Rub the stain gently with the fingers. This action loosens the stain and transfers it to the towel. Continue rubbing until the stain disappears.
4. Remove the towel. Wet a cloth with the cleaning substance and wipe around the edges of the stain. Wipe toward the center to prevent a ring from forming.
5. Allow the area to dry.

Wet treatment

Berry stains	Ice Cream
*Blood	Milk
Catchup	*Mustard
*Coffee	Soft drinks
*Egg	Tea
*Grass	Washable ink

1. Place a towel under the stained area.
2. Apply cool water to the stain.
3. Rub the stained area lightly with the fingertips to loosen the stain.
4. If the stain remains, gently rub a liquid detergent into the stained area.
5. Wet a cloth and squeeze water over the stain. This action rinses out the detergent so it does not leave a ring.
6. Remove the towel. Wipe around the edges of the area with a wet cloth.
7. Allow the area to dry.

Dry and wet treatment

Gravy	Paint	Shoe polish
Lipstick	Salad dressing	

1. Follow the steps for dry treatment.
2. After the stained area has dried use the wet treatment.

---

*Removal especially difficult if dry.

Washing methods for basic fabrics

Method		Cotton	Linen	Silk	Wool	Acetate	Triacetate	Acrylic	Anidex	Glass	Metallic	Modacrylic	Nylon	Olefin	Polyester	Rayon	Rubber	Saran	Spandex	Vinyon
Hand wash	Warm	•	•	•	•	•	•	•			•	•	•		•	•			•	•
	Cold	•		•	•										•		•			
Machine wash	Hot	•																		
	Warm	•	•			•	•	•	•	•		•	•	•	•		•	•	•	•
Tumble dry	Hot/Normal	•	•								•				•					
	Warm/Delicate	•	•			•	•	•				•	•	•	•	•			•	
Drip Dry	Flat Surface																			
	Line Dry	•		•		•				•					•	•	•	•	•	•
Dry Clean		•	•	•	•	•		•			•	•	•		•	•			•	
Do Not Use a Strong Detergent				•	•						•				•	•	•	•		
Do Not Bleach				•	•	•	•				•				•	•			•	
Iron	Low Heat Set			•	•	•			•		•	•								
	Medium Set	•						•	•				•		•	•				
	High Set	•	•				•													
No Ironing Required										•					•	•	•	•	•	•

Security

Security checklist

General security

☐ Trim shrubs so that windows and doors are in full view from the street.

☐ Make sure you've got adequate outdoor lighting, especially at side and back doors.

☐ Don't leave "hidden" house keys nearby. Most hiding spots are well known to burglars.

☐ Make sure your mailbox is large enough to conceal your mail totally or install a slot in the door.

☐ Display your house numbers prominently and make sure they're well lighted.

☐ Make sure that all exterior doors are either metal-clad or solid hardwood.

☐ Install deadbolt locks on all exterior doors. Use a thumb turn (single-cylinder) lock when there's no breakable glass within 40″ of the lock; otherwise use a key (double-cylinder) lock.

☐ Secure sliding doors and supplement window locks.

☐ Install a wide-angle peephole in your front door; don't depend on an inside chain guard to protect you when you're identifying visitors.

Before you go away

☐ Ask a trusted neighbor to park in your driveway, put garbage in your garbage can, mow the lawn or shovel the sidewalk, and occasionally check your home.

☐ Have the post office hold your mail and cancel the newspaper (rather than tell the paper company you're going on vacation).

☐ Use automatic timers to turn lights on at dusk and off at your normal bedtime. Vary the lights to be turned on. Also have a timer turn a radio on occasionally during the day.

☐ Leave your drapes in the normal position and have a neighbor close them at night, open them at daylight and reposition them every day or so.

☐ Unplug your phone or set the bell on low to prevent a potential burglar from hearing an unanswered phone ring.

☐ Tell a neighbor where you can be reached in an emergency.

☐ For long absences, ask your local law enforcement agency to keep an eye on your home.

SOURCE: Minnesota Department of Public Safety, taken from THE HOUSEHOLD HANDBOOK, Meadowbrook Press

Securing sliding doors and windows

Sliding doors
1. Drill a downward-angled hole at the top center of the door's overlapping frames. Insert a steel pin or heavy nail in the hole.

2. Place a broomstick or a length of wood in the lower track. Make sure it's snug.

3. Buy a "Charley bar" from a locksmith. It attaches to the side frame and folds down across the glass, bracing itself against the opposite frame.

4. Install a special key-operated deadbolt lock.

5. Install 1¼ inch large-head, sheet metal screws in the upper track at both ends and in the middle. They should protrude just enough to let the sliding frame clear, but not enough to allow someone to pry the sliding door from its track.

Windows
1. For traditional double-hung windows, drill a small hole at a slight downward angle through the first sash and into (but not through) the second sash. Then slip a heavy steel pin or large nail into the hole.

2. For windows that slide sideways, fasten a broomstick or a length of wood in the lower track.

3. For casement windows, remove the operator handle and store it in a convenient place. Even if someone breaks the glass, it will be difficult to reach inside and crank open the window.

SOURCE: Minnesota Department of Public Safety, taken from THE HOUSEHOLD HANDBOOK, Meadowbrook Press

Fireplace safety checklist

☑ Check to make sure the fireplace was constructed to be used as a fireplace, not just for decoration. Have it inspected to determine whether it has all necessary linings and clearances.

☐ Do not use gasoline or other flammable liquids to kindle or rekindle a fire because the flammable vapors can explode. Never use fuels near a fire; explosive vapors can travel the length of a room.

☐ Always keep the damper open while the fuel is burning to provide for efficient burning and to prevent the accumulation of poisonous or explosive gases.

☐ Do not use coal, charcoal, or polystyrene packaging in a fireplace unless the fireplace is well-ventilated.

☐ Do not treat artificial logs (made from sawdust and wax) the same way you treat real wood logs. Use only one at a time—if you use more, they can produce too much heat for some fireplaces to withstand.

☐ Always use a screen that completely covers the opening around a fireplace to keep sparks from flying out. Do not put combustible materials, such as carpets or furniture, near a fireplace.

☐ Keep children away from the fire because their clothing can easily ignite. Warn the entire family about this hazard.

☐ Check fireplaces regularly (at least once each year) to determine that all vents and chimneys are operating properly.

☐ Be sure that all ashes have thoroughly cooled before you dispose of them.

☐ Make sure the fire is out completely before retiring for the evening.

☐ Use chimney guards. Squirrel and bird nests stop up chimneys.

Home fire safety checklist

Heating and cooking

☑ Are space heaters and appliances properly installed and used?

☐ Has the family been cautioned not to use flammable liquids like gasoline to start or freshen a fire (or for cleaning purposes)?

☐ Is the fireplace equipped with a metal fire screen?

☐ Since portable gas and oil heaters and fireplaces use up oxygen as they burn, do you provide proper ventilation when they are in use?

☐ Are all space heaters placed away from traffic, and are children and older persons cautioned to keep their clothing away? Are proper clearances provided from curtains, bedding, and furniture?

Smoking

☐ Do you stop members of your household from smoking in bed?

☐ Do you check up after others to see that no butts are lodged in upholstered furniture where they can smolder unseen?

☐ Do you dispose of smoking materials carefully (and not in wastebaskets) and keep large, safe ashtrays wherever people smoke?

☐ Are matches and lighters kept away from small children?

Wiring

☐ Are all electrical cords in the open—not run under rugs, over hooks, or through door openings? Are they checked routinely for wear?

☐ Is the right size fuse used in each socket in the fuse box, and do you replace a fuse with one the same size?

Storage

☐ Children can get burned climbing on the stove to reach an item overhead. Do you store cookies, cereal, or other "bait" away from the stove?

☐ Do you keep basement, closets, garage, yard cleared of combustibles like papers, cartons, old furniture, oil-soaked rags?

☐ Are gasoline and other flammable liquids stored in closed containers (never glass jars, discarded bleach bottles or other makeshift containers) and away from heat, sparks, and children?

☐ Are old paint-laden brushes disposed of? Is paint kept in tightly closed containers?

Electrical appliance safety check

Appliance	Problem	Possible cause	Remedy
Oven	Won't heat.	Timer set at "off" or "automatic" position.	Reset timer to "manual."
		Selector switch in wrong position.	Set selector switch to "bake."
Refrigerator, freezer	Won't operate.	Temperature control set at "off" or "defrost."	If model defrosts manually, turn "on." If model defrosts automatically, check manufacturer's instructions on timing of defrost cycle.
		Use of long extension cord, smaller than No. 14 wire.	Extension cords of any kind should not be used. If there's no alternative, use a 3-wire, No. 14 (or heavier) cord.
	Motor runs too often, too long.	Dust on condenser.	Turn off or disconnect appliance. Clean condenser according to manufacturer's instructions.
		Door leaking air. Check by first closing door over dollar bill and then pulling bill out. If it pulls out easily, it's leaking air.	Clean door gasket with soap and water. Have replaced if torn or worn. Also, you may need to adjust the latch.
		Unit too near a heat source or too close to wall or cabinets.	Move unit to a different location.
	Food slow to freeze.	Freezing too much food at one time.	Freeze no more than 2–3 lbs. of food per cubic foot of freezer space in a 24-hr. period.
		Too much frost.	Defrost before ice becomes ¼" thick.
Dishwasher	Won't operate.	Door latch not completely closed.	Reclose door and latch securely.
		Cycle control not on proper setting.	Adjust control, following manufacturer's instructions.
	Dishes not clean.	Water not hot enough.	Water heat should be set to 150°.
		Dishes/cutlery not properly prepared or loaded.	Scrape dishes. Follow manufacturer's loading instructions.
		Dishwasher drain clogged.	Clean drain and strainer according to manufacturer's instructions.

Electrical appliance safety check—continued

Appliance	Problem	Possible cause	Remedy
Clothes washer	Water doesn't run into washer.	Faucets not open.	Check faucets.
		Kink in hose.	Straighten.
		Screens stopped up.	Remove hose at faucets and washer. Clean screens.
	Water doesn't drain from washer.	Kink in discharge hose.	Straighten hose.
Clothes dryer	Does not operate.	Door not firmly closed.	Reclose door firmly.
		Controls not properly set.	Check position of controls and adjust to proper setting.
	Clothes don't dry in proper time.	Dryer overloaded.	Follow manufacturer's instructions for loading.
		Lint tray full.	Clean. Empty after each use.
Room air conditioner	Fuse or circuit breaker frequently blows.	Circuit overloaded.	Remove other electrical equipment from air-conditioning circuit or have special circuit installed for unit.
	Unit operates; room not cool enough.	Dirty filter in unit.	Clean or replace filter.
		Bushes or other obstruction interfering with outdoor air flow.	Trim bushes; remove any other obstruction to at least 1′ away.
		Too much heat build-up before unit is started.	Turn unit on earlier. Keep shades drawn, windows and doors closed to reduce heat load.
		Heat or hot-water vapor from kitchen or bathroom coming into room.	Release heat or vapor through windows in kitchen or bedroom, preferably with exhaust fan.
		Round-the-clock use can cause ice to build on coils and block air flow.	Turn unit off until ice melts.

SOURCE: Edison Electric Institute, taken from THE HOUSEHOLD HANDBOOK, Meadowbrook Press

Fire extinguisher characteristics

Fire class	Extinguishing agent	Available sizes	Horizontal range, ft.	Discharge time, sec.
A	Water	1½–5 gal.	30–40	45–180
A, B	Foam	1¼–2½ gal.	35	35–60
A, B, C	Ammonium phosphate	2–3 lb.	5–20	8–25
B, C	Carbon dioxide	2½–20 lb.	2–4	15–30
B, C	Potassium bicarbonate	2–30 lb.	5–20	8–25
B, C	Potassium chloride	2–30 lb.	5–20	8–25
B, C	Potassium bicarbonate/urea	17–19 lb.	15–30	26–30
B, C	Halon 1211	2½ lb.	4–6	8–10
B, C	Halon 1301	2–4 lb.	8–12	8–12

Painting
Exterior paint: making appropriate selections

Surface	Aluminum Paint	Asphalt Emulsion	Awning Paint	Cement Base Paint	House Paint (Oil)	House Paint (Latex)	Metal Primer	Porch-and-Deck Enamel	Primer or Undercoater	Roof Cement or Coating	Spar Varnish	Transparent Sealer	Trim-and-Trellis Paint	Water Repellent Preservative	Penetrating Wood Stain (Latex or Oil)
Masonry															
Asbestos Cement					●○	○			○						
Brick	○			○	●○	○			○				○		
Cement and Cinder Block	○			○	●○	○			○				○		
Cement Porch Floor						○		○							
Stucco	○			○	●○	○			○				○		
Metal															
Aluminum Windows	○				●○	●○	○						●○		
Galvanized Surfaces	●○				●○	●○	○						●○		
Iron Surfaces	●○				●○	●○	○			○			●○		
Siding (Metal)	●○				●○	●○	●○						●○		
Steel Windows and Doors	●○				●○	●○	○						●○		
Wood															
Frame Windows	○				●○	●○			○				●○		○
* Natural Siding and Trim												○			○
* Porch Floor								○				○			○
Shingle Roof														○	○
Shutters & Other Trim					●○	●○			○				●○		○
Siding					●○	●○			○						○
Miscellaneous															
Canvas Awnings			○												
Coal Tar Felt Roof		○								○					

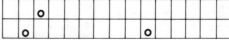

○= Paint Choice. ● = Primer or Sealer May Be Required, Check Container Label.
* May be used as a water seal. Stains will not be effective if applied over varnish.

Interior paint: making appropriate selections

Surface	Alkali Resistant Enamel	Alkyd Exterior Masonry Paint	Alkyd Flat Enamel	Alkyd Floor Enamel	Alkyd Glossy Enamel	Alkyd Semi-Glossy Enamel	Epoxy Enamel (Opaque)	Epoxy Finish (Clear)	Lacquer	Latex Exterior Masonry Paint	Latex Flat Wall Paint	Latex Floor Enamel	Latex Glossy Enamel	Latex Semi-Glossy Enamel	Pigmented Wiping Stain	Portland Cement Masonry Paint	Portland Cement Metal Paint	Shellac	Urethane Enamel (Opaque)	Urethane Finish (Clear)	Varnish
Masonry																					
Brick	•	•	•		•	•	•			•	•		•	•					•		
Cement Block	•		•		•	•	•				•		•	•		•			•		
Ceramic Tile Flooring				•		•						•							•		
Concrete	•		•	•	•	•	•				•	•	•	•		•			•		
Concrete Flooring	•			•		•						•							•		
Drywall			•		•	•	•				•		•	•					•		
Plaster			•		•	•	•				•		•	•					•		
Metal																					
Aluminum			•		•	•	•				•		•	•					•		
Galvanized Steel			•		•	•	•				•		•	•		•	•		•		
Iron and Steel			•		•	•	•				•		•	•		•	•		•		
Steel Flooring				•		•										•	•		•		
Wood																					
Flooring				•			•	•	•			•			•				•	•	•
Trim and Paneling			•		•	•	•	•	•		•		•	•	•				•	•	•
Miscellaneous																					
*Acoustical Surfaces			•								•										
Vinyl Wallcovering, Smooth, with Design			•		•	•					•		•	•							
Vinyl Wallcovering, Smooth, without Design					•	•					•										
Vinyl Wallcovering, Textured			•		•	•					•										
Wallpaper			•		•	•					•		•	•							

● = Paint Choice.
*Apply a very thin coating so that soundproof characteristics will not be seriously affected.

Wall surfaces: light reflection values

Color	Percentage of reflection	Color	Percentage of reflection
Whites		**Deep tones**	
dull or flat white	75–90	cocoa brown, mauve	24
Light tones		medium green and blue	21
cream, eggshell	79	medium gray	20
pale pink, pale yellow	75–80	**Dark tones**	
ivory	75	dark brown, dark gray	10–15
light green, blue, orchid	70–75	olive green	12
light beige, pale gray	70	dark blue, blue-green	5–10
soft pink, light peach	69	forest green	7
Medium tones		**Natural wood tones**	
pink	64	birch, beech	35–50
apricot	56–62	light maple, light oak	25–35
tan, yellow-gold	55	dark oak, cherry	10–15
yellow-green	45	black walnut, mahogany	5–15
light grays	35–50		
medium turquoise	44		
medium light blue	42		
old gold, pumpkin	34		
rose	29		

From PRACTICAL GUIDE TO HOME LIGHTING by William F. Rooney. Copyright © 1980 by Van Nostrand Reinhold Company. Reprinted by permission of the publisher.

Energy conservation

Insulation

Types	Uses	Types	Uses
Batts		**Loose fill** (blown-in)	
glass fiber	unfinished attic floor	glass fiber	unfinished attic floor
rock wool	unfinished attic rafters	rock wool	finished attic floor
	underside of floors	cellulose	finished frame walls
	open sidewalls		underside of floors
Blankets		**Loose fill** (poured-in)	
glass fiber	unfinished attic floor	glass fiber	unfinished attic floor
rock wool	unfinished attic rafters	rock wool	
	underside of floors	cellulose	
	open sidewalls	vermiculite	
		perlite	

Insulation materials: R-values

R-Value*	Batts or blankets		Loose and blown fill				
	Glass fiber	Rock wool	Glass fiber	Rock wool	Cellulose fiber	Vermic-ulite	Perlite
R-11	3½†	3	5	4	3	5	4
R-13	4	3½	6	4½	3½	6	5
R-19	6	5	8½	6½	5	9	7
R-22	7	6	10	7½	6	10½	8
R-26	8	7	12	9	7	12½	9½
R-30	9½	8	13½	10	8	14	11
R-33	10½	9	15	11	9	15½	12
R-38	12	10½	17	13	10	18	14

*Nominal R-values for various thicknesses of insulation
†Inches of thickness

Weatherstripping

Form	Installation/use	Notes
Self-adhesive foam tape	Apply to dry clean surfaces at room temperature by pressing in place on door and window jambs, stops, or sashes	Resilient sponge rubber or vinyl on paper or vinyl backing, ⅜″ to ¾″ wide. Deteriorates when exposed to weather. May last only one season
Felt or aluminum and felt	Staple to wood or glue to metal stops, sills, and sashes	Felt tears easily during use and is ineffective when wet
Vinyl	Tack, staple, screw, or glue flange of tubeshaped strip to surfaces	Durable, easy to apply
Neoprene-coated sponge rubber	Tack or staple to surfaces	Easy to install. More durable than uncoated material
Bronze metal	Tack to door and casement window jambs	Durable, easy to install, not affected by moisture and temperature
Caulking cords	Press into place on any type surface	Comes in strips; easy to apply; pliable; durable, not affected by moisture
Fiberglass strip	Various sizes with waterproof tape seals larger crack as around garage doors or may be wrapped around pipes for insulation	Durable
Waterproof tape	Seals crack. Apply half on window sash and half on stops. Seals cracks by pressing to clean dry surfaces	Not affected by moisture.
Air-conditioner weather strip	Easy to install, rectangular polyfoam strip for sealing around window mounted units and window sashes	Low cost
Magnetic vinyl	For steel door insulation	Durable

Faucet leaks: estimating costs

Drops per minute	Gallons per month	KWH per month	Cost per month	Cost per year
60	192	48	$1.68	$20.16
90	310	78	2.73	32.76
120	429	107	3.75	45.00

From HOMEMAKERS BOOK OF ENERGY SAVERS by Jean E. Laird. Copyright © 1981. Reprinted by permission of The Stephen Greene Press, Brattleboro, Vermont.

Calculating EER's (energy efficiency ratings)

Major appliances are, by government regulation, sold with energy efficiency rating information attached. The ratings help the consumer buy with an eye to maximum efficiency of use. The following formula shows how these ratings are calculated:

$$EER = \frac{Btu\ (British\ thermal\ unit)/hour}{watts} = \frac{Btu}{watt\text{-}hour}$$

Calculating hardness of water

Hard water can raise soap, clothing, and plumbing bills. To find out if water is too hard, buy tincture of green soap at a drugstore and add one drop to one half ounce (30 milliliters) of water in a bottle. Shake vigorously. Repeat the procedure, shaking thoroughly each time, until a thick layer of suds appears. If the number of drops of soap needed to form suds is

| 1 | 2 | 3 | 4 | 5 | 6 |

the hardness ratio of your water is

| 0 | 2½ | 4 | 7½ | 10 | 12¼ |

Anything above 4 calls for water softeners, at the least, and a water softening system, at best.

5 The home gardener

Whether the reader is a novice or veteran gardener, the Section 5 tables and formulas will prove to be a practical and helpful addition to his or her growing library. The section includes some of the most basic information available on both interior and exterior planting.

The beginner may want to try his or her hand at some of the recommended "easy" plants or study the care levels required for common house plants and the table that tracks most common flowers' schedule for bloom. Decorative indoor plants appear on a separate, detailed list.

If the more experienced gardener has encountered problems with some plants, and problems are a part of everyday gardening, he or she will appreciate the table that focuses on symptoms and diagnosis.

Outside the house, the family gardener is faced with tricky questions regarding climate, types of soil, mulching, etc. The tables and formulas in the second half of "Home Gardener" provide guidance in these areas. Information on when and how to plant vegetable seeds and plants is offered, as well as charts on frost dates and methods for obtaining multiple crops. A table is included on the cultivation of sprouts, now so popular as a salad ingredient.

For the apartment dweller, the "Home Gardener" offers full information on vegetable pot gardening. For the suburban or country gardener, Section 5 gives complete instructions on constructing and maintaining a compost heap, as well as examining methods for safe application of pesticides.

Section 5, in short, is designed to provide the reader with a handy and complete guide to the enjoyable and often profitable pastime of gardening.

House plants

Decorative indoor plants

Name	Mature size	Light level	Water requirement
Abutilon species (Flowering, maple)	pot, hanging plant	high	moist
Acalypha hispida (Chenille plant)	pot plant	high	moist
Achimines (Magic flower)	pot, hanging plant	high	moist, in ground dry, when dormant
Adiantum species (Maidenhair fern)	pot, hanging, terrarium plant	medium	wet
Aechmea fasciata (Bromeliad)	pot plant	medium	moist
Aeschynanthus javanicus (Lipstick plant)	pot, hanging, terrarium plant	medium	moist

Name	Mature size	Light level	Water requirement
Aglaonema commutatum (Chinese evergreen)	pot plant	low	moist
Aglaonema "Pseudo-bracteatum" (Golden aglaonema)	pot plant	low	moist
Aglaonema roebelinii (Pewter plant)	pot plant	low	moist
Aloe variegata	pot plant	very high	dry
Alternanthera beutzickiana	pot, hanging, terrarium plant	high to medium	moist
Ananas comosus (Pineapple)	pot plant	high	moist
Aphelandra squarrosa (Zebra plant)	pot, terrarium plant	high	moist
Araucaria excelsa (Norfolk island pine)	tree, floor, pot plant	high	moist
Ardisia crispa (Coral ardisia)	pot plant	medium	moist
Asparagus sprengeri (Asparagus fern)	pot plant	medium	moist
Aspidistra elatior (Cast-iron plant)	floor, pot plant	low	moist
Asplenium nidus (Bird's nest fern)	pot plant	medium	wet
Aucuba japonica (Japanese laurel)	pot plant	medium	dry
Begonia rex	pot, hanging plant	medium	moist
Begonias, other than metallica and rex	pot plant	very high	moist
Beloperone guttata (Shrimp plant)	pot, hanging plant	high	dry
Bougainvillea glabra (Bougainvillea)	pot, hanging plant	very high	dry
Brassaia actinophylla (Schefflera)	tree, floor, pot plant	medium	dry
Bromeliads (many species)	pot, hanging plant	medium	moist
Browallia speciosa (Browallia)	pot, hanging plant	high to medium	moist
Caladium (Fancy-leaved caladium)	pot plant	high	moist—dry (dormant)
Calathea species (Calathea)	pot plant	medium	moist
Campanula isophila (Star-of-Bethlehem)	pot, hanging plant	high	moist
Capsicum annum (Christmas pepper)	pot, hanging plant	high	moist
Chamaedorea elegens (Neanthe bella palm)	floor, pot plant	low	moist
Chamaedorea erumpens (Bamboo palm)	tree, floor, pot plant	low	moist
Chamaeropsis humilis (European fan palm)	tree, floor plant	high	moist
Chlorophytum (Spider plant)	pot, hanging, terrarium plant	medium	moist
Chrysanthemum morifolium (Chrysanthemum)	pot plant	very high	moist
Cissus antarctica (Kangaroo vine)	pot, hanging, terrarium plant	high	moist
Cissus rhombifolia (Grape ivy)	pot plant	medium	dry
Citrus mitis (Calamondin)	pot plant	high	dry
Clerodendrum thomsonae (Bleeding-heart vine)	pot, hanging plant	high to medium	moist
Clivia (Kaffir-lily)	pot plant	medium	dry
Codiaeum	pot plant	very high	dry
Coffea arabica (Arabian coffee tree)	tree plant	medium	moist
Coleus	pot, hanging plant	very high	wet
Columnea species (Columnea)	pot, hanging, terrarium plant	medium	moist
Cordyline terminalis (Hawaiian ti plant)	tree, floor, pot plant	medium	moist
Crassula	pot plant	very high	dry
Crossandra infundibuliformis	pot plant	medium	moist
Cryptanthus species (Dwarf bromeliad)	pot, terrarium plant	medium	dry
Cyclamen species (persicum or other species)	pot plant	high	moist—dry (dormant)
Cyperus alternifolius	Umbrella plant	medium	wet
Cyrtomium falcatum (Japanese holly fern)	pot plant	medium to low	moist
Davallis fejeensis (Figi rabbit's-foot fern)	pot, hanging plant	low	moist
Dieffenbachia amoena (Dumb cane)	floor, pot plant	medium	dry
Dieffenbachia "Exotica" (Dumb cane)	pot, terrarium plant	medium	dry

Name	Mature size	Light level	Water requirement
Dizygotheca elegantissima (Spider aralia)	floor, pot plant	high	moist
Dracaena deremensis (Green dracaena)	floor, pot plant	medium	wet
Dracaena deremensis "Warneckei" (White striped dracaena)	pot plant	medium	dry
Dracaena fragrans massangeana (Corn plant)	floor, pot plant	low	wet
Dracaena godseffiana (Gold-dust dracaena)	pot, terrarium plant	medium	wet
Dracaena marginata (Dragon tree)	tree, floor plant	medium	wet
Epiphyllum hybrids (Orchid cactus)	pot, hanging plant	high	moist, in growth dry, over winter
Episcia (Flame-violet)	pot, hanging, terrarium plant	medium	moist
Eriobotrya japonica (Japanese loquat)	tree	high	moist
Euphorbia mili (splenders) (Crown-of-thorns)	pot plant	high	dry
Euphorbia pulcherrima (Poinsettia)	pot plant	very high	dry
Exacum affine	pot, hanging plant	medium	moist
Fatsia japonica (Japanese aralia)	floor, pot plant	medium	moist
Ficus benjamina exotica (Weeping java fig)	tree	medium	moist
Ficus elastica "Decora" (Rubber plant)	tree, floor, pot plant	medium	moist
Ficus lyrata (Fiddle leaf fig)	tree, floor plant	medium	moist
Ficus philippinensis (Philippine fig)	tree, floor plant	medium	moist
Ficus repens var. *pumila* (Creeping fig)	pot, hanging plant	medium to low	moist
Ficus retusa nitida (India laurel)	tree	medium	moist
Fittonia verschaffeltii	pot, terrarium plant	medium	moist
Fuchsia	pot, hanging plant	very high	moist
Gardenia jasminoides (Gardenia)	pot plant	very high	moist
Gynura aurantiaca (Velvet plant)	pot, hanging, terrarium plant	medium	moist
Gynura sarmentosa (Velvet plant)	pot, hanging, terrarium plant	medium	moist
Haemanthus coccineus (Blood lily)	pot plant	very high	moist, during growth dry, when dormant
Haworthia species (Haworthia)	pot, terrarium plant	medium	dry
Helxine soleirolii (Baby's-tears)	pot, terrarium plant	medium	moist
Hibiscus rose-sinensis (Rose-of-China)	pot plant	very high	moist
Howeia forsteriana (Kentia palm)	tree, floor plant	low	moist
Hoya carnosa (Wax plant)	pot, hanging plant	medium	dry
Impatiens	pot, hanging, terrarium plant	very high	moist
Jacobinia obtusior (Plume flower)	pot plant	medium	moist
Kalanchoe species	pot, hanging plant	high	dry
Lantana camara (Trailing lantana)	pot, hanging plant	high	dry
Lantana montevidensis (Trailing lantana)	pot, hanging plant	high	dry
Ligustrum lucidum (Wax leaf privet)	tree, floor plant	medium	dry
Maranta leuconeura (Prayer plant)	pot, hanging, terrarium plant	medium	moist
Mimosa pudica (Sensitive plant)	pot, hanging plant	high	moist
Monstera deliciosa (Ceriman or Mexican Breadfruit)	pot plant	low	moist
Naomarica northiana (Apostle plant)	pot plant	medium	wet
Neoregelia spectabilis (Fingernail plant)	pot plant	medium	moist
Nephrolepsis exalata bostoniensis (Boston fern)	pot, hanging, terrarium plant	medium	moist
Nerium oleander (Oleander)	floor, pot plant	high	dry

Name	Mature size	Light level	Water requirement
Nertera depressa granadensis (Bead plant)	pot, terrarium plant	high	moist
Orchids (many species)	pot, hanging plant	very high	moist/dry
Pandanus veitchii (Screw-pine)	floor, pot plant	medium	dry
Passiflora species (Passion-flower)	pot, hanging plant	very high	moist
Pathenocissus benryana (Ampelopsis)	pot, hanging plant	medium	moist
Pelargonium species (Geranium)	pot, hanging plant	very high	dry
Pellionia daveauana (Trailing watermelon-begonia)	pot, hanging, terrarium plant	medium	moist
Peperomia caperata (Emerald ripple)	pot, hanging, terrarium plant	low	dry
Petunia hybrida (Cascade type)	pot, hanging plant	very high	moist
Philodendron hybrids (Self-heading philodendron)	floor, pot plant	medium	moist
Philodendron oxycardium (Common philodendron)	pot, hanging plant	low	dry
Phoenix roebelenii (Dwarf date palm)	floor, pot plant	medium	wet
Pilea micorphylla (Artillery plant)	pot, hanging plant	medium	moist
Pittosporum tobira (Mock orange)	floor, pot plant	high	dry
Plectranthus australis (Swedish-ivy)	pot, hanging, terrarium plant	medium	moist
Pleomele reflexa (Green pleomele)	floor plant	medium	wet
Podocarpus macrophylla Maki (Podocarpus)	tree, floor, pot plant	high	moist
Polyscias guilfoylei (Parsley aralia)	floor, pot plant	medium	moist
Primula malacoides (Fairy primrose)	pot plant	high	moist
Primula obconica (German primrose)	pot plant	high	moist
Punica granatum var. nana	pot plant	high	moist
Rhapis excelsa (Lady palm)	tree, floor plant	medium	wet
Rhipsalidopsis gaertneri (Easter cactus)	pot, hanging plant	high	moist, in growth dry, over winter
Rohdea japonica (Japanese rohdea)	pot plant	medium	moist
Rosa chinensis var. minima (Miniature rose)	pot plant	very high	wet
Saintpaulia species (African violets)	pot, hanging plant	very high	moist
Salvia splendens (Scarlet sage)	pot plant	very high	moist
Saxifraga stolonifera var. tricolor (Variegated strawberry-geranium)	pot, hanging, terrarium plant	very high	dry
Schlumbergea bridgesii (Christmas cactus)	pot, hanging plant	high	moist, in growth dry, over winter
Selaginella lepidophylla (Resurrection plant)	pot, terrarium plant	medium to low	moist
Senecio cruentus (Cineraria)	pot plant	high	moist
Senecio mikanioides (German ivy)	pot, hanging, terrarium plant	medium	moist
Setcreasea purpurea (Purple heart)	pot, hanging, terrarium plant	medium	dry
Sinningia species (Gloxinia)	pot, hanging plant	very high	wet
Solanum pseudo-capsicum (Jerusalem cherry)	pot, hanging plant	high	dry
Spathiphyllum "Mauna Loa" (White flag)	pot plant	medium	dry
Streptocarpus species (Cape-primrose)	pot plant	high	moist
Sygonium podophyllum (Nephthytis)	pot, hanging, terrarium plant	low	moist
Tagetes species (Marigold)	pot plant	very high	moist
Tolmiea memziezii (Piggy-back plant)	pot, hanging plant	high	moist
Tradescantia species (Wandering Jew)	pot, hanging, terrarium plant	medium	dry
Vinca major var. variegata (Periwinkle)	pot, hanging plant	high	moist

Name	Mature size	Light level	Water requirement
Zantedeschia species (Calla-lily)	pot plant	high	wet, in growth dry, when dormant
Zebrina species (Wandering Jew)	pot, hanging, terrarium plant	medium	moist
Zygocactus truncatus (Thanksgiving cactus)	pot, hanging plant	high	moist, in growth dry, over winter

Plants recommended for the beginner

Name of plant	Light level	Water requirement
Aechmea fasciata (Bromeliad)	medium	moist
Aglaonema roebelinii (Pewter plant)	low	moist
Begonia rex (Begonia)	medium	moist
Brassaia actinophylla (Schefflera)	medium	dry
Chamaedorea elegans (Neanthe bella palm)	low	moist
Chrysanthemum motifolia (Mum)	very high	moist
Cyclamen species	high	moist
Dieffenbachia amoena (Dumb cane)	medium	dry
Dracaena fragrans (Corn plant)	low	wet
Euphoria pulchettima (Poinsettia)	very high	dry
Fatsia japonica (Japanese aralia)	medium	moist
Ficus elastica 'Decora' (Rubber plant)	medium	moist
Hoya carnosa (Wax plant)	medium	dry
Maranta leuconeura (Prayer plant)	medium	moist
Nephrolepis exalta bostoniensis (Boston fern)	medium	moist
Podocarpus macrophyllus 'Maki' (Podocarpus)	high	moist
Saintpaulia species (African violet)	high	moist
Zebrina species (Wandering Jew)	medium	moist

Watering houseplants
Three ways to water your plants

Here are three different watering methods you can use. Each has its advantages and disadvantages, so it's wise to alternate methods now and then.

· **Surface watering.** Pour water slowly over the surface until it starts to run out of the bottom of the container. Be careful not to wash away the soil from the crown and top roots of the plant.

· **Bottom watering.** Pour water into a saucer underneath any pot with a bottom drainage hole. Capillary action of the plant's root system will move the water up through the potting mix until it reaches the surface. Remove excess water in the saucer in about an hour, when the soil's surface feels moist. Occasionally pour water over the surface to dissolve chemicals that tend to gather on the surface.

· **Wick watering.** When you pot the plant, insert an absorbent wick that reaches from the bottom drainage hole to the soil in the pot. Then follow the directions for bottom watering. The wick helps the plant's root system absorb moisture.

Tips on watering your plants properly

- **Before you water,** use a knitting needle to poke a few holes in the soil, allowing the water to penetrate the root ball adequately.
- **Drinking water** is usually safe to use in watering, since the chlorine level is not high enough to hurt most plants. If your water is fluoridated, however, use untreated water.
- **Ferns and African violets** are sensitive to chlorine levels in drinking water, so these plants need water that has been exposed to air overnight, allowing the chlorine to escape into the atmosphere.
- **Water plants** in the morning with room-temperature water.
- **Growing or flowering plants** need more water than resting or dormant ones.
- **Plants with hairy, thorny, or waxy leaves** need less water than thin-leaved varieties.

Houseplant problem diagnosis

Symptoms / Possible Causes		Too much light	Not enough light	High temperature	Low temperature	Overwatering or poor drainage	Not enough water	Too much fertilizer	Not enough fertilizer	Compacted soil	Drafts	Day length	Air pollution
Foliage:	tips or margins brown					•	•	•	•		•		
	bend down and curl				•						•		•
	yellowish green	•	•	•		•		•	•	•			•
	oldest drop		•	•		•	•	•	•	•	•		•
	all drop					•	•	•					•
	spots	•			•		•						
	wilt	•		•		•	•	•			•	•	
Growth:	weak, thin and soft		•	•		•			•	•			
	new leaves small		•	•		•	•	•	•	•			•
	none develops				•	•	•	•					
	plant died				•	•	•	•					
Flowers:	fail to develop or buds drop		•	•	•	•	•	•	•	•	•	•	•
	color less intense		•	•		•			•	•			
	decline too fast			•			•				•		•
	become smaller		•						•	•			
	no blooms		•	•								•	

SOURCE: New York State Cooperative Extension, taken from THE HOUSEHOLD HANDBOOK, Meadowbrook Press

Exterior planting: ornamental gardens

Trees and shrubs

Forest trees Large	Garden trees Medium	Large shrubs Small	Small shrubs Dwarf
Ash Beech Oak Lime Horse chestnut Sweet chestnut Norway maple Birch	Thorn Crab Cherry (Japanese) Laburnum Purple leaf plum *Acer hersii* *Acer ginnala*	Camellia Sumach Lilac Berberis Mexican orange Laurustinus Laurel Rhododendron	*Helichrysum lanatum* Dwarf rhododendrons Rue Cotton lavender Daphne Spanish gorse

Lombardy poplar
Dawyck beech
Cypress
Douglas fir
Incense cedar
Eucryphia 'Nymansay'
	Sweet bay
	Prunus serrulata erecta
	Certain cypress, e.g.
	  Chamaecyparis fletcheri
	Irish yew
	Prunus hillieri Spire
		Chamaecyparis elwoodii
		Picea albertiana conica
		*Crataegus monogyna
		  stricta*
		Viburnum fragrans
			Dwarf juniper
			Thuya 'Rheingold'
			Thuya plicata rogersii
			*Berberis thunbergii
			  erecta*

Weeping willow Weeping ash Weeping beech Swedish birch	Young's weeping birch Weeping pear *Buddleia alternifolia* Weeping cherry Weeping ash	*Cotoneaster multiflorus* *Cotoneaster hybridus pendulus* *Cotoneaster dielsianus* *Acer palmatum dissectum* *Escallonia langleyensis*	*Viburnum davidii* *Juniperus depressa aurea* Dwarf weeping cedar *Cotoneaster conspicuus*

Cedar of
  Lebanon } mature
Scots pine
Austrian pine
	Prunus serrulata
	Prunus 'Shiro-fugen'
	Cockspur thorn
	Dovaston yew
		*Viburnum tomentosum
		  mariesii*
		Acer palmatum dissectum
		Lonicera pileata
		Pyracantha angustifolia
			Cotoneaster horizontalis
			Cotoneaster microphyllus
			Cytisus kewensis
			Prostrate juniper
			Chaenomeles simonii

Maidenhair tree (*Gingko
  biloba*)
Scots pine (*Pinus
  sylvestris*)
Austrian pine (*Pinus nigra*)
Mock acacia
  (*Robinia pseudo-acacia*)
Liquidambar styraciflua
Tulip tree
  (*Liriodendron tulipifera*)
Monkey puzzle
  (*Araucaria araucana*)
	Magnolia soulangeana
	Parrotia persica
	Mt. Etna broom
	Strawberry tree
	Autumn cherry
	Japanese maples
	Prunus serrula tibetica
	Acer griseum
		Rhus typhina
		Cytisus battandieri
		*Clerodendron
		  trichotomum*
		Corylus avellana contorta
			Pernettya
			Miniature conifers
			Japanese azaleas
			Anchor plant
			  (*Colletia cruciata*)
			Teucrium fruticans

Successful lawn seed mix

	Percentage of total	Germination
Fine-textured grasses: Kentucky bluegrass	30.00%	75%
Red fescue	20.00%	80%
Coarse-textured grasses: Annual ryegrass	20.00%	90%
Ky 31 Tall fescue	24.00%	90%
Other ingredients: Inert matter	5.55%	
Other crop seeds	0.20%	
Weed seeds	0.25%	

Ground covers for sunny areas

Varieties	Deciduous or evergreen	Height (inches)	Comments
Crowberry *Empetrum nigrum*	E	6	Black berries in fall.
Crown vetch *Coronilla varia*	D	18	Pink flowers in summer. Fast-growing.
Ice plant *Mesembryanthemum* and other genera	E	8	Glistening foliage. Unbelievably brilliant colors. Outstanding on steep slopes.
Juniper, Chinese *Juniperus chinensis sargentii*	E	18	Very tough: dogs can't wear it down. Fairly upright.
Juniper, creeping *Juniperus horizontalis*	E	15	Prostrate. Very tough. Several fine varieties.
Juniper, shore *Juniperus coniferta*	E	12	Grows flat. Very tough.
Korean grass *Zoysia tenuifolia*	E	8	Velvety grass forming large ripples.
Lippia canescens	E	3	Blue-gray foliage. Lavender flowers.
Sandwort *Arenaria verna*	E	3	Resembles fine grass. Tiny white flowers.
Strawberry, Alexandria *Fragaria vesca*	Semi-E	6	Pretty little plants that do not spread; set close together. Delectable little fruits.
Thrift *Armeria maritima*	E	3	Dead ringer for grass. Pink flowers. Needs perfect drainage.

MAKE YOUR GARDEN NEW AGAIN by Stanley Schuler. Copyright © 1975 by Stanley Schuler.
Reprinted by permission of Simon & Schuster a division of Gulf & Western Corporation.

Common garden flowers:
blooming season and light requirements

Spring flowers		Summer flowers		Fall flowers	
Tall Varieties	**Light Needs**	**Tall Varieties**	**Light Needs**	**Tall Varieties**	**Light Needs**
Day Lily*	Full sun and partial shade	Clematis	Full sun or partial shade	Aconite	Full sun or partial shade
Gladiolus*	Full sun	Cosmos	Full sun or partial shade	Babies'-Breath	Full sun
Iris	Full sun			Clematis	Full sun or partial shade
Lupine	Full sun or partial shade	Dahlia	Full sun		
		Foxglove	Full sun or partial shade	Chrysanthemum	Full sun
Peony	Full sun or partial shade	Hollyhock	Full sun	Cosmos	Full sun or partial shade
Medium		Phlox	Full sun or partial shade	Dahlia	Full sun
Aster*	Full sun			Hollyhock	Full sun
Bleeding Heart	Full sun or partial shade	Snapdragon	Full sun	Larkspur	Full sun
Columbine	Full sun or partial shade	**Medium**		**Medium**	
		Bachelor's-Button	Full sun	Anemone	Partial shade
Daffodil	Full sun or partial shade	Chrysanthemum	Full sun	Canna	Full sun
		Coreopsis	Full sun	Chrysanthemum	Full sun
Day Lily*	Full sun and partial shade	Phlox	Full sun or partial shade	Dahlia	Full sun
Four-O'Clock*	Full sun			Daisy	Full sun
Poppy*	Full sun	Sage	Full sun or partial shade	Lily	Partial shade
Tulip	Full sun or partial shade	Zinnia	Full sun		

Spring flowers		Summer flowers		Fall flowers	
Short Varieties	Light Needs	Short Varieties	Light Needs	Short Varieties	Light Needs
Amaryllis	Partial shade	Ageratum	Full sun	Adonis	Full sun or partial shade
Columbine	Full sun or partial shade	Balsam, Garden	Full sun		
		Coleus	Full sun or partial shade	Allwood's Pink	Full sun
Crocus	Full sun or partial shade			Begonia	Partial shade
		Carnation	Full sun	Carnation	Full sun
Daisy*	Full sun or partial shade	Feverfew	Full sun or partial shade	Cockscomb	Full sun
				Colchicum	Full sun or partial shade
Forget-Me-Not*	Partial shade	Lobelia	Full sun		
Hyacinth	Full sun	Marigold	Full sun	Crocus	Full sun or partial shade
Iris	Full sun	Pansy	Full sun or partial shade		
Lily of the Valley*	Partial shade			Lily	Full sun
Pansy	Full sun or partial shade	Petunia	Full sun or partial shade	Petunia	Full sun or partial shade
Snowdrop	Partial shade	Portulaca	Full sun	Plumbago	Full sun or partial shade
Sweet William	Full sun	Sweet Alyssum	Full sun or partial shade	Sage	Full sun or partial shade
		Wallflower	Partial shade	Sweet Alyssum	Full sun or partial shade

*Blooms in all three seasons.

Exterior planting: vegetable gardens

Vegetable cultivation

Crop	Requirement for 100 feet of row			Distance apart		
	Seed	Plants	Depth for planting seed	Horse- or tractor-cultivated	Hand-cultivated	Plants in a row
			Inches	*Feet*		
Asparagus	1 ounce	75	1 –1½	4 –5	1½ to 2 feet 18 inches.	
Beans:						
Lima, bush	½ pound		1 –1½	2½–3	2 feet	3 to 4 inches.
Lima, pole	½ pound		1 –1½	3 –4	3 feet	3 to 4 feet.
Snap, bush	½ pound		1 –1½	2½–3	2 feet	3 to 4 inches.
Snap, pole	4 ounces		1 –1½	3 –4	2 feet	3 feet.
Beet	2 ounces		1	2 –2½	14 to 16 inches	2 to 3 inches.
Broccoli:						
Heading	1 packet	50– 75	½	2½–3	2 to 2½ feet	14 to 24 inches.
Sprouting	1 packet	50– 75	½	2½–3	2 to 2½ feet	14 to 24 inches.
Brussels sprouts	1 packet	50– 75	½	2½–3	2 to 2½ feet	14 to 24 inches.
Cabbage	1 packet	50– 75	½	2½–3	2 to 2½ feet	14 to 24 inches.
Cabbage, Chinese	1 packet		½	2 –2½	18 to 24 inches	8 to 12 inches.
Carrot	1 packet		½	2 –2½	14 to 16 inches	2 to 3 inches.
Cauliflower	1 packet	50– 75	½	2½–3	2 to 2½ feet	14 to 24 inches.

Crop	Requirement for 100 feet of row		Distance apart			
	Seed	Plants	Depth for planting seed	Horse- or tractor-cultivated	Hand-cultivated	Plants in a row
			Inches	*Feet*		
Celeriac	1 packet	200–250	⅛	2½–3	18 to 24 inches	4 to 6 inches.
Celery	1 packet	200–250	⅛	2½–3	18 to 24 inches	4 to 6 inches.
Chard	2 ounces		1	2 –2½	18 to 24 inches	6 inches.
Chervil	1 packet		½	2 –2½	14 to 16 inches	2 to 3 inches.
Chicory, witloof	1 packet		½	2 –2½	18 to 24 inches	6 to 8 inches.
Chives	1 packet		½	2½–3	14 to 16 inches	In clusters.
Collards	1 packet		½	3 –3½	18 to 24 inches	18 to 24 inches.
Cornsalad	1 packet		½	2½–3	14 to 16 inches	1 foot.
Corn, sweet	2 ounces		2	3 –3½	2 to 3 feet	Drills, 14 to 16 inches; hills, 2½ to 3 feet.
Cress, Upland	1 packet		⅛– ¼	2 –2½	14 to 16 inches	2 to 3 inches.
Cucumber	1 packet		½	6 –7	6 to 7 feet	Drills, 3 feet; hills, 6 feet.
Dasheen	5 to 6 pounds	– 50	2 –3	3½–4	3½ to 4 feet	2 feet.
Eggplant	1 packet	– 50	½	3	2 to 2½ feet	3 feet.
Endive	1 packet		½	2½–3	18 to 24 inches	12 inches.
Fennel, Florence	1 packet		½	2½–3	18 to 24 inches	4 to 6 inches.
Garlic	1 pound		1 –2	2½–3	14 to 16 inches	2 to 3 inches.
Horseradish	Cuttings	50– 75	2	3 –4	2 to 2½ feet	18 to 24 inches.
Kale	1 packet		½	2½–3	18 to 24 inches	12 to 15 inches.
Kohlrabi	1 packet		½	2½–3	14 to 16 inches	5 to 6 inches.
Leek	1 packet		½–1	2½–3	14 to 16 inches	2 to 3 inches.
Lettuce, head	1 packet	–100	½	2½–3	14 to 16 inches	12 to 15 inches.
Lettuce, leaf	1 packet		½	2½–3	14 to 16 inches	6 inches.
Muskmelon	1 packet		1	6 –7	6 to 7 feet	Hills, 6 feet.
Mustard	1 packet		½	2½–3	14 to 16 inches	12 inches.
Okra	2 ounces		1 –1½	3 –3½	3 to 3½ feet	2 feet.
Onion: Plants		–400	1 –2	2 –2½	14 to 16 inches	2 to 3 inches.
Seed	1 packet		½–1	2 –2½	14 to 16 inches	2 to 3 inches.
Sets	1 pound		1 –2	2 –2½	14 to 16 inches	2 to 3 inches.
Parsley	1 packet		⅛	2 –2½	14 to 16 inches	4 to 6 inches.

Crop	Requirement for 100 feet of row		Distance apart			
	Seed	Plants	Depth for planting seed	Horse- or tractor-cultivated	Hand-cultivated	Plants in a row
			Inches	*Feet*		
Parsley, turnip-rooted	1 packet		⅛– ¼	2 –2½	14 to 16 inches	2 to 3 inches.
Parsnip	1 packet		½	2 –2½	18 to 24 inches	2 to 3 inches.
Peas	½ pound		2 –3	2 –4	1½ to 3 feet	1 inch.
Pepper	1 packet	50– 70	½	3 –4	2 to 3 feet	18 to 24 inches.
Physalis	1 packet		½	2 –2½	1½ to 2 feet	12 to 18 inches.
Potato	5 to 6 pounds, tubers		4	2½–3	2 to 2½ feet	10 to 18 inches.
Pumpkin	1 ounce		1 –2	5 –8	5 to 8 feet	3 to 4 feet.
Radish	1 ounce		½	2 –2½	14 to 16 inches	1 inch.
Rhubarb		25– 35		3 –4	3 to 4 feet	3 to 4 feet.
Salsify	1 ounce		½	2 –2½	18 to 26 inches	2 to 3 inches.
Shallots	1 pound (cloves)		1 –2	2 –2½	12 to 18 inches	2 to 3 inches.
Sorrel	1 packet		½	2 –2½	18 to 24 inches	5 to 8 inches.
Soybean	½ to 1 pound		1 –1½	2½–3	24 to 30 inches	3 inches.
Spinach	1 ounce		½	2 –2½	14 to 16 inches	3 to 4 inches.
Spinach, New Zealand	1 ounce		1 –1½	3 –3½	3 feet	18 inches.
Squash: Bush	½ ounce		1 –2	4 –5	4 to 5 feet	Drills, 15 to 18 inches, hills, 4 feet.
Vine	1 ounce		1 –2	8 –12	8 to 12 feet	Drills, 2 to 3 feet; hills, 4 feet.
Sweetpotato	5 pounds, bedroots	– 75	2 –3	3 –3½	3 to 3½ feet	12 to 14 inches.
Tomato	1 packet	35– 50	– ½	3 –4	2 to 3 feet	1½ to 3 feet.
Turnip greens	1 packet		¼– ½	2 –2½	14 to 16 inches	2 to 3 inches.
Turnips and rutabagas	½ ounce		¼– ½	2 –2½	14 to 16 inches	2 to 3 inches.
Watermelon	1 ounce		1 –2	8 –10	8 to 10 feet	Drills, 2 to 3 feet; hills, 8 feet.

Average hard freeze dates by state: spring and fall

State	Last spring frost	First fall frost	State	Last spring frost	First fall frost
Alaska			**Arizona**		
Interior	June 15	Aug. 15	North	Apr. 23	Oct. 19
Coast	May 30	Sept. 30	South	Mar. 1	Dec. 1
Alabama			**Arkansas**		
North	Mar.25	Oct. 30	North	Apr. 7	Oct. 23
South	Mar. 8	Nov. 15	South	Mar. 25	Nov. 3

State	Last spring frost	First fall frost
California		
Central Valley	Mar. 1	Nov. 15
Imperial Valley	Jan. 30	Dec. 20
North Coast	Feb. 28	Dec. 1
South Coast	Jan. 30	Dec. 15
Mountain	Apr. 20	Sept. 1
Colorado		
West	May 30	Sept. 15
Northeast	May 10	Sept. 30
Southeast	Apr. 30	Oct. 10
Connecticut	Apr. 28	Oct. 10
Delaware	Apr. 15	Oct. 20
Florida		
North	Feb. 20	Nov. 30
Central	Jan. 30	Dec. 20
South	No Frost	
Hawaii	No Frost	
Georgia		
North	Mar. 30	Nov. 10
South	Mar. 10	Nov. 20
Idaho	May 30	Sept. 25
Illinois		
North	Apr. 30	Oct. 10
South	Apr. 10	Oct. 20
Indiana		
North	Apr. 30	Oct. 10
South	Apr. 20	Oct. 20
Iowa		
North	May 1	Oct. 1
South	Apr. 10	Oct. 10
Kansas		
Northwest	Apr. 30	Oct. 10
Southeast	Apr. 10	Oct. 20
Kentucky	Apr. 20	Oct. 20
Louisiana		
North	Mar. 20	Nov. 10
South	Feb. 8	Dec. 10
Maine		
North	May 30	Sept. 20
South	May 10	Oct. 10
Maryland	Apr. 20	Oct. 20
Massachusetts	Apr. 25	Oct. 25
Michigan		
Upper Peninsula	May 30	Sept. 20
North	May 20	Sept. 25
South	May 10	Oct. 10
Minnesota		
North	May 30	Sept. 10
South	May 10	Sept. 30
Mississippi		
North	Mar. 30	Oct. 30
South	Mar. 10	Nov. 10
Missouri	Apr. 20	Oct. 20
Montana	May 20	Sept. 20
Nebraska		
East	Apr. 30	Oct. 10
West	May 10	Sept. 30
Nevada		
North	May 30	Sept. 5
South	Apr. 15	Nov. 10
New Hampshire	May 20	Sept. 20
New Jersey	Apr. 20	Oct. 20
New Mexico		
North	Apr. 30	Oct. 10
South	Apr. 1	Oct. 30
New York		
East	May 1	Oct. 10
West	May 10	Oct. 5
North	May 20	Sept. 30
North Carolina		
Northeast	Apr. 10	Nov. 1
Southeast	Mar. 30	Nov. 30
North Dakota	May 20	Sept. 20
Ohio		
North	May 10	Sept. 20
South	Apr. 20	Sept. 30
Oklahoma	Apr. 1	Oct. 30
Oregon		
West	Apr. 20	Oct. 30
East	May 30	Sept. 10
Pennsylvania		
West	Apr. 20	Oct. 20
Central	May 20	Oct. 10
East	May 10	Sept. 30
Rhode Island	Apr. 20	Oct. 20
South Carolina		
Southeast	Mar. 10	Nov. 10
Northwest	Mar. 20	Nov. 20
South Dakota	May 10	Sept. 30
Tennessee	Apr. 10	Oct. 30
Texas		
Northwest	Apr. 20	Oct. 30
Northeast	Mar. 20	Nov. 20
South	Feb. 5	Dec. 10
Utah		
North	May 30	Sept. 30
South	Apr. 30	Oct. 10
Vermont	May 20	Sept. 30
Virginia		
North	Apr. 20	Oct. 10
South	Apr. 10	Oct. 20
Washington		
West	Apr. 20	Oct. 30
East	May 20	Sept. 30
West Virginia	May 5	Oct. 10
Wisconsin		
North	May 20	Sept. 20
South	May 10	Oct. 10
Wyoming		
West	June 20	Aug. 25
East	May 30	Sept. 30

Latest dates for setting out vegetables

Crop	Planting dates for localities in which average dates of first freeze is				
	Aug. 30	Sept. 10	Sept. 20	Sept. 30	Oct. 10
Asparagus*					Oct. 20–Nov. 15
Beans, lima				June 1–15	June 1–15
Beans, snap		May 15–June 15	June 1–July 1	June 1–July 10	June 15–July 20
Beet	May 15–June 15	May 15–June 15	June 1–July 1	June 1–July 10	June 15–July 25
Broccoli, sprouting	May 1–June 1	May 1–June 1	May 1–June 15	June 1–30	June 15–July 15
Brussels sprouts	May 1–June 1	May 1–June 1	May 1–June 15	June 1–30	June 15–July 15
Cabbage*	May 1–June 1	May 1–June 1	May 1–June 15	June 1–July 10	June 15–July 15
Cabbage, Chinese	May 15–June 15	May 15–June 15	June 1–July 1	June 1–July 15	June 15–Aug. 1
Carrot	May 15–June 15	May 15–June 15	June 1–July 1	June 1–July 10	June 1–July 20
Cauliflower*	May 1–June 1	May 1–July 1	May 1–July 1	May 10–July 15	June 1–July 25
Celery* and celeriac	May 1–June 1	May 15–June 15	May 15–July 1	June 1–July 5	June 1–July 15
Chard	May 15–June 15	May 15–July 1	June 1–July 1	June 1–July 5	June 1–July 20
Chervil and chives	May 10–June 10	May 1–June 10	May 15–June 15		
Chicory, witloof	May 15–June 15	May 15–June 15	May 15–June 15	June 1–July 1	June 1–July 1
Collards*	May 15–June 15	May 15–June 15	May 15–June 15	July 15–Sept. 1	July 1–Aug. 1
Cornsalad	May 15–June 15	May 15–July 1	June 15–Aug. 1	July 15–Sept. 1	Aug. 15–Sept. 15
Corn, sweet			June 1–July 1	June 1–July 1	June 1–July 10
Cress, upland	May 15–June 15	May 15–July 1	June 15–Aug. 1	July 15–Sept. 1	Aug. 15–Sept. 15
Cucumber			June 1–15	June 1–July 1	June 1–July 1
Eggplant*				May 20–June 10	May 15–June 15
Endive	June 1–July 1	June 1–July 1	June 1–July 15	June 15–Aug. 1	July 1–Aug. 15
Fennel, Florence	May 15–June 15	May 15–July 15	June 1–July 1	June 1–July 1	June 15–July 15
Garlic	(†)	(†)	(†)	(†)	(†)
Horseradish*	(†)	(†)	(†)	(†)	(†)
Kale	May 15–June 15	May 15–June 15	June 1–July 1	June 15–July 15	July 1–Aug. 1
Kohlrabi	May 15–June 15	June 1–July 1	June 1–July 15	June 15–July 15	July 1–Aug. 1
Leek	May 1–June 1	May 1–June 1	(†)	(†)	(†)
Lettuce, head*	May 15–July 1	May 15–July 1	June 1–July 15	June 15–Aug. 1	July 15–Aug. 15
Lettuce, leaf	May 15–July 15	May 15–July 15	June 1–Aug. 1	June 1–Aug. 1	July 15–Sept. 1
Muskmelon			May 1–June 15	May 15–June 1	June 1–June 15
Mustard	May 15–July 15	May 15–July 15	June 1–Aug. 1	June 15–Aug. 1	July 15–Aug. 15
Okra			June 1–20	June 1–July 1	June 1–July 15
Onion*	May 1–June 10	May 1–June 10	(†)	(†)	(†)
Onion, seed	May 1–June 1	May 1–June 10	(†)	(†)	(†)
Onion, sets	May 1–June 1	May 1–June 10	(†)	(†)	(†)
Parsley	May 15–June 15	May 15–June 15	June 1–July 1	June 15–July 15	June 1–Aug. 1
Parsnip	May 15–June 1	May 1–June 15	May 15–June 15	June 1–July 1	June 1–July 10
Peas, garden	May 10–June 15	May 1–July 1	June 1–July 15	June 1–Aug. 1	
Peas, black-eye					June 1–July 1
Pepper*			June 1–June 20	June 1–July 1	June 1–July 1
Potato	May 15–June 1	May 1–June 15	May 1–June 15	May 1–June 15	May 15–June 15
Radish	May 1–July 15	May 1–Aug. 1	July 1–Aug. 1	July 1–Sept. 1	July 15–Sept. 15
Rhubarb*	Sept. 1–Oct. 1	Sept. 15–Oct. 15	Sept. 15–Nov. 1	Oct. 1–Nov. 1	Oct. 15–Nov. 15
Rutabaga	May 15–June 15	May 1–June 15	June 1–July 1	June 1–July 1	June 15–July 15
Salsify	May 15–June 1	May 10–June 10	May 20–June 20	June 1–20	June 1–July 1
Shallot	(†)	(†)	(†)	(†)	(†)
Sorrel	May 15–June 15	May 1–June 15	June 1–July 1	June 1–July 15	July 1–Aug. 1
Soybean				May 25–June 10	June 1–25
Spinach	May 15–July 1	June 1–July 15	June 1–Aug. 1	July 1–Aug. 15	Aug. 1–Sept. 1
Spinach, New Zealand				May 15–July 1	June 1–July 15
Squash, summer	June 10–20	June 1–20	May 15–July 1	June 1–July 1	June 1–July 15
Squash, winter			May 20–June 10	June 1–15	June 1–July 1
Sweetpotato					May 20–June 10
Tomato	June 20–30	June 10–20	June 1–20	June 1–20	June 1–20
Turnip	May 15–June 15	June 1–July 1	June 1–July 15	June 1–Aug. 1	July 1–Aug. 1
Watermelon			May 1–June 15	May 15–June 1	June 1–June 15

*Plants.
†Generally spring-planted.

Planting dates for localities in which average date of first freeze is—

Oct. 20	Oct. 30	Nov. 10	Nov. 20	Nov. 30	Dec. 10	Dec. 20
Nov. 1–Dec. 15	Nov. 15–Jan. 1	Dec. 1–Jan. 1				
June 15–30	July 1–Aug. 1	July 1–Aug. 15	July 15–Sept. 1	Aug. 1–Sept. 15	Sept. 1–30	Sept. 1–Oct. 1.
July 1–Aug. 1.	July 1–Aug. 15	July 1–Sept. 1	July 1–Sept. 10	Aug. 15–Sept. 20	Sept. 1–30	Sept. 1–Nov. 1.
July 1–Aug. 5.	Aug. 1–Sept. 1	Aug. 1–Oct. 1	Sept. 1–Dec. 1	Sept. 1–Dec. 15	Sept. 1–Dec. 31	Sept. 1–Dec. 31.
July 1–Aug. 1.	July 1–Aug. 15	Aug. 1–Sept. 1	Aug. 1–Sept. 15	Aug. 1–Oct. 1	Aug. 1–Nov. 1	Sept. 1–Dec. 31.
July 1–Aug. 1.	July 1–Aug. 15	Aug. 1–Sept. 1	Aug. 1–Sept. 15	Aug. 1–Oct. 1	Aug. 1–Nov. 1	Sept. 1–Dec. 31.
July 1–20.	Aug. 1–Sept. 1	Sept. 1–15	Sept. 1–Dec. 1	Sept. 1–Dec. 31	Sept. 1–Dec. 31	Sept. 1–Dec. 31.
July 15–Aug. 15.	Aug. 1–Sept. 15	Aug. 15–Oct. 1	Sept. 1–Oct. 15	Sept. 1–Nov. 1	Sept. 1–Nov. 15	Sept. 1–Dec. 1.
June 15–Aug. 1.	July 1–Aug. 15	Aug. 1–Sept. 1	Sept. 1–Nov. 1	Sept. 15–Dec. 1	Sept. 15–Dec. 1	Sept. 15–Dec. 1.
July 1–Aug. 5.	July 15–Aug. 15	Aug. 1–Sept. 1	Aug. 1–Sept. 15	Aug. 15–Oct. 10	Sept. 1–Oct. 20	Sept. 15–Nov. 1.
June 1–Aug. 1.	June 15–Aug. 15	July 1–Aug. 15	July 15–Sept. 1	Aug. 1–Dec. 1	Sept. 1–Dec. 31	Oct. 1–Dec. 31.
June 1–Aug. 1.	June 1–Sept. 10	June 1–Sept. 15	June 1–Oct. 1	June 1–Nov. 1	June 1–Dec. 1	June 1–Dec. 31.
	(†)	(†)	Nov. 1–Dec. 31	Nov. 1–Dec. 31	Nov. 1–Dec. 31	Nov. 1–Dec. 31.
June 15–July 15.	July 1–Aug. 10	July 10–Aug. 20	July 20–Sept. 1	Aug. 15–Sept. 30	Aug. 15–Oct. 15	Aug. 15–Oct. 15.
July 15–Aug. 15.	Aug. 1–Sept. 15	Aug. 15–Oct. 1	Aug. 25–Nov. 1	Sept. 1–Dec. 1	Sept. 1–Dec. 31	Sept. 1–Dec. 31.
Sept. 1–Oct. 15.	Sept. 15–Nov. 1	Oct. 1–Dec. 1	Oct. 1–Dec. 1	Oct. 1–Dec. 31	Oct. 1–Dec. 31	Oct. 1–Dec. 31.
June 1–July 20.	June 1–Aug. 1	June 1–Aug. 15	June 1–Sept. 1			
Sept. 1–Oct. 15.	Sept. 15–Nov. 1	Oct. 1–Dec. 1	Oct. 1–Dec. 1	Oct. 1–Dec. 31	Oct. 1–Dec. 31	Oct. 1–Dec. 31.
June 1–July 15.	June 1–Aug. 1	June 1–Aug. 15	June 1–Aug. 15	July 15–Sept. 15	Aug. 15–Oct. 1	Aug. 15–Oct. 1.
June 1–July 1.	June 1–July 1	June 1–July 15	June 1–Aug. 1	July 1–Sept. 1	Aug. 1–Sept. 30	Aug. 1–Sept. 30.
July 15–Sept. 1.	July 15–Aug. 15	Aug. 1–Sept. 1	Sept. 1–Oct. 1	Sept. 1–Nov. 15	Sept. 1–Dec. 31	Sept. 1–Dec. 31.
June 15–Aug. 1.	July 1–Aug. 1	July 15–Aug. 15	Aug. 15–Sept. 15	Sept. 1–Nov. 15	Sept. 1–Dec. 1	Sept. 1–Dec. 1.
(†)	(†)	Aug. 1–Oct. 1	Aug. 15–Oct. 1	Sept. 1–Nov. 15	Sept. 15–Nov. 15	Sept. 15–Nov. 15.
(†)	(†)	(†)	(†)	(†)	(†)	(†)
July 15–Aug. 15.	July 15–Sept. 1	Aug. 1–Sept. 15	Aug. 15–Oct. 15	Sept. 1–Dec. 1	Sept. 1–Dec. 31	Sept. 1–Dec. 31.
July 15–Aug. 15.	Aug. 1–Sept. 1	Aug. 15–Sept. 15	Sept. 1–Oct. 15	Sept. 1–Dec. 1	Sept. 15–Dec. 31	Sept. 1–Dec. 31.
	(†)		Sept. 1–Nov. 1	Sept. 1–Nov. 1	Sept. 1–Nov. 1	Sept. 15–Nov. 1.
Aug. 1–30.	Aug. 1–Sept. 15	Aug. 15–Oct. 15	Sept. 1–Nov. 1	Sept. 1–Dec. 1	Sept. 15–Dec. 31	Sept. 15–Dec. 31.
July 15–Sept. 1.	Aug. 15–Oct. 1	Aug. 25–Oct. 1	Sept. 1–Nov. 1	Sept. 1–Dec. 1	Sept. 15–Dec. 31	Sept. 15–Dec. 31.
June 1–July 1.	June 1–July 10	June 1–July 20	June 15–Aug. 15	July 1–Sept. 1	July 15–Sept. 1	July 15–Sept. 1.
June 1–July 1.	June 10–July 10	June 20–July 20	July 1–Aug. 1	July 15–Aug. 15	Aug. 1–Sept. 1	Aug. 1–Sept. 1.
June 1–15.	June 1–15	June 1–July 1	June 1–July 1	June 1–July 1	June 1–July 1	June 1–July 1.
June 1–July 1.	June 1–July 1	June 1–July 1	June 1–July 1	Aug. 1–Sept. 1	Aug. 15–Oct. 1	Oct. 1–Nov. 1.
July 15–Aug. 15.	Aug. 1–Sept. 15	Sept. 1–Oct. 15	Sept. 1–Nov. 15	Sept. 1–Nov. 15	Oct. 1–Dec. 1	Oct. 1–Dec. 31.
June 15–July 20.	July 1–July 15	July 15–July 30				

Raising sprouts

Type	Rinses/day	Harvest sprout length (in.)	Sprout time (days)	Approximate yield	Comments
Alfalfa	2	1–2	3–5	3 T. = 4 c.	Easy to sprout. Pleasant, light taste.
Almonds	2–3	¼	3–5	1 c. = 1½ c.	Similar to unsprouted nuts. Crunchy, nutty flavor.
Amaranth	3	¼	2–3	3 T. = 1 c.	Mild taste. Sprouts smell like corn silk.
Anise	6	1	2	3 T. = 1 c.	A strong, anisey flavor. Good if used sparingly.
Barley	2–3	sprout is length of seed	3–4	½ c. = 1 c.	A chewy texture and pleasant taste. Not sweet. Toasting enhances flavor.
Beans (all kinds except those listed individually in chart)	3–4	1	3–5	1 c. = 4 c.	Taste like unsprouted beans. For tender sprouts, limit germination time to 3 days.
Buckwheat	1	¼–½	2–3	1 c. = 3 c.	Simple to sprout. Buy raw, hulled groats for sprouting.
Chia	1	¼–1	1–4	2 T. = 3–4 c.	Hard to sprout, because of their tendency to become gelatinous. Sprinkling rather than thorough rinsing can help prevent this problem. Their strong flavor adds zip to any dish.
Clover (red)	2	1–2	3–5	1½ T. = 4 c.	Similar to alfalfa sprouts.
Corn	2–3	½	2–3	1 c. = 2 c.	Sweet corn taste, with chewy texture. Difficult to find untreated kernels for sprouting.
Cress	2	1–1½	3–5	1 T. = 1½ c.	A gelatinous seed. A strong, peppery taste.
Fenugreek	1–2	1–3	3–5	¼ c. = 1 c.	Spicy taste, good in curry dishes. Bitter if sprouted too long.
Flax	2–3	1–2, greened	4	2 T. = 1½–2 c.	Tend to become gelatinous when wet. Sprinkle rather than rinse. Sprouts have a mild flavor.
Garbanzos	4	½	3	1 c. = 3 c.	A raw bean flavor. Best lightly cooked.
Lentils	2–4	¼–1	3	1 c. = 6 c.	Chewy bean texture. Can be eaten raw or steamed lightly.
Millet	2–3	¼	3–4	1 c. = 2 c.	Similar to barley sprouts.
Mung beans	3–4	1½–2	3–5	1 c. = 4–5 c.	Easy to sprout. Popular in oriental dishes. Sprouts begin to lose their crispness after 4 days of storage.
Mustard	2	1–1½	3–4	2 T. = 3 c.	Spicy, tangy taste, not unlike fresh English mustard.
Oats	1	lead sprout is length of seed	3–4	1 c. = 2 c.	Only unhulled oats will sprout. Water sparingly; too much water makes sprouts sour.
Peas	2–3	sprout is length of seed	3	1½ c. = 2 c.	Taste like fresh peas. Best when steamed lightly.
Pumpkin	2–3	¼	3	1 c. = 2 c.	Hulled seeds make best sprouts. Light toasting improves flavor.
Radish	2	⅛–2	2–6	1 T. = 1 c.	Sprouts taste just like the vegetable.
Rice	2–3	sprout is length of seed	3–4	1 c. = 2½ c.	Similar to other sprouted grains. Only whole-grain brown rice will sprout.
Rye	2–3	sprout is length of seed	3–4	1 c. = 3½ c.	Easy to sprout. Very sweet taste, with crunchy texture.
Sesame	4	sprout is length of seed	3	1 c. = 1½ c.	Only unhulled seeds will sprout. Delicious flavor when young; sprouts over 1/16" turn bitter.

Type	Rinses/ day	Harvest sprout length (in.)	Sprout time (days)	Approximate yield	Comments
Soybeans	4–6	1–2	4–6	1 c. = 4–5 c.	Difficult to sprout because they ferment easily. Need frequent, thorough rinses. Should be cooked before eating for optimum protein availability.
Sunflower	2	sprout no longer than seed	1–3	½ c. = 1½ c.	Good snacks, especially if lightly roasted. Become bitter if grown too long.
Triticale	2–3	sprout is length of seed	2–3	1 c. = 2 c.	Similar to wheat sprouts.
Vegetable seeds	2	1–2	3–5	1 T. = 1–2 c.	Usually easy to sprout. Best eaten raw.
Wheat	2–3	sprout is length of seed	2–4	1 c. = 3½–4 c.	Simple to sprout. Very sweet taste.

Adapted from HOME FOOD SYSTEMS © 1981 by Rodale Press, Inc. Permission granted by Rodale Press, Inc., Emmaus, PA 18049

Pot gardening: vegetables
Equipment

Tools. Hose or watering can; trowel, gardening fork, or hand cultivator; artists' brush.
Materials. Containers, soil or potting mix, seeds, seedlings, or plants, fertilizer, water.

Instructions

Beans. Plant bush beans in a large pot or box. Plant pole beans to grow onto a balcony railing.

Cabbage. Small, early varieties are best. Grow single cabbages in 8-inch pots.

Corn. Small varieties grow successfully in washtubs.

Cucumbers. Cucumbers can be grown as hanging plants or trained to grow upwards from a pot, tub, or tire planter. Choose a bush or small-space variety.

Lettuce. Lettuce needs lower temperatures and does well in partial shade; it performs well in any container. Grow leaf lettuce or butterhead lettuce as single plants in 4-inch pots.

Green onions. Plant onion sets in any container; you can plan on harvesting 8 to 10 green onions from an 8-inch flower pot.

Green peppers. Grow individual plants in any large pot or container—1 cubic foot of soil is adequate.

Root crops. Beets, carrots, and turnips can be grown in any container at least 8 to 10 inches deep; radishes can be grown in 4 inches of soil. Be sure to keep the soil moist. Choose the shorter, more compact varieties of root crops.

Squash. Bush-type summer squash, such as zucchini and pattypan, grows well in washtubs, tire planters, or any medium or large container. Vining-type winter squashes can be trained to grow along a railing, but you may have to make slings to support the vegetables.

Tomatoes. Dwarf tomatoes can be grown in 1 cubic foot of soil; standard tomatoes need 2 to 3 cubic feet of soil. Small-fruited tomatoes do well in hanging baskets or staked along with other vegetables in a planter. Plant tomatoes where they will get full sun.

Strawberries. Strawberries in containers do not fruit as heavily as ground-planted ones, but you will still harvest a few. Plant them in strawberry jars, large planters, or hanging baskets.

Herbs. Most herbs do excellently in containers of any size. Some herbs, such as mint, should be contained to keep them from growing rampant.

Note. If your garden is up too high, you may not have any insects, and you will have to pollinate by hand. Use a clean, fat artists' brush to transfer pollen from blossom to blossom; consult a gardening manual for precise instructions.

DO IT YOURSELF AND SAVE MONEY by the Editors of CONSUMER GUIDE®, published by Harper & Row, New York.

Lawn and garden care

Making compost

Compost can easily be made using two bins. Fill one with alternating layers of organic material 6 to 12 inches thick and garden soil 1 inch thick. Then add chemicals to each layer at the following rates:

Chemical	Rate in cups per bushel of organic material*	Chemical	Rate in cups per bushel of organic material*
Method 1		**Method 2**	
Ammonium sulfate	1	Mixed fertilizer 5-10-5.	3
or		Ground dolomitic limestone†	⅔
Ammonium nitrate	½		
Ground dolomitic limestone†	⅔		
or			
Wood ashes†	1½		
Superphosphate	½		
Magnesium sulfate (epsom salts)**	¹⁄₁₆ (1 tbs)		

*Packed tightly by hand.
†For acid compost (for azaleas and rhododendrons) omit lime, limestone, and wood ashes.
**Add epsom salts only if dolomitic limestone is unavailable and ordinary limestone is used (at the same rate).

Calculating fertilizer needs

Measurement	Weight of fertilizer to apply when the weight to be applied per acre is			
	100 pounds	400 pounds	800 pounds	1,200 pounds
Space between rows, and row length (feet)				
2 wide, 50 long	0.25	1.0	2.0	3.0
2 wide, 100 long	.50	2.0	4.0	6.0
2½ wide, 50 long	.30	1.2	2.4	3.6
2½ wide, 100 long	.60	2.4	4.8	7.2
3 wide, 50 long	.35	1.4	2.8	4.2
3 wide, 100 long	.70	2.8	5.6	8.4
Area (square feet):				
100	.25	1.0	2.0	3.0
500	1.25	5.0	10.0	15.0
1,000	2.50	10.0	20.0	30.0
1,500	3.75	15.0	30.0	45.0
2,000	5.00	20.0	40.0	60.0

Pesticides: how to use them

Types of formulations

Active ingredients are the chemicals that do the work. *Inert ingredients* make the product easier to apply. Active ingredients + inert ingredients = pesticide formulation. Listed below are the most common kinds of formulations.

Dry formulations

Dusts. Dust formulations are made by adding the active ingredient to fine inert powder. Dusts must be used dry.

Granules. Granular formulations are made by adding the active ingredient to coarse particles (granules) of some inert material. Granular particles are much larger than dust particles.

Wettable powders. Wettable powder formulations are made by combining the active ingredient with a fine powder and a wetting agent. They look like dusts, but they are made to mix with water. These formulations need continuous agitation to maintain a suspension.

Soluble powders. A soluble powder formulation is made from an active ingredient that dissolves in water.

Liquid formulations

Emulsifiable concentrates. An emulsifiable concentrate can be mixed with water to form an emulsion in your spray tank.

Flowables. A flowable can be mixed with water to form a suspension in your spray tank.

Aerosols. These are low concentrate solutions, usually applied as a fine spray or mist indoors. Some are sold in pressurized cans.

131

Ultra low volume solutions. These formulations may contain only the active ingredient itself. They require special application equipment.

Solutions. These formulations are ready to use. They are often used on livestock and in barns.

Liquefied gases. These fumigant formulations turn into a gas when they are applied. Some of them have to be packaged in pressure containers.

Baits. A bait formulation is made by adding the active ingredient to an edible or attractive substance.

When to use

Preemergence. These are used before crops or weeds emerge. May also refer to use after crops emerge or are established, but before weeds emerge.

Preplant. Preplants are used before the crop is planted.

Postemergence. These are used after the crop or weeds have emerged.

How to use

Band. Application to a strip over or along each crop row.

Broadcast. Uniform application to an entire, specific area.

Dip. Complete or partial immersion of a plant, animal, or object in a pesticide.

Directed. Aiming the pesticide at a portion of plant, animal, or structure.

Drench. Saturating the soil with a pesticide; oral treatment of an animal with a liquid pesticide.

Foliar. Application to the leaves of plants.

In-furrow. Application to or in the furrow in which a plant is planted.

Over-the-top. Application over the top of the growing crop.

Pour-in. Pouring the pesticide along the midline of the back of livestock.

Sidedress. Application along the side of a crop row.

Soil incorporation. Application to the soil followed by use of tillage implements to mix the pesticide with the soil.

Spot treatment. Application to a small area.

Pesticides: safety checklist

☑ Pesticides used improperly can be injurious to humans, animals, and plants. Follow the directions and heed all precautions on the labels.

☐ Store pesticides in original containers under lock and key—out of the reach of children and animals—and away from food and feed.

☐ Apply pesticides so that they do not endanger humans, livestock, crops, beneficial insects, fish, and wildlife. Do not apply pesticides when there is danger of drift, when honeybees or other pollinating insects are visiting plants, or in ways that may contaminate water or leave illegal residues.

☐ Avoid prolonged inhalation of pesticide sprays or dusts; wear protective clothing and equipment if specified on the container.

☐ If your hands become contaminated with a pesticide, do not eat or drink until you have washed. In case a pesticide is swallowed or gets in the eyes, follow the first-aid treatment given on the label and get prompt medical attention. If a pesticide is spilled on your skin or clothing, remove clothing immediately and wash skin thoroughly.

☐ Do not clean spray equipment or dump excess spray material near ponds, streams, or wells. Because it is difficult to remove all traces of herbicides from equipment, do not use the same equipment for insecticides or fungicides that you use for herbicides.

☐ Dispose of empty pesticide containers promptly. Have them buried at a sanitary land-fill dump or crush and bury them in a level, isolated place.

☐ NOTE: Some states have restrictions on the use of certain pesticides. Check your state and local regulations. Also, because registrations of pesticides are under constant review by the Federal Environmental Protection Agency, consult your county agricultural agent or state extension specialist to be sure the intended use is still registered.

Spray equipment chart

Type of equipment	Description	Advantages	Disadvantages
Low-volume, compressed air sprayer	Hand-operated, capacity 2 to 5 gallons, adjustable nozzle	Inexpensive, variety of uses	Small capacity, limited to trees 20 feet tall
Hydraulic "knapsack" sprayer	Hand-operated, capacity 4 to 6 gallons, pump pressure up to 150 pounds per square inch	Inexpensive, variety of uses	Small capacity, limited to trees 25 to 30 feet tall
Garden-hose-powered siphon sprayer	Nozzle and siphon attached to jar, uses domestic water supply, capacity 4 to 6 gallons (concentrated mix)	Inexpensive, easy to operate, variety of uses	Small capacity, limited by water outlets, range limited by water pressure
Power hydraulic sprayers, suburban type	Gas- or electric-powered, capacity 12 to 15 gallons, pump pressures 20 to 150 pounds per square inch	Suitable for larger trees, large tank capacity	Expensive (rental possible)

6 Miscellany

The final section of TABLES AND FORMULAS contains critically important and useful information applicable in many different situations. The
subjects covered range from factors to consider in choosing a college
or university to a listing of the federal agencies that provide aid to
consumers.

Federal student aid is offered in various forms. It takes some study and
expertise to apply for such aid successfully. The tables that appear in
Section 6 offer guidance, indicating who can qualify for such aid, what
programs exist, and the records necessary for successful application.

Travel and transportation occupy the next subsection. Safe driving has
its do's and don't's, as does safe cycling. Each is covered in a separate
table. Other travel information ranges from data on U.S. national parks
and recreation facilities to international travel tips and checklists. For the
world traveler, a chart detailing key vaccinations is included.

The final area examined by TABLES AND FORMULAS is government
services, agencies, and regulations. The reader will find the various regulations pertaining to each of the 50 states' small claims courts fascinating
and possibly useful. Also offered is the timetable by which veteran's benefits are distributed. U.S. postal rates are summarized as well as various
services offered by the post office. And finally, a table listing all federal
agencies from which consumers can request aid and information is included.

Education

Choosing a college or university: a checklist

☑ **Administration.** How accessible is the school administration to the student body? Do students have a voice in administrative decision-making? Is
there a forum for students in which to air their gripes? How does the administration define *in loco parentis*? What types of restrictions does it place on student
activities?

☐ **Admissions.** On what bases are admissions decisions made? What factors
does the admissions office consider to be most important? Is there an attempt to admit a diverse student body in age, interests, race, culture, religion,
and geographic background?

☐ **Counseling and guidance.** What kind of counseling facilities are available to students? How accessible are the facilities and people who provide academic and psychological counseling? Is peer counseling available? What types of programs are available to ease the transition newcomers must make? Is counseling available on future educational alternatives?

☐ **Curriculum.** What types of academic requirements does the institution have? Are all students required to take certain "core" courses or to take courses in a variety of areas? What types of offerings are available to students who must meet these requirements? What requirements are there for specific majors? Do students have the opportunity to take a variety of courses? Is it difficult to arrange tutorials, part-time study, visiting semesters, auditing, external degree programs, field work, and other independent courses of study?

☐ **Environment.** What types of educational, social, cultural and athletic opportunities are available to the students? Do large numbers of students leave campus on weekends? What type of relationship does the institution have with the surrounding community? Is it accessible to other educational or cultural institutions?

☐ **Faculty.** Are faculty members available outside the class? Do they hold frequent office hours? Are they willing to meet informally with students or only to talk about specific problems? Do students have access to well-known scholars? What size are most classes? How are faculty members and courses evaluated? Is the emphasis on publishing and academic research and/or teaching? Do students have any input in the evaluation process?

☐ **Finances.** What is the institution's current and expected financial position? How is it dealing with inflationary pressures? If there are cutbacks, who feels the brunt of these? How accountable is the institution? What types of financial aid are available? Does the institution help students take advantage of different programs?

☐ **Food service.** What choices does the food service offer in hours, menus, alternative meal plans and dietary options? Is there a clear emphasis on good nutrition?

☐ **Housing.** What types of housing options are available both on- and off-campus? What type of rooming situation could a first-year student expect to have? How does this change in later years? Are dormitories coeducational or single-sex? Are there alternative options? How are roommates selected? Are the housing facilities and other buildings well maintained?

☐ **Jobs.** What types of counseling and placement facilities are there to help students find employment both in school and after graduation? Are there programs to arrange internships and volunteer employment?

College and university information

Listed below are samplings of organizations and free or inexpensive publications, which should be of interest and help to the family or individual seeking information on colleges or universities.

- College Board Publication Orders, Dept. C-12,
  Box 2815, Princeton, New Jersey 08540
- "Don't Miss Out." Octameron Associates,
  P.O. Box 3437, Alexandria, Virginia 22302
  ($1.25)
- "Meeting College Costs." College Board.
  Free from high school counselors, updated annually.
- "Need a Lift?" American Legion,
  P.O. Box 1055, Indianapolis, Indiana 46206
  (50¢)
- "Selected List of Postsecondary Education Opportunities for Minorities and Women."
  Carol Smith, Department of Health, Education, and Welfare, Office of Education, Regional Office Building 3, Room 4082,
  Washington, D.C. 20202
  (Free)
- "Student Guide." Public Documents Distribution Center, DEA—84,
  Pueblo, Colorado 81009
  (Free)

From SYLVIA PORTER'S NEW MONEY BOOK FOR THE 80'S by Sylvia Porter. Copyright © 1975, 1979 by Sylvia Porter. Reprinted by permission of Doubleday & Company, Inc.

Federal student aid: five programs

Pell Grants
Pell Grants are awarded to students who need money to pay for their education or training after high school. A Pell Grant is not a loan, so you don't have to pay it back. To get a Pell Grant, you must be an *undergraduate* who does not already have a Bachelor's degree. You must also go to school at least half-time.

Supplemental Educational Opportunity Grants (SEOG)
SEOG's are also grants; you don't have to pay them back. To get an SEOG, you must be an *undergraduate* who does not already have a Bachelor's degree. Usually you must be going to school at least half-time. However, some schools award SEOG's to a few students who are less than half-time.

College Work-Study (CW-S)
CW-S jobs let you earn money to put toward your school expenses. These jobs are for both *undergraduate* and *graduate* students. Usually you must be going to school at least half-time. However, some schools award a few CW-S jobs to students who are less than half-time.

National Direct Student Loans (NDSL)
NDSL's are low interest loans made through your school's financial aid office. You must repay this money. These loans are for both *undergraduate* and *graduate* students who are going to school at least half-time.

Guaranteed Student Loans (GSL)
GSL's are low interest loans made to you by a lender such as a bank, credit union, or savings and loan association. You must repay this money. These loans are for both *undergraduate* and *graduate* students who are going to school at least half-time.

Federal student aid: qualifications

To receive financial aid from government programs you must:
- be a U.S. citizen or an eligible noncitizen
- be registered for the draft with Selective Service if you are a man who is at least 18 years old and born after December 31, 1959 and who is not a current member of the active armed forces
- have financial need; the U.S. Department of Education and your school will use the information you put on this form to determine your need.
- attend a school that takes part in one or more of the programs
- be enrolled at least half-time (except for CW-S and SEOG)
- be working toward a degree or certificate (except for GSL)
- be making satisfactory academic progress (as defined by your school)

Federal student aid: required records

Get together these records for yourself and your family:
- U.S. income tax return (IRS Form 1040, 1040A, or 1040EZ) for previous year
- State and local income tax returns for previous year
- W-2 Forms and other records of money earned in previous year
- Records of nontaxable income, such as welfare, social security, AFDC or ADC, or veterans benefits
- Current bank statements
- Current mortgage information
- Records of medical or dental bills that were paid in previous year
- Business and farm records
- Records of stocks, bonds, and other investments

Travel

Safe driving: do's and don't's

Do's

Fasten your safety belt snugly before starting the engine.

Drive defensively—always think ahead.

Obey all traffic regulations.

Drive at a safe speed.

Reduce speed at night, in bad weather, in heavy traffic.

Yield the road to emergency vehicles that flash a light or sound a siren. Pull to the right and stop.

Drive in the passing lane only when passing.

Allow vehicles behind you to pass when drivers indicate they want to do so, and if passing conditions are favorable.

Signal by hand or light your intention to slow down, stop, turn, pass, or change lanes.

At intersections yield right of way. . .
1. to pedestrians;
2. to drivers ahead of you;
3. to the driver on the right if you both arrive at an intersection at the same time;
4. to through traffic, if you are turning left.

Don't's

Never pass a car unless you have plenty of open road ahead. Come back into line only after the car you have passed is visible in your rear-view mirror.

Never pass a stopped bus without taking special precautions. A passenger may step into your path from in front of the bus.

Never park with any part of your car in a driving lane.

Never coast with gears in neutral.

Never weave from lane to lane in traffic.

Never drive past a **STOP** sign without stopping, even though there is no traffic and even though the car ahead of you has halted and moved on.

Never pull into traffic until your car's engine is running smoothly.

Never park a car facing traffic. It confuses other drivers, especially at night and is illegal in most places.

Never drive with your bright lights on when other cars are approaching or when following another car.

Bicycle safety rules: do's and don't's

Do's

Use hand signals

Walk across busy intersections

Obey traffic signs

Keep to the right

In groups or pairs, ride in single file

Don't's

Don't ride double

Don't stunt

Don't hitch rides

National recreation areas

Name	Area		Location	Outstanding features
	In acres	In hectares		
Amistad	62,452	25,273	Texas	U.S. part of Amistad Reservoir on Rio Grand
Bighorn Canyon	120,280	48,676	Montana, Wyoming	Reservoir created by Yellowtail Dam
Chattahoochee River	8,515	3,446	Georgia	Sites along a 48-mile (77-kilometer) stretch of the river
Chickasaw	9,500	3,845	Oklahoma	Cold mineral springs; Lake of the Arbuckles
Coolee Dam	100,059	40,492	Washington	Franklin D. Roosevelt Lake, formed by Grand Coulee Dam
Curecanti	42,114	17,043	Colorado	Blue Mesa and Morrow Point reservoirs
Cuyahoga Valley	32,460	13,136	Ohio	About 20 miles (30 kilometers) of Cuyahoga River from Akron, Ohio to Cleveland, Ohio
Delaware Water Gap	71,000	28,733	New Jersey, Pennsylvania	Scenery along Delaware River
Gateway	26,172	10,591	New Jersey, New York	Park in urban harbor area
Glen Canyon	1,236,880	500,548	Arizona, Utah	Lake Powell, formed by Glen Canyon Dam
Golden Gate	38,677	15,652	California	Urban recreational park

Name	Area In acres	In hectares	Location	Outstanding features
Lake Chelan	61,890	25,046	Washington	Snow-fed Lake Chelan in forested valley
Lake Mead	1,496,601	605,653	Arizona, Nevada	Lake Mead, formed by Hoover Dam; Lake Mohave, formed by Davis Dam
Lake Meredith	44,994	18,208	Texas	Lake Meredith on Canadian River
Ross Lake	117,574	47,581	Washington	Lakes and forested valleys among snow-capped peaks
Santa Monica Mountains	150,000	60,703	California	Beaches, uplands and highlands
Whiskeytown-Shasta-Trinity	42,497	17,198	California	Whiskeytown Reservoir, formed by Whiskeytown Dam

U.S. national park system

Name	Number	Area In acres	In hectares
Types of areas			
National battlefield parks	3	6,685	2,705
National battlefield sites	1	1	0.4
National battlefields	10	10,571	4,278
National Capital Park	1	6,468	2,618
National cemeteries		1,616	654
National historic sites	63	17,410	7,046
National historical parks	26	144,716	58,564
National lakeshores	4	196,894	79,680
National Mall	1	146	59
National memorials	22	8,234	3,332
National military parks	10	34,490	13,958
National monuments	78	4,598,729	1,861,039
National parks	48	46,111,881	18,660,814
National parkways	4	161,623	65,407
National preserves	12	19,643,550	7,949,462
National recreation areas	17	3,661,671	1,481,826
National scenic riverways	10	524,254	212,158
National scenic trail	1	52,034	21,057
National seashores	10	598,089	242,038
National Visitor Center	1	18	7
Parks (other)	10	32,026	12,960
White House	1	18	7
Total	333	75,811,124	30,679,670

U.S. national parks

Name	Area In acres	In hectares	Location	Outstanding features
Acadia	38,632	15,634	Maine	Highest land on Atlantic Coast of the United States; rugged coastline
Arches	73,379	29,695	Utah	Giant rock arches, windows, and towers formed by erosion
Badlands	243,302	98,461	South Dakota	Rugged ravines, ridges, and cliffs; prehistoric animal fossils
Big Bend	708,118	286,565	Texas	Chisos Mountains and Desert in big bend of Rio Grande

Name	Area		Location	Outstanding features
	In acres	In hectares		
Bryce Canyon	35,835	14,502	Utah	Oddly shaped, beautifully colored rock formations in horseshoe-shaped basins
Canyonlands	337,570	136,610	Utah	Canyons, mesas, and sandstone spires; 1,000-year-old Indian rock carvings
Capital Reef	241,904	97,895	Utah	Colorful ridge 60 miles (97 kilometers) long with white dome-shaped rock
Carlsbad Caverns	46,755	18,921	New Mexico	Huge underground caves with strange rock formations
Channel Islands	124,740	50,480	California	Large sea lion breeding place; nesting sea birds; animal fossils
Crater Lake	160,290	64,867	Oregon	Lake in dead volcano; colorful lava walls almost 2,000 feet (610 meters) high
Everglades	1,398,800	566,074	Florida	Subtropical wilderness with plentiful wildlife
Glacier	1,013,595	410,187	Montana	Many glaciers and lakes among towering Rocky Mountain peaks
Grand Canyon	1,218,375	493,059	Arizona	Canyon 1 mile (1.6 kilometers) deep with brightly colored walls and rock shapes
Grand Teton	310,516	125,661	Wyoming	Rugged Teton peaks; winter feeding ground of large elk herd
Great Smoky Mountains	517,379	209,376	North Carolina, Tennessee	High Mountains; large hardwood and evergreen forests
Guadalupe Mountains	76,293	30,875	Texas	Fossil limestone reef; evergreen forest overlooking desert
Haleakala	28,655	11,596	Hawaii	Inactive volcano with large, colorful crater
Hawaii Volcanoes	229,177	92,745	Hawaii	Two active volcanoes; rare plants and animals
Hot Springs	5,826	2,358	Arkansas	Mineral springs at base of Hot Springs Mountain
Isle Royale	571,796	231,398	Michigan	Island wilderness with large moose herd and wolves
Kings Canyon	460,136	186,210	California	Mountain wilderness of giant sequoia trees
Lassen Volcanic	106,372	43,047	California	Dormant volcano; steep domes of lava
Mammoth Cave	52,452	21,227	Kentucky	Huge cave with 212 miles (341 kilometers) of corridors; underground lakes, rivers, and waterfalls
Mesa Verde	52,085	21,078	Colorado	Prehistoric Indian cliff dwellings
Mount McKinley	1,939,493	784,885	Alaska	Highest mountain in North America; wildlife
Mount Rainier	235,404	95,265	Washington	Greatest single-peak glacier system in United States
North Cascades	504,781	204,278	Washington	Mountain wilderness with glaciers, lakes, waterfalls, and jagged peaks
Olympic	908,781	367,771	Washington	Oceanside mountain wilderness with rain forest and elk
Petrified Forest	93,493	37,835	Arizona	Ancient, rock-hard wood; Indian ruins; Painted Desert
Redwood	109,027	44,122	California	World's tallest known tree in coastal redwood forest
Rocky Mountain	263,809	106,760	Colorado	More than 100 peaks over 11,000 feet (3,350 meters) high
Sequoia	403,023	163,098	California	Giant sequoia trees; Mount Whitney
Shenandoah	194,825	78,843	Virginia	Blue Ridge Mountains; hardwood forest; Skyline Drive
Theodore Roosevelt	70,416	28,496	North Dakota	Badlands along Little Missouri River and part of President Theodore Roosevelt's ranch
Virgin Islands	14,697	5,948	Virgin Islands	White beaches; tropical plants and animals
Voyageurs	219,128	88,678	Minnesota	Beautiful northern forests of aspen, birch, pine, and spruce; more than 50 lakes
Wind Cave	28,292	11,449	South Dakota	Limestone caverns; prairie wildlife

Name	Area In acres	In hectares	Location	Outstanding features
Wrangell-St. Elias	8,147,000	3,296,974	Alaska	Country's largest collection of glaciers and peaks over 16,000 feet (4,977 meters)
Yellowstone	2,219,823	898,330	Idaho, Montana Wyoming	World's greatest geyser area; canyons and waterfalls; wide variety of wildlife
Yosemite	760,917	307,932	California	Mountain scenery with deep gorges and high waterfalls
Zion	146,551	59,307	Utah	Colorful canyons and mesas

International travel: clothing sizes
Men

Suits, Sweaters and Overcoats

American and British		34	36	38	40	42	44	46	48
European:		44	46	48	50	52	54	56	58

Shirts

American and British:		14	14½	15	15½	16	16½	17	17½
European		36	37	38	39	40	41	42	43

Socks

American and British			9½	10	10½	11	11½	12	12½
European			39	40	41	42	43	44	45

Shoes

American	7	7½	8	8½	9	9½	10	10½	11	11½
British	6½	7	7½	8	8½	9	9½	10	10½	11
European	39	40	41	42	43	43	44	44	45	45

Men's hats

American	6⅝	6¾	6⅞	7	7⅛	7¼	7⅜	7½	7⅝
British	6½	6⅝	6¾	6⅞	7	7⅛	7¼	7⅜	7½
European	53	54	55	56	57	58	59	60	61

Women

Dresses, suits and coats

American		8	10	12	14	16	18
British		30	32	34	36	38	40
European		36	38	40	42	44	46

Blouses and sweaters

American	32	34	36	38	40	42	44
British	34	36	38	40	42	44	46
European	40	42	44	46	48	50	52

Dresses and coats (Children's and junior misses)

American	2	4	6	8	10	13	15
British & European	1	2	5	7	9	10	12

Stockings

American and British	8	8½	9	9½	10	10½	11
European	35	36	37	38	39	40	41

Shoes

American	5	5½	6	6½	7	7½	8	8½	9
British	3½	4	4½	5	5½	6	6½	7	7½
European	35	35	36	37	38	38	38½	39	40

International travel: temperatures*

	Dec.	Jan.	Feb.	Mar.	Apr.	May	June	July	Aug.	Sept.	Oct.	Nov.
Africa												
Addis Ababa, Ethiopia	60	62	63	65	66	65	62	60	60	61	61	60
Canary Islands	66	64	64	65	66	67	70	72	74	74	73	70
Cape Town, South Africa	68	70	70	69	63	59	56	55	56	58	62	65
Leopoldville, Congo	77	77	79	79	79	77	73	70	73	77	79	77
Caribbean												
Antigua	77	76	76	77	78	79	80	80	81	81	80	79
Bahamas	74	72	72	73	75	78	81	82	82	82	80	76
Barbados	78	77	76	77	78	80	81	80	80	80	80	79
Bermuda	65	63	63	63	65	70	75	79	80	78	74	69
Dominican Republic	76	75	76	76	77	79	80	80	81	80	79	78
Haiti	77	76	77	78	79	80	82	82	82	81	80	78
Jamaica	78	77	77	77	79	80	82	82	82	81	81	79
Netherlands Antilles	82	79	80	80	81	83	83	83	83	84	83	82
Puerto Rico	76	75	75	75	77	79	80	80	81	81	80	79
Trinidad and Tobago	79	78	78	79	80	81	80	80	80	80	80	80
Virgin Islands	77	77	77	77	78	80	81	82	82	81	81	79
Central America												
Guatemala City, Guatemala	61	61	63	66	66	68	66	66	66	66	65	63
Mexico City, Mexico	54	54	57	62	65	67	66	64	64	63	60	58
Panama City, Panama	79	79	80	81	82	80	78	80	80	79	78	78
San Jose, Costa Rica	67	67	68	69	71	71	71	69	70	70	69	68
San Salvador, El Salvador	73	73	75	76	77	76	76	76	76	75	75	73
Europe												
Amsterdam, Netherlands	38	36	37	41	47	54	60	62	62	57	50	42
Athens, Greece	52	48	49	53	60	69	76	81	81	75	67	58
Belgrade, Yugoslavia	35	33	35	46	54	63	68	72	72	66	54	43
Brussels, Belgium	38	35	38	42	49	55	61	64	64	60	50	43
Copenhagen, Denmark	36	32	32	35	42	51	59	62	61	56	48	40
Dublin, Ireland	41	41	41	42	45	50	56	59	58	54	48	44
Frankfurt, Germany	33	31	33	38	40	56	62	65	63	58	48	39
Geneva, Switzerland	32	29	33	38	47	56	62	65	64	57	48	39
Helsinki, Finland	28	23	22	28	37	46	55	62	59	50	41	32
Lisbon, Portugal	53	50	52	55	59	62	70	70	72	69	63	57
London, England	41	39	40	43	48	54	60	63	62	57	50	44
Luxembourg, Luxembourg	38	35	38	42	49	55	61	64	64	60	50	43
Madrid, Spain	42	41	44	48	53	61	68	74	75	66	56	47
Moscow, Russia	13	10	13	22	36	51	58	62	54	49	36	24
Oslo, Norway	27	25	26	32	41	51	58	64	60	53	42	33
Paris, France	40	37	40	44	50	57	62	66	65	60	52	43
Reykjavik, Iceland	33	33	42	48	48	49	50	52	50	46	41	34
Rome, Italy	47	44	48	52	58	64	71	77	76	71	62	53
Sofia, Bulgaria	40	38	37	37	57	60	68	73	73	56	48	40
Stockholm, Sweden	29	27	27	30	39	49	58	63	60	53	43	35
Vienna, Austria	35	32	34	42	49	58	63	66	65	58	49	39
Warsaw, Poland	29	26	28	35	46	63	66	66	64	57	48	36
Far East												
Bangkok, Thailand	78	80	82	84	87	86	85	84	84	83	83	80
Calcutta, India	67	67	71	80	86	87	85	84	84	83	81	74
Colombo, Ceylon	79	79	79	81	82	82	81	81	80	81	80	79
Hong Kong	63	60	59	64	71	77	82	83	83	80	77	70
Karachi, Pakistan	69	67	70	75	84	87	85	82	82	82	81	76
Manila, Philippines	76	75	76	80	81	82	82	80	80	80	80	77
Peking, China	27	27	29	38	54	69	77	81	77	68	46	36
Tokyo, Japan	42	39	39	45	55	62	70	76	79	73	62	52

*Average daily temperatures

Reprinted with the permission of the American Society of Travel Agents, Inc. from WHAT EVERY OVERSEAS TRAVELER SHOULD KNOW, copyright © 1982.

International travel: checklist

Before the trip

☑ **Be sure to pack properly.**
Whether traveling domestically or internationally, when packing, don't forget to take: a sufficient supply of your prescribed medications, some extra cash in addition to traveler's checks, a pair of comfortable walking shoes, an extra pair of glasses, sunglasses, an umbrella, headache and motion remedies, a travel alarm clock, and film for your camera.

☐ **Make sure your luggage is properly identified.**
The Civil Aeronautics Board now requires that all luggage be properly identified with your name and address inside and out. Be sure all your bags are properly tagged for your own protection.

☐ **Be sure and cancel routine services for the duration of your trip.**
For as long as you will be traveling away from home, stop all routine services—newspapers, milk, laundry, and refuse collection. Ask the post office to put a hold on your mail until you return.

☐ **Notify the local authorities.**
Advise the local police of your planned absence and ask them to periodically check your premises. Recheck the expiration dates on your insurance policies. Prior to leaving, set the timers for lights in your home to go on and off throughout the evening hours.

☐ **Do comparative shopping.**
To ensure that you get a bargain, do some comparative shopping on any items you plan to buy for your trip.

During the trip

☐ **Keep travel documents accessible.**
Keep all your travel documents (passports, visas, etc.) in one place, preferably on your person, for easy accessibility. Remember, never leave any personal valuables or cash lying about; most hotels have a safe-deposit box for such articles.

☐ **Know about the place you are visiting.**
When traveling to a destination, especially outside the United States, learn about the area you are visiting—the customs, climate, food, and facilities, etc. If you require any special diet or medical facility check with the hotel or your travel agent as to its availability.

☐ **Reconfirm your flights.**
Remember when traveling domestically or internationally reconfirm your flights and leave sufficient time for making all connections.

☐ **Document all inconveniences.**
If anything goes awry on your trip, document all inconveniences, listing what went wrong, where and when. Upon your return, contact your travel agent.

☐ **If you are a minor carry a letter of consent.**
If you are a minor and are planning on traveling domestically or internationally, you should carry a letter of consent for traveling signed by one or both of your parents.

International travel: vaccinations

No vaccinations are required for direct travel from the United States to most countries. Certain vaccinations are required only by some countries in Africa and Asia, and French Guiana in South America. No vaccinations are required to return to the United States.

Type	Doses	Comments
Cholera	1	Certificate valid for 6 months beginning 6 days after 1 injection of vaccine or on the date of revaccination if within 6 months of first injection.
Yellow Fever	1	Certificate valid for 10 years beginning 10 days after primary vaccination or on the date of revaccination if within 10 years of first injection.

International travel: packing checklist

For him

- [x] 1 suit—synthetic or knit
- [ ] 2 sports jackets (one a blazer), 2 pairs of slacks
- [ ] 1 raincoat
- [ ] 6–8 shirts—permanent press
- [ ] 6 sets of underwear—wash and wear
- [ ] 2 pairs of pajamas—wash and wear
- [ ] 6 pairs of socks
- [ ] 3–6 neckties
- [ ] 2–3 pairs of shoes
- [ ] 1 light sweater—long sleeve

For her

- [ ] 3 sets of lingerie
- [ ] 1 small purse for evening use
- [ ] 6 pairs hose
- [ ] 2 suits
- [ ] 1 casual dress for sightseeing
- [ ] 2 pairs of slacks
- [ ] 1 topcoat (all weather)
- [ ] 2 blouses (wash and wear), 1 skirt
- [ ] 1 or 2 cocktail dresses
- [ ] 1 sweater
- [ ] 2 nightgowns (wash and wear), 1 robe
- [ ] 1 pair of slippers
- [ ] 2 pairs of low-heeled walking shoes, 1 pair "after 5" shoes

In general

☐ Passport

☐ Visas—if needed

☐ Drivers License

☐ Travelers Checks

☐ Credit cards

☐ Money—including small denominations of foreign currency

☐ Documents

☐ Ball point pen and refills (fountain pens leak on airplanes)

☐ Foot powder

☐ Headache remedy

☐ Antidote for diarrhea

☐ Extra glasses—or prescription

☐ Insect repellent

☐ Plastic bags (for damp laundry, anything that might leak)

☐ Spot remover

☐ Sunglasses

☐ Sunburn lotion

Reprinted with the permission of the American Society of Travel Agents, Inc. from WHAT EVERY OVERSEAS TRAVELER SHOULD KNOW, copyright © 1982.

Weather

Determining wind chill factors

wind/speed	Temperature (F)											
Calm	40	30	20	10	5	0	−10	−20	−30	−40	−50	−60
	Equivalent Chill Temperature											
5	35	25	15	5	0	−5	−15	−25	−35	−45	−55	−70
10	30	15	5	−10	−15	−20	−35	−45	−60	−70	−80	−95
15	25	10	−5	−20	−25	−30	−45	−60	−70	−85	−100	−110
20	20	5	−10	−25	−30	−35	−50	−65	−80	−95	−110	−120
25	15	0	−15	−30	−35	−45	−60	−75	−90	−105	−120	−135
30	10	0	−20	−30	−40	−50	−65	−80	−95	−110	−125	−140
35	10	−5	−20	−35	−40	−50	−65	−80	−100	−115	−130	−145
40	10	−5	−20	−35	−45	−55	−70	−85	−100	−115	−130	−150

Danger	Increasing Danger (Flesh may freeze within 1 min.)	Great Danger (Flesh may freeze within 30 seconds)

How to build and use a hygrometer

To Make a Hygrometer, cut a hole about 2½ inches from the bottom of an empty milk carton and fill the carton with water up to the opening. Fasten two thermometers to the carton, one with the bulb just above the hole. Wrap cloth around this bulb and push it through the hole into the water.

To Determine Relative Humidity, allow the hygrometer to stand for 15 minutes in a breeze away from direct sunlight. Read both thermometers and use the temperatures to find the humidity on the chart, *below.* Read across from the wet-bulb readings. Read downward from the dry-bulb readings. For example, if the dry-bulb thermometer reads 70° F. and the wet-bulb thermometer reads 60° F., the relative humidity is 55 per cent.

Wet-bulb temperatures °F.	\ Dry-bulb temperatures °F. 56	58	60	62	64	66	68	70	71	72	73	74	75	76	77	78	79	80	82	84	86	88
38	7	2																				
40	15	11	7																			
42	25	19	14	9	7																	
44	34	29	22	17	13	8	4															
46	45	38	30	24	18	14	10	6	4	3	1											
48	55	47	40	33	26	21	16	12	10	9	7	5	4	3	1							
50	66	56	48	41	34	29	23	19	17	15	13	11	9	8	6	5	4	3				
52	77	67	57	50	43	36	31	25	23	21	19	17	15	13	12	10	9	7	5	3	1	
54	88	78	68	59	51	44	38	33	30	28	25	23	21	19	17	16	14	12	10	7	5	3
56		89	79	68	60	53	46	40	37	34	32	29	27	25	23	21	19	18	14	12	9	7
58			89	79	70	61	54	48	45	42	39	36	34	31	29	27	25	23	20	16	14	11
60				90	79	71	62	55	52	49	46	43	40	38	35	33	31	29	25	21	18	15
62					90	80	71	64	60	57	53	50	47	44	42	39	37	35	30	26	23	20
64						90	80	72	68	65	61	58	54	51	48	46	43	41	36	32	28	25
66							90	81	77	73	69	65	62	59	56	53	50	47	42	37	33	30
68								90	86	82	78	74	70	66	63	60	57	54	48	43	39	35
70									95	91	86	82	78	74	71	67	64	61	55	49	44	40
72											95	91	86	82	79	75	71	68	61	56	50	46
74													96	91	87	83	79	75	69	62	57	51
76															96	91	87	83	76	69	63	57
78																	96	91	84	76	70	64
80																			92	84	77	70
82																				92	84	77
84																					92	85
86																						92

Government services, agencies, and regulations

Small claims court, by state

State	Type of court	Maximum claim	Minimum age	Lawyers: permitted/or required	Appeals permitted by plaintiff	defendant	Typical filing and service costs
Alabama	Small Claims	$500	21	Permitted	yes	yes	$10–$15
Alaska	Small Claims	1000	18	Corps: Required Others: Permitted	yes	yes	7–15
Arizona	Justice Court	999	21	Corps: Required Others: Permitted	yes	yes	3–6
Arkansas	Municipal Court	100–300	([12])	Permitted	yes	yes	10
California	Small Claims	750	([13])	Not permitted	no	yes	2–5
Colorado	Small Claims	500	18	Not permitted	yes	yes	7–10
Connecticut	Common Pleas	750	21	Permitted	no	no	6–15
Delaware	Justice of Peace	1500	19	Permitted	yes	yes	10
District of Columbia	Small Claims	750	21	Permitted[1]	yes	yes	2–10
Florida	Small Claims	1500–2500[14]		Permitted	yes	yes	5–10
Georgia	Small Claims or Justice of Peace	200–300	18	Permitted	([2])	([2])	2–15
Hawaii	Small Claims	300	21	Permitted[3]	no	no	7
Idaho	Small Claims	500	21	Not permitted	yes	yes	5–10
Illinois	Small Claims (State)	1000	18	Corps: Required	yes	yes	7–11
	Cook County[4]	300		Others: Permitted			
Indiana	Small Claims	3000	21	Corps: Required Others: Permitted	yes	yes	6–10
Iowa	District Court	1000	19	Permitted	yes	yes	3–5
Kansas	Small Claims	300	18	Not permitted	yes	yes	10
Kentucky	Small Claims[5]	500	18	Permitted	yes	yes	6.50
Louisiana	City Courts	25	21	Permitted	no	no	10–20
	Justice of Peace	300					
Maine	Small Claims	800	21	Permitted	yes	yes	5
Maryland	District Court	500	21	Permitted	yes	yes	5–10
Massachusetts	Small Claims	400	21	Permitted	no	yes	2–3
Michigan	Small Claims	300	21	Not Permitted	no	no	7–12
Minnesota	Conciliation Court	500–1000	21	Not permitted[9]	yes	yes	3
Mississippi	Justice of Peace	500	None	Permitted	yes	yes	6
Missouri	Small Claims	500	21	Permitted	yes	yes	9–11
Montana	District Court	1500	19	Permitted	yes	yes	2.50
Nebraska	Small Claims	500	19	Not permitted	yes	yes	4
Nevada	Small Claims	300	([12])	Permitted	yes	yes	5–7
New Hampshire	Small Claims	500	21	Permitted	yes	yes	3
New Jersey	Small Claims	500	21	Permitted	yes	yes	3–5
New Mexico	Small Claims[6]	2000	18	Permitted	yes	yes	6–14
New York	Small Claims	1000	21	Permitted[7]	yes	yes	3–4
North Carolina	Small Claims	500	18	Permitted	yes	yes	7–12
North Dakota	Small Claims	200–500	18	Permitted	no	no	3
Ohio	Small Claims	300	21	Permitted	yes	yes	2.75
Oklahoma	Small Claims	600	([12])	Permitted	yes	yes	5–10
Oregon	Small Claims	500	21	Not permitted[8]	no	yes	15
Pennsylvania	Small Claims	1000	None	Permitted	yes	yes	6–12
Rhode Island	Small Claims	300	21	Corps: Required Others: Permitted	no	yes	2
South Carolina	Magistrate Court	200–3000	21	Permitted	yes	yes	varies
South Dakota	Magistrate Court	1000	18	Permitted	no	no	2–4
Tennessee	Justice of Peace	3000	18	Permitted	yes	yes	25 bond
Texas	Small Claims	150–200	18	Permitted	yes[10]	yes[10]	5–8

State	Type of court	Maximum claim	Minimum age	Lawyers: permitted/or required	Appeals permitted by plaintiff	defendant	Typical filing and service costs
Utah	Small Claims	200	([12])	Permitted	no	yes	5–7
Vermont	Small Claims	250	18	Permitted	yes	yes	3–6
Virginia	District Court	5000	None	Permitted	([10])	([10])	3–5
Washington	Small Claims	300	18	Not permitted	no	([11])	3–5
West Virginia	Magistrate Court	1500	18	Permitted	yes	yes	7.50
Wisconsin	Small Claims	500	21	Permitted	yes	yes	5–7
Wyoming	Justice of Peace	200	21	Permitted	yes	yes	2–6

[1]Law students allowed to represent parties; [2]Appeals allowed only for amounts over $50; [3]Lawyers not permitted in security deposit cases; [4]Lawyers not permitted in Cook Co. Pro Se Court. Corporations, partnerships and associations not permitted to use court; [5]In Jefferson Co., Consumer Court, for consumer plaintiffs only; [6]Small Claims Court in Albuquerque only; [7]Corporations, assignees, partnerships, associations, and insurers not permitted as plaintiffs; [8]Lawyers may appear only with consent of judge; [9]Lawyer permitted in Minneapolis and St. Paul only; [10]Appeals allowed only for amounts over $20; [11]Appeals allowed only for amounts over $100; [12]Minimum age is 18 for females, 21 for males; [13]Minimum age 18 for married individuals, 21 for single individuals; [14]Lawyer required for claim over $1,500.

Veterans' benefits timetable

You have (after separation from service)	Benefits	Where to apply
10 years or until Dec. 31, 1989, whichever comes first	GI education: The VA will pay you while you complete high school, go to college, or learn a trade, either on the job or in an apprenticeship program. Vocational and educational counseling is available.	Any VA office
10 years	Veterans Educational Assistance Program: The VA will provide financial assistance for the education and training of eligible participants under the voluntary contributory education program. Vocational and educational counseling is available upon request.	Any VA office
12 years, although extensions are possible under certain conditions	Vocational Rehabilitation: As part of a rehabilitation program, the VA will pay tuition, books, tools, or other expenses and provide a monthly living allowance. Employment assistance is also available to help a rehabilitated veteran get a job. A seriously disabled veteran may be provided services and assistance to increase independence in daily living.	Any VA office
No time limit	GI loans: The VA will guarantee your loan for the purchase of a home, mobile home, or condominium.	Any VA office
No time limit	Disability compensation: The VA pays compensation for disabilities incurred in or aggravated by military service. Payments are made from date of separation if claim is filed within 1 year from separation.	Any VA office
1 year from date of mailing of notice of initial determination	Appeal to Board of Veterans Appeals: Appellate review will be initiated by a notice of disagreement and completed by a substantive appeal after a statement of the case has been furnished.	VA office or hospital making the initial determination
No time limit	Medical care: The VA provides hospital care covering the full range of medical services. Outpatient treatment is available for all service-connected conditions, or nonservice-connected conditions in certain cases. Alcohol and drug dependency treatment is available.	Any VA office
Time varies	Burial benefits: The VA provides certain burial benefits, including interment in a national cemetery and partial reimbursement for burial expenses.	VA National Cemetery having grave space, any VA office
Within 2 years of discharge or before Oct. 1, 1984, whichever is later	Readjustment counseling: General or psychological counseling is provided to assist in readjusting to civilian life.	Any Vet Center, VA office, or hospital
Within 90 days of separation	One-time dental treatment: The VA provides one-time dental care for certain service-connected dental conditions.	Any VA office or hospital

You have (after separation from service)	Benefits	Where to apply
No time limit	Dental treatment: Treatment for veterans with dental disabilities resulting from combat wounds or service injuries and certain POWs and other service-connected disabled veterans.	Any VA office or hospital
1 year from date of notice of VA disability rating	GI insurance: Low-cost life insurance (up to $10,000) is available for veterans with service-connected disabilities. Veterans who are totally disabled may apply for a waiver of premiums on these policies.	Any VA office
120 days or 1 year with evidence of insurability; or up to 1 year if totally disabled	Veterans Group Life Insurance: SGLI may be converted to a 5-year nonrenewable term policy. At the end of the 5-year term, VGLI may be converted to an individual policy with a participating insurance company.	Office of Servicemen's Group Life Insurance, 212 Washington St. Newark, NJ 07102 or any VA office
No time limit	Employment: Assistance is available in finding employment in private industry, in Federal service and in local or state employment service.	Local or state employment service, U.S. Office of Personnel Management, Labor Department. Any VA office
Limited time	Unemployment Compensation: The amount of benefit and payment period vary among States. Apply after the separation.	State employment service
90 days	Reemployment: Apply to your former employer for employment.	Employer
30 days	Selective Service: Male veterans born in 1960 or later years must register.	At any U.S. Post Office; overseas at any U.S. Embassy or Consulate

U.S. and Canadian legal holidays

The United States has nine federal legal public holidays (1983). Canada celebrates eight legal public holidays in all provinces and territories.

Day	Celebrated Where	Date
New Year's Day	Canada, all provinces; U.S., all states	January 1
Washington's Birthday (President's Day)	U.S., all states	Variable, based on Feb. 22
Good Friday	Canada, all provinces; U.S., all states	Variable, based on Easter
Easter Monday	Canada, all provinces	Variable, based on Easter
Victoria Day	Canada, all provinces	Variable, based on May 25
Memorial Day	U.S., most states	May 30 or last Monday in May
Canada Day (Dominion Day)	Canada, all provinces	Officially marked July 1
Independence Day	U.S., all states	Officially marked July 4
Labor Day	Canada, all provinces; U.S., all states	First Monday in Sept. First Monday in Sept.
Thanksgiving Day	Canada, all provinces	Second Monday in Oct.
Columbus Day	U.S., most states	Second Monday in Oct.
General Election Day	U.S., some states	First Tuesday after first Monday in Nov.
Remembrance Day (U.S. Veterans day)	Canada, all provinces; U.S., all states	Officially marked Nov. 11
Thanksgiving Day	U.S., all states	Fourth Thursday in Nov.
Christmas Day	Canada, all provinces; U.S., all states	Dec. 25
Boxing Day	Canada, all provinces, except Quebec	Dec. 26

Gun ownership regulations

	Waiting period	Purchase requirements	Registration
Alabama	48 hours, pistol	Application, criminal history check	Partial
Alaska	None	None	None
Arizona	None	None	None
Arkansas	None	None	None
California	15 days, all transactions	Application; criminal history check	Partial
Colorado	None	None	None
Connecticut	2 weeks	Application; criminal history check	Partial
Delaware	None	None	None
Florida	None	None	None
Georgia	None	None	None
Hawaii	None	Permit to purchase	Full; every person within 48 hours
Idaho	None	None	None
Illinois	72 hours, handguns, 24 hours, others	Firearms owner's identification card	None
Indiana	7 days	Application, criminal history check	Prohibited
Iowa	None	Permit to purchase	Partial
Kansas	None	None	None
Kentucky	None	None	None
Louisiana	None	Applications to transfer, both parties	Full; Dept. of Public Safety
Maine	None	None	None
Maryland	7 days	Application; police review	Partial
Massachussetts	None	Firearms identification card	None
Michigan	10 days	License to purchase (both dealer and md'f sales)	Full
Minnesota	7 days	Transferee permit; criminal history check	None
Mississippi	None	None	Full
Missouri	None	Permit to purchase	Partial
Montana	None	None	None
Nebraska	None	None	None
Nevada	None	None	None
New Hampshire	None	None	Partial
New Jersey	7 days	Permit to purchase	Partial

License or permit to carry a firearm	Dealer requirements	Saturday night special	Mandatory minimum sentences
License to carry a concealed handgun	License, ledger	None	None
None	None	None	Unlawful possession of firearms by convict; not to exceed 5 years
None	None	None	None
None	None	None	None
License to carry a concealed handgun; fingerprints	License, ledger	None	Additional sentence for person armed in commission of a felony
License to carry concealed firearms	Ledger	None	None
Permit to carry openly or concealed	License, ledger	None	None
License to carry a concealed firearm	License, ledger	None	5 years for use of firearm in commission of a felony
License to carry	None	None	None
License to carry a firearm openly, fingerprints	License	None	Sentences for carrying concealed firearm and for carrying a firearm in commission of crime
License to carry; registration	License	Prohibited	None
License to carry a concealed firearm	None	None	Sentence for having firearm during assault on another person
Firearm owner's identification card	Ledger	Prohibited	Sentences concern person convicted of felony in which firearm is used in commission of offense
License to carry	License	None	None
License to carry concealed firearm. Training program	License, ledger	None	None
None	None	None	None
None	None	None	None
None	Registration	None	Sentences for person using firearm when committing crime of violence
License to carry a concealed firearm	Ledger	None	None
License to carry a handgun, requires "good and substantial reason" and evidence of training	License	None	1 year for unlawful carrying, 5 years for use of firearm in crime of violence
Firearms identification card, license to carry openly and concealed, fingerprints and photo	License, ledger	None	1 year for unlawful carrying, sentence for use of firearm in felony
License to carry, fingerprints, registration	License, ledger	None	Additional 2 years for felony by person carrying or possessing firearm
Permit to carry, proof of ability to use pistol safely	License, ledger	Prohibited	Sentences for possessing firearms when committing violent crime
None	Ledger	None	None
None	Ledger	None	Sentences for using firearm in crime
License to carry a concealed firearm	None	None	None
None	None	None	None
License to carry concealed firearm	None	None	None
License to carry in a motor vehicle	License, ledger	None	None
Firearms identification card for rifles and shotguns, license to carry handguns	Retail dealers license and ledger	None	Additional sentences for committing or attempting to commit violent crime with firearm

151

Gun ownership regulations—*continued*

	Waiting period	Purchase requirements	Registration
New Mexico	None	None	None
New York	None	License to carry or possess	Full
North Carolina	None	Permit to purchase	None
North Dakota	None	License to carry	Partial
Ohio	None	None	None
Oklahoma	None	None	None
Oregon	5 days	Application, criminal history check	Partial
Pennsylvania	48 hours	Application; criminal history check	Partial
Rhode Island	72 hours handgun	Application, criminal history check	Prohibited
South Carolina	None	Application	Partial
South Dakota	48 hours	Application	Partial
Tennessee	15 days	Application, criminal history check	None
Texas	None	None	None
Utah	None	None	None
Vermont	None	None	None
Virginia	None	Permit to purchase (counties with dealers)	None
Washington	72 hours	Application; police review	Partial
West Virginia	None	None	None
Wisconsin	48 hours	None	None
Wyoming	None	None	None
District of Columbia	48 hours	Application	Full

License or permit to carry a firearm	Dealer requirements	Saturday night special	Mandatory minimum sentences
None	None	None	None
License to possess, carry, repair, and dispense	License, ledger	None	1 year for carrying loaded, unlicensed handgun in public place
None	License	None	Use of firearm in robbery is felony, sentence specified
License to carry, valid reason	License, ledger	None	Sentence with no parole for person committing felony with firearm
None	None	None	None
None	None	None	None
License to carry a concealed firearm	License, ledger	None	Sentences for person who commits felony while armed and without permit to carry
License to carry a concealed firearm	License, ledger	None	None
License to carry a concealed firearm, handgun safety course	License, ledger	None	Sentences for committing or attempting to commit violent crime while armed
License to carry a concealed firearm; proficiency test	License, ledger	Prohibited	Sentences for committing or attempting to commit violent crime with firearm
License to carry	License, ledger	None	None
License to carry	License	None	5 years for use of firearm in crime
None	License, ledger	None	None
License to carry a concealed firearm; fingerprints	Ledger	None	None
None	Ledger	None	None
License to carry a concealed firearm	License in certain counties, ledger	None	None
License to carry a concealed firearm	License, ledger	None	Additional sentences for using firearm in crime
License to carry openly or concealed	License, ledger	None	None
None	None	None	None
License to carry	Ledger	None	None
None	License	None	None

NEXT DAY EXPRESS MAIL SERVICE:

GUARANTEED SERVICE BETWEEN MAJOR U.S. CITIES OR YOUR MONEY BACK.*

Articles received by 5 p.m. at a postal facility offering Express Mail Service will be delivered by 3 p.m. the next day or, if you prefer, your shipment can be picked up as early as 10 a.m. the next business day.

Rates include Insurance, Shipment Receipt, and Record of Delivery at the destination post office.

Express Mail Service is available for any mailable articles up to 70 lbs.

Consult Postmaster for other Express Mail Services and rates.

*The Postal Service will refund, upon application to originating office, the postage for any Express Mail shipments not meeting the service standard except for those delayed by strike or work stoppage.

FIRST-CLASS

LETTER RATES:

1st ounce... 20¢
Each additional ounce... 17¢

For Pieces Not Exceeding (oz.)	The Rate Is	For Pieces Not Exceeding (oz.)	The Rate Is
1	$0.20	7	$1.22
2	0.37	8	1.39
3	0.54	9	1.56
4	0.71	10	1.73
5	0.88	11	1.90
6	1.05	12	2.07

FOR PIECES OVER 12 OUNCES SEE FIRST-CLASS ZONE RATED (PRIORITY) MAIL RATES

CARD RATES:

Single postal cards sold by the post office..............................	13¢ each.
Double postal cards sold by the post office..............................	26¢ (13¢ each half.)
Single post cards......................	13¢ each.
Double post cards (reply-half of double post card does not have to bear postage when originally mailed)........	26¢ (13¢ each half.)
Presort rate...........................	Consult Postmaster
Business reply mail....................	Consult Postmaster

SECOND-CLASS
(Newspapers and periodicals with second-class mail privileges.)

For copies mailed by the public, the rate is:

Weight up
to and
Including

1 ounce	19¢	5 ounces	65¢
2 ounces	35¢	6 ounces	75¢
3 ounces	45¢	7 ounces	85¢
4 ounces	55¢	8 ounces	95¢

Each additional two ounces over 8 ounces, add 10¢.

THIRD CLASS

Circulars, books, catalogs, and other printed matter; merchandise, seeds, cuttings, bulbs, roots, scions, and plants, weighing less than 16 ounces.

0 to 1 oz	$0.20	Over 6 to 8 ozs	0.95
Over 1 to 2 ozs	0.37	Over 8 to 10 ozs	1.05
Over 2 to 3 ozs	0.54	Over 10 to 12 ozs	1.15
Over 3 to 4 ozs	0.71	Over 12 to 14 ozs	1.25
Over 4 to 6 ozs	0.85	Over 14 but less than 16 ozs	1.35

BULK RATE
CONSULT POSTMASTER

FOURTH CLASS

(PARCEL POST) ZONE RATES
CONSULT POSTMASTER FOR WEIGHT AND SIZE LIMITS

NONMACHINABLE SURCHARGE:
A parcel mailed to a ZIP Code destination outside the BMC service area for your post office is subject to a surcharge of $0.50 in addition to the rate shown in this table if:

  A. It is nonmachinable according to the standards prescribed in Domestic Mail Manual section 753 or

  B. It weighs more than 35 pounds.

  C. Note: The nonmachinable surcharge for a 35 pound parcel sent to Zone 8 is 31¢ instead of 50¢.

WITHIN (INTRA-BMC) BMC DISCOUNT:
A parcel mailed to a ZIP Code destination shown below is for delivery within the BMC service area for your post office and is eligible for a discount of $0.14 from the rate shown in this table.

WITHIN (INTRA-BMC) BMC ZIP CODE DESTINATIONS FOR YOUR POST OFFICE ARE:

STAMPS, ENVELOPES, AND POSTAL CARDS

ADHESIVE STAMPS AVAILABLE

Purpose	Form	Denomination and prices
Regular postage	Single or sheet	1, 2, 3, 4, 5, 6, 7, 10, 11, 12, 13, 14, 15, 16, 17, 18, 19, 20, 25, 28, 30, 35, 37, 40 & 50 cents, $1, $2 and $5
	Book	6 at 20 = $1.20 20 at 20 = $4.00
	Coil of 100	20 cents. (Dispenser to hold coils of 100 stamps may be purchased for 10¢ additional)
	Coils of 500	1, 2, 3, 5, 6, 10, 12, 13, 15, 16, 17, 18, 20, cents and $1
	Coil of 3,000	1, 2, 3, 5, 6, 10, 12, 13, 15, 16, 17, 18, 20 and 25 cents
International Airmail postage	Single or sheet	28, 35 and 40¢

ENVELOPES AVAILABLE

	Denomination	Selling price each
		Less than 500
Regular	20¢	24¢

POSTAL CARDS AVAILABLE

Kind	Selling price each
Single	13¢
Reply (13¢ each half)	26¢

SPECIAL SERVICES — DOMESTIC MAIL ONLY

INSURANCE

For Coverage Against Loss or Damage
Fees (in addition to postage)

Liability	Fee
$0.01 to $20	0.45
20.01 to 50	0.85
50.01 to 100	1.25
100.01 to 150	1.70
150.01 to 200	2.05
200.01 to 300	3.45
300.01 to 400	4.70

REGISTRY For Maximum Protection and Security

Value	Fees in addition to postage	
	For articles covered by Postal Insurance	For articles not covered by Postal Insurance
$0.01 to 100.00	3.30	3.25
$100.01 to 500.00 500.01 to 1,000.00 For higher values, consult Postmaster	3.60 3.90	3.55 3.85

Miscellany

ADDITIONAL SERVICES

CERTIFIED MAIL (in addition to postage)	$0.75

CERTIFICATE OF MAILING *(For Bulk mailings, see Postmaster)*	$0.40

ADDITIONAL SERVICES FOR INSURED, CERTIFIED AND REGISTERED MAIL

Restricted Delivery*	$1.00
Return Receipts*	
Requested at time of mailing:	
Showing to whom and when delivered	$0.60
Showing to whom, when, and address where delivered	$0.70
Requested after mailing:	
Showing to whom and when delivered	$3.75

*Not available for mail insured for $20 or less

COD

Consult Postmaster for fee and conditions of mailing

SPECIAL DELIVERY FEE (In addition to required postage)

Class of Mail	Weight		
	Not more than 2 pounds	More than 2 pounds but not more than 10 pounds	More than 10 pounds
First Class	$2.10	$2.35	$3.00
All other classes	2.35	3.00	3.40

SPECIAL HANDLING   Third and Fourth Class Only (In addition to required postage)

10 pounds and less	$0.75
More than 10 pounds	1.30

MONEY ORDERS   For safe transmission of money

$0.01 to 25.00	$0.75
25.01 to 50.00	1.10
50.01 to 500.00	1.55

Federal agencies and addresses

Civil Aeronautics Board
Congressional, Community and
  Consumer Affairs
1825 Connecticut Ave., NW
Washington, D.C. 20428

Commission on Civil Rights
Office of Information
Washington, D.C. 20425
(202)-254-6697

**Consumer Product Safety
  Commission**
Washington, D.C. 20207*

Comptroller of the Currency
Consumer Examinations Division
490 L'Enfant Plaza, SW
Washington, D.C. 20219
202-447-1600

**Department of Agriculture
  (Food)**
Office of Consumer Affairs
Washington, D.C. 20250

Department of Commerce
Consumer Affairs Division
Washington, D.C. 20230
(202)-377-5001

Department of Energy
Federal Energy Regulatory
  Commission
825 N. Capitol Street, NE
Washington, D.C. 20426
(202)-357-8055

**Department of Health and
  Human Services**
Office of Consumer Affairs
1009 Premiere Building, NW
Washington, D.C. 20201

**Department of Housing and
  Urban Development**
Washington, D.C. 20410
202-755-8702

Department of Interior
Office of Consumer Affairs
Washington, D.C. 20240

Department of Justice
Office of Consumer Affairs
Main Justice Building
Washington, D.C. 20530

Department of Labor
Office of Consumer Affairs
Washington, D.C. 20210

Department of State
Office of Public Affairs
Washington, D.C. 20520

Department of Transportation
Consumer Liaison
Washington, D.C. 20590

**Environmental Protection
  Agency**
Office of Public Affairs (A107)
401 M Street, SW
Washington, D.C. 20460

**Equal Employment Opportunity
  Commission**
Washington, D.C. 20506

Federal Aviation Administration
Department of Transportation
Washington, D.C. 20591

**Federal Communications
  Commission**
Consumer Assistance Office
1919 M Street, NW
Washington, D.C. 20554
202-632-7000

**Federal Deposit Insurance
  Corporation**
Consumer Programs
550 17th Street, NW
Washington, D.C. 20429

Federal Home Loan Bank Board
1700 G Street, NW
Washington, D.C. 20552
202-377-6000

**Federal Insurance
  Administration**
Washington, D.C. 20472

Federal Reserve Board
Division of Consumer and
  Community Affairs
Washington, D.C. 20551

Federal Trade Commission
6th and Pennsylvania Avenue, NW
Washington, D.C. 20580

Food and Drug Administration
Office of Consumer Affairs
5600 Fishers Lane
Rockville, Maryland 20857
301-443-3170

Government Printing Office
Superintendent of Documents
Customer Information Branch
Washington, D.C. 20402

Internal Revenue Service
Taxpayer Service Division
Washington, D.C. 20224

**Interstate Commerce
  Commission**
Compliance and Consumer
  Assistance
Washington, D.C. 20423

**National Highway Traffic Safety
  Administration**
Public and Consumer Affairs
Department of Transportation
Washington, D.C. 20590

**Securities and Exchange
  Commission**
Office of Consumer Affairs
Washington, D.C. 20549

Small Business Administration
Office of Consumer Affairs
1441 L Street, NW
Washington, D.C. 20416

U.S. Postal Service
Consumer Advocate
Washington, D.C. 20260

Veterans Administration
Central Office
Public and Consumer Affairs (06
  CA)
810 Vermont Avenue, NW
Washington, D.C. 20420

---

*There are Federal Information Centers around the country. The CPSC will send information on request.